HB71 .M83 1995
Mulberg, Jon, 1960-
Social limits to econom

P9-DUN-098

WITHDRAWN

MURDOCK LEARNING RESOURCE CTR
GEORGE FOX COLLEGE
NEWBERG, OREGON 97132

SOCIAL LIMITS TO ECONOMIC THEORY

Economics seems incapable of providing an adequate description of the economic world, let alone dealing with such pressing social problems as widespread poverty and the destruction of the environment. *Social Limits to Economic Theory* critically examines the current asocial nature of economic theory. As an alternative it considers the prospects for a new, progressive political economy based on notions of community and justice, and incorporating environmental and ethical considerations. In demonstrating that modern economics is far from being a value-free science, *Social Limits to Economic Theory* sheds much light on the hidden history of economics. It thus serves as an excellent introduction to critical non-orthodox economics. Particular attention is focused on the Austrian and Institutional schools as well as on the philosophy of economics and the green social and political economy.

This book will be of interest to anyone concerned with critiques of economics or with its ethical and environmental dimension.

Jon Mulberg currently lectures in government at the University of Ulster. Previously he lectured in sociology at the Universities of Bath and Plymouth. He was a finalist in the International Sociological Association's second worldwide competition and has published in *Political Studies* and other journals. He has been involved in the green movement for many years and has stood in several local elections.

SOCIAL LIMITS
TO ECONOMIC
THEORY

Jon Mulberg

London and New York

MURDOCK LEARNING RESOURCE CTR
GEORGE FOX COLLEGE
NEWBERG, OREGON 97132

First published 1995
by Routledge
11 New Fetter Lane, London EC4P 4EE

Simultaneously published in the USA and Canada
by Routledge
29 West 35th Street, New York, NY 10001
Jon Mulberg has asserted his moral right to be identified as the
author of this work.

© 1995 Jon Mulberg

Typeset in Garamond by
Ponting–Green Publishing Services, Chesham, Bucks
Printed and bound in Great Britain by
T.J. Press (Padstow) Ltd, Padstow, Cornwall

All rights reserved. No part of this book may be
reprinted or reproduced or utilized in any form or by
any electronic, mechanical, or other means, now
known or hereafter invented, including photocopying
and recording, or in any information storage or
retrieval system, without permission in writing
from the publishers.

British Library Cataloguing in Publication Data
A catalogue record for this book is available from
the British Library.

Library of Congress Cataloging in Publication Data
A catalogue record for this book has been requested

ISBN 0–415–09298–1 (hbk)
ISBN 0–415–12386–0 (pbk)

To my parents,
who have waited

1-14-96

CONTENTS

Preface and acknowledgements   ix

INTRODUCTION AND OVERVIEW   1

1 THE POLITICS OF POSITIVE ECONOMICS   10
   Positive science   10
   Positive economics   16
   Social theory of positivism   29

2 FROM UTILITY TO WELFARE: THE TRAJECTORY
   OF ORTHODOX ECONOMICS   37
   Utilitarianism   38
      Bentham   38
      Jevons   40
      Edgeworth   45
   Neo-classics   47
      Marshall   47
      Pigou   56
   Ordinalists   60
      Pareto   60
      Robbins   63
      Hicks   64
      Samuelson   65
      Welfare economics   68

3 1930s' MARKET SOCIALISM   74
   Market socialism   74
   Austrian critique   81
   Normative theory   93

4 AMERICAN INSTITUTIONALISM 100
Determinist theories 101
  Veblen 101
  Mitchell 110
  Ayres 116
Purposive theories 121
  Commons 121

5 NEW INSTITUTIONALISM 128
Game theory 131
Transaction-cost analysis 133
Evolutionary theories of the firm 136
Critique 137

6 NEW SOCIAL MOVEMENTS 145
The green movement 146
  Hirsch 146
  Environmental economics 150
New market socialists 156
  Positive freedom 156
  Market limitations 159
  Participation 163
Summary and conclusion 169

Notes 175
References 184
Index 194

PREFACE AND
ACKNOWLEDGEMENTS

I now view this book as part of an ongoing project retaliating to the ideas of the Right, which have informed the rhetoric if not the policies of governments worldwide throughout the last twenty years, and which have caused misery and untold damage not only to my country but throughout the world. However the project did not start out as that. It actually started as a Ph.D. dissertation in 1984 on the definition of economics, which was in turn influenced by an earlier interest in the environment. Both issues quickly snowballed into wide-ranging questions of the legitimacy of economics and the possibility of a green political economy. Then, as now, answers led to more questions.

In 1984 there was very little interest in many of the questions of environment and market socialism which I posed, certainly little interest within British academia. The fact that these are now on the agenda is due to the dedication of many writers and activists, and I have a great deal for which to thank my colleagues in the green movement. Much of the material used in the second half of this book did not exist in 1984, and the project has been something of a voyage of discovery for me. I hope the reader also gets some of the sense of adventure that I felt.

One of the problems with producing a book of any length is that inevitably much will have been published during the period of writing. I am aware that this is the case here, and have also found several instances where an author I have cited has recently changed his or her mind. I cannot guarantee to have found out about all of these, and apologise to any authors unfairly slighted.

An author engaged on a ten-year project incurs too many debts of gratitude to mention them all, but I would like to single out a few people. Simon Clarke, Tony Elger and Ken Penney helped with the doctoral thesis. The participants at a number of conferences, including the EAEPE and IRNES conferences, were helpful. My colleagues at the University of Bath provided a pleasant working atmosphere. Tony Ashford gave me some vital references on the Coase theory. Sue, Ann and Max made life bearable in Plymouth. The late Mary Farmer read the book on behalf of the publishers and made many helpful suggestions; her death is a loss to us all.

I would also like to thank the medical staff at Edgware General and Harefield Hospitals, in particular Mr Maiwand, for keeping me alive.

In addition, my parents have given support and practical help throughout, in sickness and in health. Their telephone number is more like a helpline for many people. This book is dedicated to them.

INTRODUCTION AND
OVERVIEW

Hutchison: What alarms me is that we are not building on the advances of the 1930s. In some respects, we are going back to the 1930s. The barbarians really *were* at the gates then, and in some ways they still are . . .

Caldwell: Who are the barbarians? . . .

Hutchison: The barbarians in the 1930s that I was concerned about were the Nazis. They had a pseudo race science which I saw taught in German universities. Today there are dogmatists of a different sort . . .

Caldwell: My point is that the criterion you used against the Nazis can also be used against much of economic theory as well . . .

Hutchison: Then let it be so used.

Caldwell: But do you simply apply it less harshly against theories you happen to like? I'd like to see the criterion employed more equitably, and then there'd not be much of economics left.

Hutchison: I wouldn't say that. But if a lot has to go, then let it go.

(DeMarchi 1988, p. 36)

Twenty-four years ago, one of the world's leading economists made a stunning public criticism of his own profession. Making his presidential address to the American Economic Association in 1970, Wassily Leontief claimed not only that in economics

Much of current academic teaching and research has been criticised for its lack of relevance.

but also that this criticism is not entirely unfounded:

The uneasiness . . . is caused not by the *irrelevance* of the practical problems to which present day economists address their efforts, but rather by the palpable *inadequacy* of the scientific means with which they try to solve them.

(Leontief 1971 p. 1; emphasis in original)

1

This is a strong rebuke. The president of one of the leading professional associations is claiming that economics is *palpably* inadequate (my emphasis) to deal with relevant practical problems. Neither did it end there. The whole question of the value of economics in the understanding of contemporary problems was raised again the following year by Phelps-Brown in his presidential address to the Royal Economic Association:

> My starting point is the smallness of the contribution that the most conspicuous developments of economics in the last quarter of a century have made to the solution of the most pressing problems of the times.
>
> (Phelps-Brown 1972 p. 1)

So a year after the president of the leading American association claimed that economics was inadequate to solve practical problems, the president of the leading British association also claimed that economics was useless for policy advice. Even stronger criticism was to come. In the same year that Phelps-Brown delivered his admonition of the economics profession, Worswick claimed in his presidential address to the British Association that much economics has no empirical reference at all:

> Anyone who has attempted to keep pace with even some small part of the enormous output of theoretical literature must have asked himself at times, what is it actually *about*?

He continues:

> Facts hardly ever occur in this literature: the nearest we get is what Professor Kaldor has called stylized facts, which sometimes means no more than conventional assumptions without which determinate solutions of theoretical problems could not be obtained.
>
> (Worswick 1972 p. 77; emphasis in original)

When even the leading practitioners of economics attack their own profession, it might be thought that economists would take notice. But twenty years on nothing much seems to have changed. In a recent address to the British Association, Paul Ormerod claimed that economics is unable to provide satisfactory explanations even for simple everyday economic behaviour:

> why are people operating in, say, financial markets, paid far more than, say, school teachers or academic economists? There are answers to this question, but none of them involves the 'fundamental' principle of supply and demand. Indeed, orthodox economics is quite unable to answer a simple question such as this, except by resorting to definitions of supply, demand and price that degenerate into meaningless tautology.
>
> (Ormerod 1992a p. 12)

Economics is not only charged by Ormerod with being unable to offer explanations for commonplace behaviour. He also claims that the ability of economists to predict economic variables, which must surely be the main justification for the pervasive influence of economics upon public policy, has been thrown into serious doubt. According to Ormerod 'the forecasting record of (economic) models, never brilliant, has deteriorated since the mid 1980s' and 'in virtually every western country, serious errors have been made in forecasts' (Ormerod 1992a p. 12).

The discipline of economics has therefore been subject to constant censure not only from outside the discipline, but also by economists themselves. It would seem that economics can neither explain nor predict. Yet these criticisms are now over twenty years old. Why has nothing changed?

It could be suggested that one of the reasons that these criticisms of economics have had little effect is because the complainants themselves continue to practise what they are preaching against. There is actually little difference between the economics of Phelps-Brown or Worswick and that of the rest of the profession. The pleas for more realism in the models and theories are largely ignored by those doing the pleading. However, this is not simply a matter of hypocrisy or of leading economists preaching counsels of perfection.

The contention of this book is that it is impossible for economics as presently constituted to alter its theoretical structure and its applied modelling to take account of the lack of realism which pervades the discipline at present, and also that such realistic theories and models would not solve the majority of the problems which the discipline faces. Indeed, an economics which does contain realistic models would not look anything like economics as currently practised. This book will suggest that the lack of realism in economics is a defensive strategy which has been invoked to avoid the political conclusions to which economic theory would otherwise lead. This has resulted in an orthodox economic theory which is at best useless and at worst vacuous.

In this book I will argue that what is regarded as the 'science' of economics is in fact a palpably political discipline, and that economic theory must necessarily contain a political theory. I will deny that economics is in any sense a neutral science, and indeed we will see that the very idea of a neutral social science is problematic. We will also see that the economic cannot be separated from the social and the political, and that both economic theory and economic policy are as much political and social as purely 'economic'. Indeed, this book will deny that there is such a thing as a science of 'economics' *per se*, but will suggest instead that only a social and political economy can be seen to be viable. Questions of economic theory, we will suggest, are really questions within political and social theory.

The starting point for our argument is that the usual justification for economics, that it is a 'positive', politically neutral, empirical science which enables us to understand and predict economic behaviour, contradicts the actual policy recommendations which economists arrive at. Because, as we shall see, a neutral policy science is impossible; any such science must have an inherent political theory. Unfortunately, the political theory which is implied in the notion of a positive social science is one of economic planning, not *laissez-faire* or even some sort of mixed-economy, 'reformed' *laissez-faire*. Economists who support *laissez-faire* have therefore to reconcile their stance with the strictures of a positive, empirical science. We shall see that this cannot be done, and in actual fact economics does not practise positive science at all. The empirical input to the science is negligible, if not non-existent (the statistical work done by economists seems to draw nothing from, and contribute little to, economic theory). However, any attempt to make economics more 'realistic', we will maintain, will require a radical reworking of the entire discipline and will have considerable political consequences.

In fact, it is possible to employ positive economic models to show how a centrally planned economy could operate. A number of these models were developed by 'market socialists' in the 1930s, and used the same standard assumptions about market behaviour and price feedback to show how the state could employ the sort of objective, empirical knowledge about the economy which positive economics claims to be able to obtain to enable the state to plan economic production and distribution. If economics is neutral and objective, it is far from clear why economic planning cannot ensue. These questions will occupy the first part of the book.

A defence of *laissez-faire* would therefore require a different approach to economics, which is not justified by recourse to positive, empirical science. The most successful approach of this sort, and one which has informed much of the political rhetoric of the last fifteen years, is that of the Austrian school. The Austrians expressly denied the legitimacy of a positive, empirically based social science. Their theory is explicitly political, and the Austrian critique tarred both the market socialists and the orthodox economics from which it was derived with the same brush. We will see that in order to defend *laissez-faire*, economists have to ditch the idea that economics can yield objective knowledge. However, the price of doing so is high. Economics can no longer be practised in the same way, and indeed, if we deny the idea of an objective science then all the aggregate macroeconomic indicators such as GNP, unemployment or even inflation would also have to be abandoned.

Although I will suggest that the Austrian school's critique of orthodox economics is convincing, this does not mean that we need accept their political and social theory. Given that the critique of objective social science involves the abandonment of objective economic aggregates, we then have to show how economic activity can be optimally organised. The Austrian/libertarian view is that this organisation will occur spontaneously, without any inter-vention by the state. We will be raising criticisms of this view, and will see that deliberate control over the social, legal and political institutions which constitute the economy is both possible and necessary in order for the economy to function. The debate therefore shifts away from the workings of markets, and focuses upon the formation and structure of social and political institutions. These matters will occupy us in the second part of the book.

Much of the argument in the initial chapters is concerned with the concept of 'positive' science. Although this conception of science is now largely discredited, it remains the popular idea of science, and more to the point it continues to be defended by most orthodox economists. The positive view of science is that scientific knowledge

- is value free;
- is based on empirical observation and testing;
- enables prediction of (and thereby control of) the external world.

Many critiques of positivism have emerged since the 1950s, concerning both scientific practice and also the content of scientific knowledge. The main thrust of the work of Thomas Kuhn (Kuhn 1962) is that scientists do not actually practise positive science, because the scientific theories which are employed determine what is to count as evidence. The theories are only questioned during 'revolutions' in the scientific community, not during periods of 'normal' science. However, our main concern in this book will be with the criticisms of the positive view of what ought to constitute scientific knowledge rather than studies of scientific practice. In essence, we will be raising the criticism that the three elements of positivism mentioned above – value-neutrality, observation and testing, and prediction and control – contradict each other. The contradiction pointed out by philosophers of science such as Benton (1977) and Keat and Urry (1975) is that between the desiderata of prediction and control and the emphasis within positivism upon empirical data and testing. They point out that the emphasis on exclusively empirical data means that the positive scientist is unable to consider causal relationships. Causal explanation, it is claimed, will necessarily involve going beyond observation, and will necessitate the use of non-empirical concepts and theories which cannot be brought to test against empirical evidence. Prediction, we will see, actually involves going beyond empirical knowledge.

The second contradiction in the positivist philosophy we will consider is the claim that a neutral science can be concerned with prediction and control. We will see that this specification for science is itself non-neutral, since the very idea that science should be employed for control is *ipso facto* a political statement, and such a science will involve an inherent political theory. In social science, this political theory is the theory of social planning; the very opposite of *laissez-faire*.

So in fact we shall see in Chapter 1 that the positivist methodology has difficulty squaring with market-led theories of the economy. We will trace two consequences of this. In Chapter 1 we will consider the methodological arguments of economists concerning the practice of positive economic science; that is to say, we will consider the attempts at the philosophical level to reconcile economics with the strictures of positivist philosophy.

Chapter 2 looks at the attempts at reconciling positivism and economics at the theoretical level. We will see how the methodological debate maps directly on to questions of economic theory. Recall that a part of our argument is that all social science theories, contrary to the protestations of positivists, necessarily contain a political theory, and that the political theory of positivism – planning – does not square with the market-based theories of orthodox economics. We will see how successive generations of economists have attempted to reconcile *laissez-faire* with the strictures of a positivist philosophy which has not methodological individualism and *laissez-faire*, but instead has social planning as an inherent political theory.

Although our main concern will be with the constitution of economic knowledge rather than the practice of economists, there are overlaps between the two. One of the more interesting aspects of the Kuhnian critique of positive science is the claim that scientists tend to reinterpret the history of their disciplines. Kuhn's conception of the progression of scientific knowledge was that it 'jumps', as it were, between incommensurate paradigms between which no dialogue is possible. Between these paradigm-shifts (scientific revolutions) comes period of 'normal' science within the dominant paradigm, where problems within the paradigm are solved incrementally. Since the paradigms are incommensurate, the history of the science has to be reinterpreted as leading up to the current paradigm.

We shall suggest that this is what has occurred in economics. The history of economic thought has been rewritten in terms of the contemporary theories. In fact, the forerunners of modern economics were working within entirely different philosophies and were concerned with different problems, and indeed in some instances may not have recognised the problems presently under deliberation as even belonging to their discipline. Chapter 2 will trace the history of economic thought as being essentially a response to methodological dilemmas concerning the conclusions as to the viability of planning and the desirability of policies leading to egalitarian distributions of income and wealth. Economic thought was driven by its inherent political theory, not by the wish to provide incremental solutions to problems within the discipline, although the theoretical innovations were often presented or interpreted in this manner. We will see in Chapter 2 that once the hidden history of economic thought is brought to light, the political and social limits will become apparent.

The political basis of economic theory came to the fore in the 1930s debate over market socialism which forms the subject matter of Chapter 3. The 1930s market socialists simply took the positive economists at their word. They reasoned that if economic theory were indeed politically neutral, then it could legitimately be used as a tool for a socialist society. Since, as we will see, economists attempt to abstract economic theory from questions of distribution, which are considered political, it would appear to be perfectly legitimate to impose a politically determined, egalitarian distribution set on to the economy. Furthermore, if the economic variables are all objectively (nay, scientifically) measurable and predictable, and since economic theory was by then encompassing cybernetic-type feedback whereby 'incorrect' pricing would be signalled by the market mechanism, the 1930s theorists suggested that the state could itself use markets to engage nationalised industries in state-controlled production.

It would therefore seem to be impossible to defend both positive economics and *laissez-faire* simultaneously. The main responses in the 1930s debate came not from orthodox economics but from the Austrian school, which explicitly rejected the idea of positive social science. Although the criticisms of market socialism raised by the Austrians are cogent, they apply with equal force to orthodox economics. The Austrians, in contrast to the neutral, predictable world of the orthodoxy, stress the unpredictable and political nature of the economic. Inequality is justified by the Austrians as a necessary reward for risk-taking and anticipation – for entrepreneurship. They point out that there would be no need for entrepreneurs in the predictable world of the orthodoxy. The economic problem, they assert, is actually not one of 'scientific' prediction, but rather of anticipating and reacting to change in an economic world where regularities do not exist.

This by itself is insufficient, and the Austrians do not stop here. Having broken with the positivist tenet of predictability, they also break with the notions of objectivity and value-neutrality. Economic valuations, according to Austrian theory, are subjective and can only be known through trade. They then invoke political and social theories (libertarianism) in order to show that these subjective valuations, as shown through the market, are the optimum set for the distribution of income and wealth. The Austrians invoke a concept of rationality as a transcendental theory of human behaviour, and also employ political theories for distributive efficiency (an evolutionary theory of entrepreneurial talent) and distributive justice (negative freedom).

The 1930s debate therefore causes us to leave the ground that is usually associated with economics, and to discuss topics more often associated with political philosophy and social psychology. The challenges to the libertarian/ Austrian theory have come mainly from these fields. In Chapter 4 we discuss the social psychology of pragmatism, which informed many of the American institutional school who denied that action was guided by rationality. They claimed instead that most action was guided by ingrained habits and beliefs. These were termed institutions, and it was the ability to control institutions that was the determining factor in society. Whereas the Austrian/libertarian theorists claimed that the 'natural order' was one of liberty and individualism, for this brand of institutionalism the world inevitably tended to be dominated by institutional manipulation and social control.

Actually the other, more purposive wing of American institutionalism had a more direct effect on the Austrian school. This wing of institutionalism is best represented by the economist J.R. Commons. Commons' contribution was to show how the activity in markets – the process of market exchange – was underpined by legal statutes of contract and property. Commons used the term 'institutions' to describe precisely the set of centrally imposed rules which were necessary for the efficient operation of individual economic interactions. The analysis posed a challenge to Austrian theory because it appeared that the market exchange mechanism which formed such a major part of their theory was reliant upon the state to oversee its efficient operation, and was therefore still dependent upon politically contingent notions of justice. It seems that, since the legislature must set up a body of contract law which is implemented by a judiciary, individuals are reliant upon the state for the sort of individualism desired by the Austrians to exist at all. To consider an individualist political theory under these circumstances would be impossible.

Chapter 5 considers the next development in this debate, and traces several lines of counter-argument to the position of the American institutionalists. I have used the collective noun 'new institutionalists' to describe the varied theorists attempting such a response. What they have in common is a belief that the sort of laws and rules described by Commons would arise as it were spontaneously from the unhindered activity of interacting individuals. They attempt to show that although there is a need for laws and rules, these need not be imposed by a state, but will – and should – emerge as and when necessary. So the need for trade-mark rules, for example, does not necessitate their imposition by the state. It is, according to the new institutionalists, perfectly feasible and certainly more desirable that these rules will *de facto* emerge from the operation of markets – through the emergence of certification organisations, for example.

We will see in Chapter 5 that some of the theories of the new institutionalists are somewhat incredible, but that the entire approach tends to be *post hoc* in nature. The new institutional economist only sees with hindsight. Furthermore, this school is only really offering an effective defence of Austrian theories concerning distributive efficiency. They do not successfully combine this with a defence of distributive justice, which is where the debate of the 1990s is heading. This debate is led by a group of theorists who I have called the 'new market socialists', although many of their ideas could also be adopted by ecofeminists. While accepting much of the Austrian critique of totally planned economies, the new market socialists reject the libertarian political theory of the Austrian school. They suggest that the state is needed in order for market mechanisms to function at all, and that questions of distributive justice are such that market-led solutions are unlikely or insufficient.

The new market socialists reject the libertarian's exclusive focus on negative freedom (freedom from coercion), and suggest this must be coupled with positive freedoms (capacity for action). They suggest that even when markets are operating well, they will be subject to considerable limitations. In particular, they do not work well when product data are insufficient; such as with health services; or when resources are not traded, such as environmental resources. There may also be resources or activities which are desirable but which do not take the form of commodities, such as housework and child-rearing, and will therefore not be allocated by the market exchange mechanisms.

Although many of the current criticisms of economists have centred on their inability to predict accurately macroeconomic variables, we can see that it is far from clear what these variables tell us when they are calculated. The microfoundations of the macroeconomic aggregates are unclear, and indeed are non-existent if one adopts the Austrian schema. This would mean that the ability to predict and control, which is the *raison d'être* usually suggested for positive science, would not be possible – indeed, this is explicit in the work of many leading Austrians. We would then be led to question the political and social theory with which positive social science is associated. While the political theory of positivism is bound up with concepts of political control through policy scientists, the social theory is bound up with the conceptions of modernity and industrialism as an explanation of social organisation. The concept of society as individualist and rationally organised, driven by the industrial development of science and technology is very much a product of the sort of ideas of prediction and control that are the basis of positivism. The denial of positivism would also enable the development of new social theories, theories which are not technologically driven and are based on ideas of caring, dialogue and community. These ideas have formed the basis of many of the new social movements of the last two decades, and will form the subject matter of Chapter 6.

Our immediate task is therefore to rehearse the main features of the positivist philosophy of science, and to show how this affects orthodox economic theory. We begin this task in Chapter 1.

1

THE POLITICS OF POSITIVE ECONOMICS

POSITIVE SCIENCE

One of the greatest misnomers in the English language must surely be the term 'natural science'. It is hard to imagine anything less natural than that which passes for present-day science. To call the study of nuclear fission or chemical weaponry 'natural science' is to virtually negate the meaning of the word 'natural'.

Neither should it be imagined that the term is appropriate because science studies nature. For the most part it does nothing of the sort. In fact, modern science usually hides itself away from nature in laboratories and attempts to keep nature well away from the scientific experiments. Indeed, much modern science is not very good at either understanding or working with nature. Rather the aim appears to be to try and dominate nature, which then means that nature can be ignored.

This becomes particularly significant when we start to discuss the idea of a social 'science', and to debate whether or not the social world can be investigated in the same manner as the physical world. We shall see that the usual view of social science, that it should employ the same value-free, empirically based techniques that supposedly characterise physical science, is often justified precisely by this appeal to domination and control. However, we will also see that this justification for social science leads to a dilemma, because the concepts of value-neutrality and domination are contradictory.

Before we discuss the question of methodological unity, of whether or not social science can adopt the same methods as physical science, we need to be clear what exactly is understood by the term 'science'. It is far from obvious what being 'scientific' actually involves, and we will begin by outlining different conceptions of what constitutes 'science', and explain why the popular, classic conception of science is inadequate. Although inadequate, the classic (positivist) view of science is nonetheless still defended by economists, and the second section of this chapter will discuss whether it is possible to square the discipline of economics with the maxims of positivist science. We will see that a value-free social science cannot be sustained, and that such a science has an inbuilt political theory. The third section will discuss the political theory of positivism, and the consequences of this theory for economics.

A useful starting point for our discussion is Keat and Urry's tripartite classification of the conceptions of science. This classification will come under strain later, but will serve our purposes for now. The authors outline three positions – positivism, realism and conventionalism (Keat and Urry 1975 p. 4). Positivism they classify as the belief that science consists of the attempt to obtain 'predictive and explanatory knowledge' of the world as it exists. This is achieved by theorising the existence of regularities, which enable prediction and explanation. These theories are objectively tested by observations and experiments (ibid.).

Realists also believe in science as empirical and objective, but posit a difference between explanation and prediction, the former being primary. This involves going 'beyond' regularities to the causal mechanisms involved, which may well necessitate positing 'unobservable entities' (ibid. p. 5).

Conventionalists reject the concept of empirical and objective science (ibid.). As a result, the goals of science become a matter of debate, and conventionalists tend not to share common views on what scientific knowledge consists of.

We can see that a belief in objectivity in science is therefore insufficient to distinguish positive science. In addition, the positivist will put forward claims about the content of explanation and its relation to prediction, the process of observation and the role of theory. Fay cites four essential features of modern positivism: the limited account of explanation, the foundation of knowledge in the language of neutral observation, the ideal of value-free science and the assertion of the methodological unity of all sciences (Fay 1975 p. 13). Our interest for the first part of this chapter will be on the first two of these features.

The positivist view of explanation is that it is limited to the discovery of regularities: to explain something is simply to show that it is the result of a regular pattern. We do not attempt to go 'behind' the empirical regularities in order to discover the 'essence' of phenomena (Keat and Urry 1975 p. 4). For the positivist, explanation and prediction are congruent: explanations consist only of data which lead to correct predictions, and predictions are the only way of confirming the validity of explanations. In addition, the second feature of positivism is that the explanations and predictions are the result of empirical observation, and that this observation is neutral. Only what can be observed is to be regarded as scientific, and non-observable entities do not form any part of the brief of the scientist.

Before we consider this view of science, it might be as well to enquire as to the status of the philosophies of science themselves. Positivists suggest that science consists of, among other things, explanatory and predictive knowledge of the world. Is this suggestion itself explanatory and predictive? It would not appear to be possible to give a positivist account of what is actually a criterion for science – to attempt to do so is to fall into an infinite regress. Modern positivism has moved away from a theory of scientific meaning towards what Kolakowski (1972) calls a 'normative attitude' to knowledge, towards the postulation of criteria for the demarcation of science from non-science. But if the positivist philosophy consists in fact of normative criteria, these criteria have to be justified normatively. Why have positive science at all? What does science achieve that religion, say, does not?

Habermas suggests that all knowledge has 'practical intent', and serves 'social practice' in the reproduction of the species. He identifies two areas of social practice: labour, where humans interact with nature in the process of production, and interaction, where social coordination occurs. For Habermas both of these are necessary; all production and existence is social. Each category of social practice has a distinct type of knowledge associated with it. Interaction requires knowledge of appropriate social norms, whereas labour requires 'purposive–rational' knowledge (Habermas 1969 pp. 93 ff.) We could therefore suggest that knowledge for labour is of an instrumental nature. It is designed for control over our external environment.

What is occurring in modern capitalist societies, what Habermas refers to as the 'discourse of modernity', is that the latter form of instrumental knowledge is dominating the former, so that social norms are increasingly decided by instrumental rationality. Habermas refers to this as the 'scientization of politics' (ibid. ch. 6). We will return to this later in the chapter.

The notion of positive science being justified instrumentally appears uncontentious. Positive science is desirable because it gives us knowledge which enables us to improve our lot. This is the point of the exercise. The question is whether this knowledge can be extended to social science. Fay believes that it would be the claim of many social scientists that

> just as the natural sciences have provided men with a certain kind of knowledge by which they can control their natural environment, thereby making it more hospitable and productive, so also the knowledge gained from social science will enable men to control their social environment, thereby making it more harmonious and congruent with the needs and wants of its members.
>
> (Fay 1975 p. 14)

Social science is therefore required in order to obtain instruments for social improvement. The positivists' claim is that two elements within positive science make it uniquely placed to provide these instruments. Firstly, they claim that the value-neutrality of positivism means that only positive science can provide objective knowledge of society, and that this is superior to subjective viewpoints. They also claim that the ability to predict gives us instrumental knowledge which would otherwise be lacking (ibid. p. 21).

The normative justification for the demarcation of science from non-science along positive lines is that it gives us control over our environment. It is able to do this because it gives us the ability both to predict the future and to understand the present in an objective manner.

We will have more to say on the emphasis on objectivity later in the chapter. Our interest for the present is in the idea of 'knowledge'. We suggest that the positivist insistence on knowledge as being exclusively based on observation places severe restrictions on the ability to understand and consequently to predict. The justification for positivism in instrumental terms (in terms of instruments for control) tended to suggest that the science would in some manner enhance our predictive ability beyond that of mere chance, which would usually be taken to mean that science could offer us causal knowledge. We would justify a prediction by explaining the causes of the phenomena under investigation.

This requirement of causal explanation creates considerable friction within the positivist philosophy, given the insistence on a limited account of explanation and of observation being the foundation of knowledge. Although the idea of causality is now accepted as implied by explanation (Hempel 1966 p. 52–3), many of what we would usually regard as explanations involve non-observational entities – viruses, magnetism, electrical resistance, friction or even (from economics) satisfaction. That is to say, we require theories and theoretical terms to develop causal analysis. Of course, the introduction of theories marks a significant weakening of the positivist position, and it is far from clear how they should be treated. Mach believed that positive science should have no interest in theory – theories may be useful heuristic devices for the practising scientist, but are of no consequence for the science itself (Caldwell 1982 p. 23). That is, we should restrict ourselves to the discovery of regularities. This appears to make non-trivial science next-to-impossible though, since we would have no method of deciding which empirical regularities to consider, and which experiments to perform. We also need to be able to interpret our observations; the regularities we observe will require theories to explain them (Hempel 1966 p. 70).

The modern positivists usually accept the centrality of explanation: 'To explain the phenomena of the physical world is one of the primary objectives of the natural sciences' (ibid. p. 47). In fact, one of the central claims of positivists is the symmetry between explanation and prediction (Keat and Urry 1975 p. 11, Caldwell 1982 p. 29). This is because of the form of explanation now adopted, known as the 'covering law' model. Covering laws are conditional statements; given the antecedent condition, we can conclude the explanandum. The explanandum can be predicted given knowledge of the existence of the antecedent conditions, and the covering law can be used as an a posteriori explanation of the explanandum (Keat and Urry 1975 p. 11). The explanations can therefore be tested by their predictions. Hempel refers to this form of explanation as 'deductive–nomological' (Benton 1977 p. 55; Fay 1975 p. 32). Nonetheless, some form of theoretical analysis is still required to enable consideration of the covering laws, since we have to distinguish our causal explanations from accidental generalisations.[1] To do this we would require in particular counter-factual conditionals (Hempel 1966 p. 56).[2] But counter-factual conditionals can seldom be observed without controlled experiment, which is not usually possible in social science.

Perhaps we can get round the problem of conditional statements by placing less emphasis on deductive explanation. The other mode of explanation frequently discussed Hempel calls 'inductive–statistical'. We can perhaps explain an event inductively by reference to its frequency of past occurrences. We might explain, for example, the fact that inflation rose as unemployment fell by the fact that this has occurred in, say, 90 per cent of all past cases.

It is important to note that this mode of explanation is not a logical probability, which is a question of the confirmation of an hypothesis, but is a statistical probability, a 'quantitative relation between repeatable *kinds of events*: a certain kind of outcome ... and a certain kind of random process' (Hempel 1966 p. 63 emphasis on original).

Given this definition, we may question whether a statistical 'explanation' is possible (Keat and Urry 1975 p. 13). Indeed, in the above quotation from Hempel the process is described as random. A poker hand which I deal to myself is not 'explained' by its probability; if I deal four aces I would not normally be inclined to 'explain' this event to the other players. I was lucky, that is all there is to it. In this sense, explanation is precluded.[3] What can perhaps be explained is the pattern of repeatable events.[4] Of course, as the analysis becomes exhaustive, the hypotheses become more like a covering law model: the overall probabilities tend to unity, and the two types of probability outlined by Hempel tend to merge.

The inductive model cannot, then, offer explanations of events. It can enable us to make predictions on the basis of regularities though. This would therefore appear to give two choices: to either break with the requirement of explanation or to adopt a weak version of deductive explanation involving theory. Theories are usually regarded by positivists as containing two types of principles: their own internal tautologies and 'bridge principles' (sometimes called 'correspondence rules'). The bridge principles link the theoretical terms to observable entities. It is this that gives a theory its 'explanatory power' and its testability (Hempel 1966 p. 74). This is a fairly significant departure from the concept of testability therefore; the theory as a whole is never tested. The only test is of the implications of the theory in terms already (antecendently) available. This makes testing problematic, since we must assume the correctness of the correspondence rules. The explanation as a whole is never tested against observation.

It would appear that the positivist philosophy as a whole cannot be sustained. We must either accept theoretical concepts which violate the principle of observation-based knowledge or abandon the congruency of explanation and prediction.

We have already mentioned the idea of inductive/statistical reasoning that does not offer explanation. In fact we can go either way – predictions that do not explain or explanations that do not predict. Of the latter, the most common form are those known as 'functional' explanations, which broadly consist of explaining processes in terms of the function played in achieving an end-state. We shall see how there is a tendency for social explanation to adopt this form. The main question in an examination of functional explanations is the domain of the theory. As special theories these forms of explanation may have some legitimacy, but as general theories, and as social theories, counter-factual conditionals cannot be supported, and functional explanations of this level tend towards bland assertions of the inevitability of the *status quo* . The whole idea of control, which was one of the reasons for our interest in positivism, is lost when one adopts evolutionary/functional analysis – indeed, there is a strong tendency towards deterministic theories. We will come across this mode of reasoning later, in the works of Veblen and of the Austrians.

The alternative route is to view theories as simply instruments to obtain predictions: we are no longer concerned with explanation at all. Theories could be completely false; as long as they generate accurate predictions they will continue to be employed. This methodological instrumentalism[5] was mooted by Friedman – we will consider it in greater detail later in the chapter. We would note in passing that neither of these views fits in well with the tripartite classification mentioned earlier. It is unclear whether methodological instrumentalism is a form of positivism or conventionalism, whereas functionalism appears to straddle the positivist/realist boundary.[6] As we shall see, this often makes these arguments difficult to grasp while, on the other hand, those who present these methodological viewpoints may end up contradicting the philosophical tradition they purport to uphold.

We have seen how the observation that the stipulations of positive science cannot themselves be justified positivistically has opened up cracks that have spread throughout the entire structure. A positive philosophy of science has to be justified normatively in terms of control, yet such control requires causal explanations which contradict the tenets of positivism. We are either forced to admit theoretical concepts and move towards realism or to move away from positivism either in the direction of conventionalist instrumental theories or towards determinist evolutionary theory.

We will now turn our attention to economic theory, and look at the effect of these problems upon economics. Chapter 2 will trace how the methodological problems outlined here have determined the trajectory of economic theory from the utilitarians to modern theory. The next section of the present chapter will look at the methodological debates as applied to economic science, or to use Fay's term, the economic 'metatheory'. The final section of this chapter will show how the metatheory adopted by economists introduces unwarranted limitations on the method and scope of the substantive economic analysis.

POSITIVE ECONOMICS

Although the idea of positive science has been largely discredited, the position is still defended by economists. Such a defence is highly problematic, and in fact we will see in this section how attempts to reconcile economic practice with positivist philosophy has led economists to adopt a tautological theory.

The problems of positive explanations in social science are compounded by the fact that the causes are often motivational in nature. A positivist social explanation would therefore often be teleological – it would explain action in terms of its final objective. This form of explanation was introduced by J.S. Mill in the guise of his means/end dichotomy, which corresponded with the distinction between fact and value. The scientist could consider the best means for a given end, but could make no judgements upon the ends themselves. By this method Mill incorporated the requisite teleological explanation into his analysis (Myrdal 1933 p. 206).

Myrdal points out a problem for economists adopting this line. If we do adopt the end/means formulation, 'we arrive, not at the *laissez-faire* inherent in the philosophy of natural law, but at some kind of "economic planning"' The consequence is a need for justification of *laissez-faire*:

> This does not mean that non-intervention may not be looked upon as a more appropriate policy to promote a given end than any alternative. But it is never a foregone conclusion. It can be seen to be the case only after the consequences of all possible courses have been explored. Modern economic liberals attempt to prove the desirability of non-intervention in this manner. By acknowledging that this kind of proof is required, they accept the end–means scheme, and the element of planning inherent in it.
>
> (Myrdal 1933 p. 207)

The additional complication created by the need for teleological social explanation under positivism is that economists are then required to explain why *laissez-faire* should be an optimal policy. If ends are given, and furthermore if means are known and can be tested empirically, then all the ingredients for successful economic planning are in existence. If the economic variables are predictable, and given that positivism is indeed justified in terms of control, it would seem, *ceteris paribus*, that planned economies would be possible and even desirable. In order to show why this should not be the case, economists would have to make manifest why empirical data concerning the economy can only be obtained through markets. The later classics and the marginalist economists who followed were therefore set two tasks to justify *laissez-faire*: to show that their conclusion is empirically based, and also to show that no non-market knowledge of policy instruments is possible. To complete both these tasks simultaneously was to prove impossible.

Myrdal notes that this dichotomy of means and ends was required as an outgrowth of the philosophy of natural law. Under this philosophy the propelling cause was identified with the final cause;[7] there was a direct connection between is and ought. What 'is' existed because it ought to. The end and means were both known a priori . The early classics would therefore have no need for the means/end dichotomy. This only occurred when propelling cause and final cause were distinguished (Myrdal 1933 p. 207), which awaited the development of the utilitarian philosophy, and the distinction was explicit in Mill. He distinguished between the art of economics – the production of effects, and the science of economics – the classification of causes (Mill 1836 p. 151). The utilitarianism of Mill was therefore not yet a full-blown positivism, but contained some remnants of the natural law philosophy. Moreover, 'It was then still believed' according to Myrdal

> that ends can be established scientifically, the only difference being that proof of those ends was required; proof was no longer seen to lie in 'the nature of things'. As before, ends were thought to be a proper subject of research, requiring, however, special methods for their discovery.
>
> (Myrdal 1933 p. 208)

In spite of the fact/value dichotomy, the identification of hedonism with positivism came after Mill; Mill's method was aprioristic. He believed that the entire science of political economy 'reasons from *assumed* premises – from premises which might be totally without foundation in fact, and which are not pretended to be universally in accordance with it'. This has the consequence that the conclusions 'are only true . . . in the abstract' (Mill 1836 p. 144, original emphasis). We must allow, Mill explains, for possible deviations when considering actual cases (ibid. p. 150). The procedure is one of deduction from abstract premises with assumptions that *ceteris* remain *paribus* . Indeed, this a priori mode of investigation is the only mode for the 'moral sciences', of which political economy is one. *A posteriori* investigations are only useful as an aid to deduction in that they enable us to verify truth (ibid. p. 153). It is also required to put the science into practice, since abstractions do not hold (ibid. p. 155). However, as Blaug puts it, 'Mill cannot bring himself to equate a failure to verify a prediction with a refutation of the underlying theory' (Blaug 1980 p. 65), the discrepancy may be because *ceteris* are not *paribus* (cf. Mill 1836 p. 154).

Utilitarian political economy is therefore saved from the possibility of having to test its actions by being imbued with a knowledge of ultimate causes. This line was continued by Cairnes (1875), who reasserted the position taken by Mill. The economist begins with a knowledge of ultimate causes, but Cairnes insists that these premises are real (Cairnes 1875 p. 87). Political economy is therefore deductive, and is hypothetical because it is conditional. Verification is aimed only at establishing the existence of antecedent conditions, not at the testing of theories.

The first edition of Cairnes was published before Jevons' *Theory of Political Economy*, and Cairnes only makes a few disparaging comments on the *Theory* in the preface to the second edition. Cairnes had very little time for the mathematics of Jevons, or at least for his view that economic knowledge would be advanced in this way. By the time of John Neville Keynes' essay on methodology (Keynes 1890), mathematics was established as an appropriate technique for the analysis of economics. Furthermore, the philosophy of utilitarianism was proving an embarrassment for reasons we shall see in the next chapter, and by the time of Marshall was virtually abandoned. Neville Keynes' *Scope and Method* was contemporary with the work of Marshall – they were colleagues at Cambridge – and can therefore be said to represent the end of the 'classical' methodology, marking a transition from the classical methodology to the new marginalism.

The inability to operationalise utilitarianism created a need for methodological adjustment to maintain the positivist philosophy of science. The changes that Keynes made were subtle but notable. Firstly, it was no longer possible to avoid empirical input. Induction was now to be used both in the testing of theories and in their derivation. Political economy 'must both begin with observation and end with observation' (Keynes 1890 p. 227). The matter of *ceteris* not being *paribus* was simply another problem of this particular discipline (ibid. p. 233).

There were many other subtleties associated with the gradual abandonment of utilitarianism. Keynes outlines the Senior–Mill–Cairnes tradition of separating the positive science from the normative art of economy, but qualifies this with the notion that the normative art is social (ibid. p. 75). The science of political economy was concerned with individuals within society, and since morals were no longer regarded as scientific, political economy was a social rather than a moral science (ibid. p. 88). 'Economic human' remained an abstraction, but one which was close to reality (ibid. p. 124).

This last was fairly illustrative of the nature of Keynes' methodology. In line with the move away from utilitarianism, we no longer have knowledge of ultimate causes *à la* Mill or Cairnes, but an assertion that economic motives are predominant, but with – as Blaug notes – only 'casual empiricism' offered as evidence (Blaug 1980 p. 55). The problem stems from the fact that ends are no longer regarded as known, but must be derived. For Mill the abstraction of economic behaviour from all other aspects of behaviour was an irrelevance – all were scientific. Since both ends and means are still known, the definition of economic science is arbitrary, and indeed Mill readily admits that his definition of 'economic human' is arbitrary (Mill 1836 p. 144). For Keynes this is not the case. Since ends are not known, any abstraction may divorce economics from reality. This is why (following Marshall) he is hesitant about the application of the conclusions of political economy – *ceteris* may not be *paribus*.

The central problem was how to obtain a social ethic from a positive methodological individualism. This will inevitably break some of the positivist tenets. The utilitarian philosophy – which we consider in more detail in the next chapter – claimed that this could be accomplished because ethics could be measured scientifically. As it became obvious that this could not be achieved, the only method of maintaining both a positivist analysis and a value-free science was to avoid considering ethics. We shall see in the next chapter that the social ethic cannot be obtained. In metatheoretical terms, the dilemma was between the positivist criteria of observation and of limited explanation, and the normative justification in terms of environmental control, because the latter places a limit on the minimum scope of positive science: we must be able to derive policy instruments from our social science in order to justify the practice. The positivist dilemma which emerged with the fall of utilitarianism was precisely how to deal with the ethical behaviour which the utilitarians tried to make scientific.

As the positivist methodology came to be established in Britain and much of Europe and the US, the methodological problems associated with positivism remained stubbornly resistant to attack. The methodological debates which occurred could be viewed as squabbles over which defensive strategy to adopt to try to protect the positivist position. The first innovation was influenced by the Austrians, who actually never adopted positivism. Robbins' *Nature and Significance of Economic Science* (1935 [1932]) attempted to deal with the problem of abstraction by positing scientific behaviour as a necessary condition of economic action. Economic action is instrumental in nature, and consists of adopting means for a given end. However, there is a further requirement for sufficiency – there must be a multiplicity of ends and a scarcity of means. This scarcity will then involve behaviour in the form of choosing between means (Robbins 1935 p. 14). In keeping with the positivist prescription, Robbins suggests that economics is neutral between ends (ibid. p. 24).

The identification of economics with scientific teleology is drawn from Robbins' contact with the Austrian school (Caldwell 1982 pp. 103 ff.). However, Robbins appears reluctant to keep the Austrians company along their entire methodological path (ibid. p. 103).[8] He does not embrace praxeology (he claims never to have been able to understand Mises' position; see Robbins 1935 p. xiv) or embrace other aprioristic epistemological positions, but rather attempts to remain within the positivist framework – indeed he accepts Popperian falsification (ibid.).[9] Since a prioristic knowledge of human behaviour is rejected, we must conceive of explanation in observational terms. As Robbins notes, valuation is not itself observable (Robbins 1935, p. 87). What is required is a method of transforming this theoretical term into observational terms which can either be observed or, for Hicks, are intuitively obvious. This is, of course, the essence of the positivist concept of correspondence rules

But the praxeology of the Austrians was aprioristic, not positivistic.[10] It is far from clear what the status of Robbins' rationality postulate is. Robbins himself believes that his sense of rationality is 'simply one of a number of assumptions of a psychological nature which are introduced into economic analysis of various stages of approximation to reality' and that 'Economic man' is simply an 'expository device' which can be used to gain knowledge which can then be applied to real, more complex situations (Robbins 1935 p. 94).

This is not the case though. The assumption of so-called rational choice in human behaviour is not simply an heuristic device that can be relaxed when applying the theoretical analysis to 'real' humans.

> It is worth emphasising that the assumption of rationality is not simply another *ceteris paribus* condition. Even if all outside influences were eliminated and all observed values of variables adjusted to fit the theory, irrational behaviour . . . would render prediction impossible.
>
> (Hollis and Nell 1975 p. 53)

The original means/end dichotomy of Mill, it will be recalled, was to distinguish between science and art. Following this, Robbins' rationality 'assumption' was also used as a *definition* of economic science. Any behaviour outside of this assumption would be beyond the purview of economics also. 'We may put this new qualification by saying that economics is the study of rational economic man' (ibid.). We cannot consider an abstract 'rational' economic human, and then compare with a real 'irrational' economic human, because economic action has been defined as rational action. Any 'irrational' behaviour would therefore be regarded as non-economic, and ignored.

The utilitarians tried to deal with morality by reducing it to scientific measurement. What Robbins appears to do is simply ignore this moral element, thereby rendering what is left 'scientific', but also vacuous: it cannot be applied to or observed in any concrete situation. By identifying the subject matter with an abstraction, Robbins has made the analysis analytic.

This would, of course, mean that Robbins would not be able to draw policy conclusions from his theories. Curiously enough he seems perfectly happy to admit this, possibly because he is unaware of the analytic nature of his theories. Although in 1935 he believed that 'without economic analysis it is not possible rationally to choose between alternative systems of society' (1935 p. 155), by 1981 he believed 'that all recommendations of policy involve judgements of value' and that 'in the application of Economic Science to problems of policy, I urge that we must acknowledge the introduction of assumptions of value essentially incapable of scientific proof' (ibid. p. xxxi). It was the vacuous nature of the 'approximation to reality' which prompted Hutchison's critique. Hutchison does not believe that the game is being played according to the positivist methodological rules. The legitimate use of theory to help test definitions was rendered inoperative by tautologous definitions and unspecified *ceteris paribus* assumptions. Hutchison complained that the Robbins definition effectively excludes all facts. He claims that, since Robbins excludes the choice of ends and technical and social considerations from the subject matter of economics, 'All facts, that is, are excluded, for technical, social, and psychological facts presumably comprise that entire possible factual material for the social scientist' (Hutchison 1938 p. 54). Furthermore, the 'hypothetical method' of economics resulted in analytic propositions (ibid. p. 36). Unspecified *ceteris paribus* assumptions achieved the same result, because they rendered the theory untestable (ibid. pp. 40 ff.). Indeed, Hutchison believes that this sort of qualification should be reserved for inductive theories. (ibid. pp. 46).

What Hutchison is after is – following Popper – economic propositions that are falsifiable. He claims that scientific propositions would 'forbid' the occurrence of some events. This economics does not do. Following from this, prediction was not possible.

> There is finally the view to which the fullest and most penetrating discussion of Economic Prognosis led up: that all prognosis of economic events is impossible. It was clearly seen that the prognostic content of propositions of pure theory was nil, but owing to the misconceived notions of exactness and necessity . . . all prognoses based on empirical regularities were objected to as in principle inexact and liable at any moment to be falsified. If all prognosis was really impossible, then . . . Economics would be . . . an idle science but a true one.
>
> (Hutchison 1938 p. 64)

Economics, according to Hutchison, depends on the discovery of regularities. He regarded it as an empirical science (ibid. p. 164), but thought that current practice limited the science to tautologies. Furthermore, policy initiatives would necessarily go beyond economics

> No one, statesman or individual, can act on purely economic advice. *All state economic policy involves politics* . . . only advice and policy which is based on an estimate of the political, sociological, and economic effects *together* of a policy or measure can be sensibly acted on.
>
> (Hutchingson 1938, p. 165; emphasis in original)

Of course, the entire problem with the discovery of regularities is the need for theoretical constructs for their understanding. While Hutchison is correct about the emptiness of Robbins' scheme, he offers nothing to put it in its place. Which regularities are non-trivial? On what basis do we judge the social and political effects of policy recommendations? The answers are not apparent, and Hutchison does not enlighten us.

Our argument in the first part of this chapter was that the sort of empirically based science that Hutchison appears to be advocating could not be sustained. We also noted at the beginning of this section how the positivist formulation tends not to *laissez-faire* but rather to economic planning. This appears to be the consequence of the Hutchison methodology, and was the very antithesis of the orthodox programme. Clearly the justification of *laissez-faire* requires that the charges laid by Hutchison be refuted. While Knight's bellicose review of Hutchison's book reasserted the Robbins definition of economics along with Austrian praxeology (Knight 1940 p. 154), the orthodox response was a move towards methodological instrumentalism. This line is taken by Friedman (1953) and Machlup (1955). We shall break slightly with the historical order and begin with the latter work, since it directly responds to Hutchison.

We mentioned the possibility of sliding into instrumentalism earlier during our review of positivism. Instrumentalists abandon the idea of explanation, and are concerned only with prediction. Machlup believes in theories, but these have no particular significance – they are, to use Popper's term, conjectures: 'No fixed lines can be drawn between theories, hypotheses and mere hunches' (Machlup 1955 p. 3). Since all conjectures have equivalent standing, Machlup believes that identifying one as a 'fundamental' postulate is an arbitrary process (ibid. p. 4). This is especially the case since Machlup does not propose to test any of the hypotheses. Rather, we are to draw empirical conclusions from these hypotheses or hunches, and then to 'confront these conclusions' with empirical data. That is, we are to use the principle of correspondence rules (ibid.). We are then to test whether an assumed change leads to the predicted change under certain conditions or not. If so, we can regard the test as a confirmation. However, we only test the occurrence of the assumed change, and the correct conclusions. We need not test for the existence of the conditions: 'Regarding them, a casual, perhaps even impressionistic, empiricism will do' (ibid.). That is, given a theory 'If A, then *ceteris paribus* B', we can test 'If A then B'. If this occurs, we assume *ceteris* were probably *paribus* (ibid. pp. 13–14).

However, Machlup appears to have gone a stage beyond positivism. He is no longer simply translating theoretical terms into observational terms, which is what bridge principles are about. He is missing out a part of the theory, which is whether the conditions under which the theoretical laws apply actually held during the test. The twist in the argument (to use what later became a cliché) is that these conditions are actually held to be irrelevant: indeed, they may even be knowingly unrealistic. 'When a simpler hypothesis, though obviously unrealistic, gives consistently satisfactory results', Machlup contends, 'one need not bother with more complicated, more realistic hypotheses' (ibid., p. 169). That is, the real test of the theory is the generation of 'satisfactory' results, whatever this means. Again, in the 'Rejoinder' Machlup states:

> We can, to repeat, test empirically whether the outcome of people's actions is most of the time reasonably close to what one would expect

if people always acted as they are unrealistically assumed to act. Again, the 'indirect verification' or justification of the postulate lies in the fact that it gives fairly good results in many applications of the theory.

(Machlup 1956 p. 488)

If these results are not forthcoming, presumably any *ad hoc* modifications to the 'hunches' could be made. Machlup views theory as a 'machine' which is 'a construction of our mind', and that 'Something goes in . . . and something comes out' (Machlup 1955 p. 12). The 'mental machine' as it were, can be altered to suit our purpose. Since the theory is only a machine to generate deductions, we would only stop using the machine when a replacement arrived. A theory will only be rejected when a better theory is available (ibid. 1955 p. 11). The position corresponds to that of methodological instrumentalism.

There is, however, one group of fundamental assumptions which according to Machlup cannot be verified (1956, p. 437). These are the 'ideal types' of action and (citing Weber and Schutz) Machlup maintains that these postulates of human action, of which the fundamental assumptions of economic theory are one, 'are not subject to a requirement of independent empirical verification, but instead to a requirement of understandability in the sense in which man can understand the actions of fellowmen' (1955 p. 17).[11] This view Machlup opposes to what he terms 'ultra-empiricism', of which Hutchison is cited as a practitioner. An ultra-empiricist requires the direct testing of all assumptions (ibid. 1955 p. 7). Machlup believes he has shown this is unnecessary and undesirable – or even impossible.

Hutchison's most telling reply is that the only 'fundamental assumption' of any note is that of rationality (1956 p. 479). He also observes that successive generations of economists have attempted to reformulate value theory in testable form. This suggests an unwillingness of economists to accept a priori postulates (ibid. 1956 p. 482).[12] Beyond this the two protagonists appear to be talking past each other, with the debate over 'ultra-empiricism' being largely semantic: for Hutchison this is possibly something like the German Historical school, for Machlup it represents Popperian positivism.

Machlup, then, adopts a sort of 'limited' methodological instrumentalism. Theories are simply mental machines to deduce change, and are really no better than hunches. We should proceed 'as if' they were true (1956 p. 487). However, there is also a fundamental postulate of rationality which is not subject to verification (1955 p. 16).[13] Friedman also believes in methodological qualifications, and uses 'as if' formulations of theories, but appears to go further than Machlup. It will be recalled that Friedman's essay predates Machlup's by two years. Friedman is still concerned to refute both the 'empty economic boxes' charge of Clapham,[14] and the charge of tautology by Hutchison and others. His response is to adopt an extreme version of methodological instrumentalism.

23

Friedman maintains that a theory contains two elements. The first element is that of language, and this Friedman accepts is indeed a set of tautologies. Its function is to serve as a 'filing system' (Friedman 1953 p. 7). Friedman also accepts that 'economic theory must be more than a structure of tautologies if it is to be able to predict and not merely describe the consequences of action; if it is to be something different from disguised mathematics' (ibid. p. 11). The second element of theory is therefore 'a body of substantive hypothesis', the validity of which is judged by its predictive power (ibid. p. 8). For Friedman, this exhausts the possibilities. The only relevant empirical test is that of the implications of the theory. Hypotheses do not, Friedman suggests, have assumptions as such (ibid. p. 14) – the so-called assumptions may indeed be widely inaccurate and yet form the basis of useful substantive hypotheses (ibid. p. 20).[15] The only relevant point is 'whether the theory works', which for Friedman 'means whether it yields sufficiently accurate predictions' (ibid. p. 15). This completes the task of economics, which is 'to provide a system of generalizations that can be used to make correct predictions about the consequences of any change in circumstances' (ibid. p. 4).

This appears straightforward. Nonetheless, Friedman attempts to justify his position. The reason for the lack of relationship between the realism of 'assumptions' and the significance of the hypothesis, he explains, is that an hypothesis abstracts 'the common and crucial elements' of phenomena, and is therefore 'descriptively false' in its assumptions (ibid. p. 14). We therefore are to proceed 'as if' the hypothesis were true (ibid. p. 16 ff.).

Should the hypothesis fail to yield true, meaningful predictions, it should presumably be replaced. The construction of hypotheses is, for Friedman, exogenous. This is a creative act which cannot be formalised (ibid. p. 43). He might also add that the derivation of hypotheses is, as for Popper, an irrelevance. If it works it is of use, no matter where the hypotheses came from.

It may well have been Friedman's justification of the instrumentalist position which caused so much confusion in the secondary literature. Viewed in terms of orthodox positivism, the position is untenable. Musgrave points out that Friedman fails to distinguish between three different types of assumption. The main sense in which Friedman is using the term is what Musgrave calls ' negligibility assumptions'. That is to say, a theory ignores some aspects of a group of phenomena because these aspects have little effect on the conclusions. We may act as if they were not there (Musgrave 1981 p. 373). We cannot say from this that the assumptions are unrealistic, though. We are not assuming that these aspects are not existent – which would be, as Friedman put it, 'descriptively false'. We are simply saying that their presence is irrelevant (Musgrave 1981 p. 379–80, cf. Melitz 1965 p. 40).

This difference is significant because of the other forms of assumptions which can be made. We may also assume a domain for the applicability of a theory. The realism of domain assumptions is significant, because it specifies when the theory will 'work', and when it will not (Musgrave 1981 p. 381). We will see this clearer later on, when we discuss the difference between testing and prediction. We may particularly note that it is possible to delimit the domain in such a way as to make the theory untestable – which is the opposite effect to that posited by Friedman (Musgrave 1981 p. 382, cf. Nagel 1963 p. 215).[16]

Indeed, we can use a theory whose assumptions are known never to hold. Musgrave calls these 'heuristic assumptions' and they are used in employing a method which Musgrave calls 'a method of successive approximation' (Musgrave 1981 p. 383). Nagel seems to consider 'ideal types' in this set (Nagel 1963 p. 215).[17] Only in this sense could the use of assumptions be regarded as 'descriptively false'. Yet Friedman has stated that the derivation of hypotheses – including presumably heuristic devices – is not a matter of concern for positive science. Both Nagel and Musgrave believe that Friedman commits an error by not distinguishing between these various senses of 'unrealistic' assumptions. It is not particularly legitimate to claim that the truth of assumptions is irrelevant because assumptions abstract from reality. Mason points out that an abstraction is different to a false statement (Mason 1980 p. 242). Friedman's justification for ignoring the assumptions of a theory cannot be sustained.

What is not clear is exactly why this justification was thought necessary in the first place. Nagel believes that

> the essay is marked by an ambiguity that perhaps reflects an unresolved tension in his views on the status of economic theory. Is he defending the legitimacy of unrealistic theoretical assumptions because he thinks theories are at best only useful instruments, valuable for predicting observable events but not to be viewed as genuine statements whose truth or falsity may be significantly investigated? But if this is the way he conceives theories (and much in his argument suggests that it is), the distinction between realistic and unrealistic theoretical assumptions is at best irrelevant, and no defense of theories lacking in realism is needed. Or is he undertaking that defense in order to show that unrealistic theories cannot only be invaluable tools for making predictions but that they may also be reasonably satisfactory explanations of various phenomena ... But if this is his aim (and parts of his discussion are compatible with the supposition that it is), a theory cannot be viewed ... as a 'simple summary' of some vaguely delimited set of empirical generalisations with distinctly specified ranges of application.
>
> (Nagel 1963 p. 218, cf. McLachlan and Swales 1982 p. 22)

If we forgo the possibility of offering explanation for economic phenomena, and focus solely on prediction, then Friedman's stance can be recovered (Coddington 1972 p. 4). This is the argument of Boland (1979). He suggests that Friedman's position is indeed one of instrumentalism. Furthermore, he claims that instrumentalism cannot be logically assailed, it 'is its own defense and its only defense' (Boland 1979 p. 522), a position accepted by Rotwein (1980 p. 1553). Rotwein does not accept that Friedman does indeed take an instrumentalist stance, however. He points out Friedman's concern with science, whereas we could classify the instrumentalist position as a sort of 'engineering' approach. Hirsch and DeMarchi also believe that Boland's categorisation

> certainly carries it too far. He ... makes it appear as if science is no concern whatsoever to Friedman. This is not true. It seems rather that Friedman passionately wanted to contribute to economic science, because he felt, as Dewey did, that to be useful, economics had to be scientific.
>
> (Hirsch and DeMarchi 1984 p. 783 fn. 6)

In addition, Hammond points out that in the other methodological essays in the *Essays*, the realism of theories is regarded as an important question (Hammond 1990 p. 204).

It is clear that Friedman did not want to go completely down the instrumentalist path. This creates the tension and ambiguity that Nagel perceived. After all, he did title his essay 'The Methodology of *Positive* Economics', in a volume called '*Essays in* Positive *Economics*'. This suggests an unwillingness to accept the conventionalist elements implied within instrumentalism: what Caldwell terms a 'methodological instrumentalism'. This position is ostensibly taken to avoid the problem of theoretical entities. However, it does not solve the problem of theory-laden observation. Friedman seems to regard empirical data as unproblematic, whereas we have seen that the opposite is the case (cf. Coddington 1972 p. 9).

In addition the inductive problem is not avoided; a problem which the pragmatist philosophy of John Dewey did attack. Hoover notes an ambiguity in this respect. He cites Boland's argument that 'For Friedman, an instrumentalist, hypotheses are chosen because they *are successful* in yielding true predictions' (Boland 1979 p. 511, emphasis in Hoover 1984). Indeed, Friedman himself states that 'the only relevant test ... of a hypothesis is comparison of its predictions with experience' (Friedman 1953 p. 8). This implies that a preconceived theory is confirmed only because it *has* been successful (Hoover 1984 p. 790). But Friedman also states that 'the goal of a positive science' is to predict phenomena 'not yet observed' (Friedman 1953 p. 7), that is, predictions that *will* be successful (Hoover 1984 p. 790). We cannot attempt both to predict the future and test the accuracy of the prediction at the same time (McLachlan and Swales 1982 p. 21). The Humean problem of induction was precisely the inability to extrapolate past regularities into the future. The past predictive success of a theory does not guarantee future success.

Yet this successful prediction of the future is clearly what Friedman had in mind, since normative questions and policy conclusions are dependent upon positive economics (Friedman 1953 p. 5). One notes in this respect the difference in the use of theories between Friedman and Machlup. Machlup appears to adopt a 'two-stage' technique of testing followed by application. 'Once we have confidence in the whole theoretical system' then, he states

> we are willing to apply it to concrete cases even where only one of the two 'changes', in the 'cause' or the 'effect', is identifiable in practice, rather than both.

This is not the case while we are testing, however

> For purposes of verification of the entire theory, however, we shall have to identify both the phenomena represented by the Assumed Change and the Deduced Change.
>
> (Machlup 1955 p. 14)

Machlup here seems to have somewhat abandoned science in favour of an 'engineering'-type approach. He is not, it would seem, concerned with universal conditionals and so on, but simply with finding tools that will probably work in the future. Boland and Frazer suggests that methodological instrumentalism is therefore applicable for short-run or most practical problems (Boland 1980 pp. 1555 ff.). Yet it is unclear exactly which 'practical problems' we are supposed to solve: we do not have much in the way of examples to follow. The snag with an engineering-type approach is that while it may be able to deal well with 'negligibility' assumptions, it is particularly susceptible to domain problems. Recall that the Robbins 'rational economic man' was only an 'expository device' – an heuristic assumption. We noted that Robbins actually denied the legitimacy of policy applications. Of course, it was Robbins' rationality postulate (which Hutchison calls 'The Assumption') which Machlup in particular was at such pains to defend. To use an assumption in an inapplicable domain will, of course, lead to false predictions. And to use an ideal type – an assumption which has no applicable domain – as a negligibility assumption is an invitation to theorists to get up to all sorts of chicanery. The Friedman methodology leads to mythology (Mason 1980 p. 242).

Indeed, it will be recalled that the main methodological dilemma for the orthodox economists was to derive a positive science – which would inevitably lead to the development of policy instruments – and at the same time show that these tools should not be used for planning. Machlup and (especially) Friedman's methodology appears to lead directly to this planning conclusion. The Robbins rationality assumption was designed to avoid the conclusion that planning is desirable, and to justify *laissez-faire* . In spite of their professed indifference to theories, Friedman and Machlup are actually closely tied to the rationality postulate and the models derived from it as a means of escape from the legitimacy of planning. This is what occurs in Friedman's essay, according to Mason:

> The Chicago assumption of 'perfect competition' has the advantage of permitting rigorous – though unrealistic – analysis
>
> (Mason 1980 p. 242)

and has the effect of

> introducing ideological bias through the back door and avoiding the moral problems of unequal economic power.
>
> (Jones 1977 p. 358, cited in Mason ibid.)

The use of rationality therefore breaks the conditions of objectivity:

> in short, the scope of positive economics is drawn so as to be a normative defense of neo-classical analysis, and the concept of a testable theory is confused with the untestable agglomeration of neoclassical doctrine.
>
> (Mason 1980, p. 242)

Actually, if 'The Assumption' of rationality is dropped, one could be forgiven for wondering what is left. As we mentioned in section one, the point about causal knowledge is precisely that it helps us to increase the accuracy of our predictions beyond that of mere guesswork, and indeed in the same year that Friedman's essay was published, Schoeffler's influential book *The Failures of Economics* pointed out that, in fact, economists were not actually very good at predicting. Similar conclusions had been drawn by Mitchell earlier.[18]

Certainly all was not well, yet it is unclear which way orthodox economics could now turn. The use of correspondence rules to transform theoretical terms appears to have serious failings, and the conventionalist consequences of instrumentalism were unacceptable, yet a purely methodological instrumentalism was not valid. Nor did a retreat into a pragmatic 'engineering' methodology help. Samuelson's answer was to turn to empiricism.

This debate began with Samuelson's critique of Friedman. Samuelson maintains an essentially positivist critique.[19] The net result is similar to Hutchison's position, that Friedman 'is fundamentally wrong in thinking that no realism in the sense of factual inaccuracy even to a tolerable degree of approximation is anything but a demerit for a theory or hypothesis' (Samuelson 1963 p. 233).

Machlup responded to Samuelson in much the same way as he responded to Hutchison, claiming that Samuelson 'rejects *all theory* '(Machlup 1964 p. 733 original emphasis). For Machlup the point is

> we never deduce a consequence from a theory alone. We always combine the postulated relationships (which constitute the theory) with an assumption of some change or event and then we deduce the

consequence of the *conjunction* of the theoretical relationships and the assumed occurrence.

(ibid. p. 733; emphasis in original)

Samuelson does not wish to accept the 'rational choice' theory of Robbins, since his own 'revealed preference' approach did not rely on a priori axioms.[20] However, rather than following Hutchison, Samuelson decides to adopt an extreme empiricist approach.

Scientists never 'explain' any behaviour, by theory or by any other hook. Every description that is superseded by a 'deeper explanation' turns out upon careful examination to have been replaced by still another description, albeit possibly a more useful description that covers and illuminates a wider area.

(Samuelson 1964 p. 737)

That is to say that 'An explanation . . . is a better kind of description, and not something that goes ultimately beyond description' (Samuelson 1965 p. 1165).

Caldwell views this position as an error (Caldwell 1982 p. 194), and certainly an anachronistic empiricist position cannot be sustained. Theories cannot, as Samuelson claims, be reduced to 'basic sentences'.[21] Observational terms are not neutral but are theory-laden (Wong 1973).

In addition, the whole justification for positive social science was that it could deliver policy prescriptions. Clearly, a science based on Samuelson's metatheory would not be able to do this. In fact, such a science of description would be pointless.

The philosophy of economics has therefore run aground on the same rocks as the positivist philosophy it tried to take on board. The idea of a methodological unity of the sciences runs into the immediate problem that much social science is motivational, and will therefore require teleological explanation. This teleological explanation cannot be squared with the requirement of observation and the need for causal explanation to justify the positivist position, leading either to analytic theory which cannot be observed, or to a sort of 'methodological' instrumentalism which is unsustainable – particularly if *laissez-faire* is to be maintained.

SOCIAL THEORY OF POSITIVISM

In fact, the need for a justification of the positivist metatheory is something of an Achilles' heel for the philosophy, for it leads to a weakness in the concept of value-neutrality, which was the cornerstone of the entire programme. Towards the end of the previous section we looked at methodological instrumentalism. This position could be arrived at through an extension of the Popperian critique. Karl Popper's philosophy, based on the refutation of theories, was born out of a dissatisfaction with the philosophy of logical positivism, in particular with the responses to the Humean problem of induction. Popper believes that theories do not obtain meaning 'in themselves', but obtain meaning *a posteriori* through the failure to refute them. This means that the way theories are constructed is immaterial – they could indeed, be conjectures. Popper believed the method of construction of a theory 'is irrelevant to the logical analysis of scientific method' (Popper 1934 p. 31). Unlike Friedman, however, Popper did not regard theories as an irrelevance, but thought them a vital part of scientific explanation.[22] It was only the method of construction he was unconcerned with. Popper was explicitly critical of instrumentalism, as he believed that 'ordinary language is full of theories' and that 'observation is always *observation in the light of theories* '(Popper 1934 p. 59 n. 1 original emphasis).

In spite of Friedman's invocation of falsification (Friedman 1953 p. 23) the positions of Friedman and Popper are therefore different.[23] Popper does not maintain that theories are irrelevant, but only that the method by which the scientist arrives at the theory is irrelevant. Theories themselves are of great importance to science. The reason for Popper's emphasis on theory is fundamental, and rests on the normative attitude to knowledge we mentioned at the start of the chapter. Popper believed that the positivist philosophy should not be regarded as a criterion of meaning but as a criterion of demarcation between science and non-science. As we noted earlier, the positivist prescription cannot itself be positive.

> Positivists usually interpret the problem of demarcation is a *naturalistic* way; they interpret it as if it were a problem of natural science. Instead of taking it as their task to propose a suitable convention, they believe they have to discover a difference, existing in the nature of things, as it were, between empirical science on the one hand and metaphysics on the other.
>
> (Popper 1934 p. 35; emphasis in original)

Popper's metatheory was explicitly conventionalist:

> My criterion of demarcation will accordingly have to be regarded as a *proposal for an agreement or convention.* As to the suitability of any such convention opinions may differ; and a reasonable discussion of these questions is only possible between parties having some purpose in common. The choice of that purpose must, of course, be ultimately a matter of decision, going beyond rational argument.
>
> (Popper 1934 p. 37; emphasis in original)

This conventionalist aspect of Popper's position is often overlooked, but the conventionalist attitude to metatheory cannot be avoided by the philosophers of economics either. As McLachlan and Swales point out, all the methodological prescriptions of the economists are themselves normative. It is therefore apparent that we require a normative discussion on metatheory before any science can take place. Yet, once we allow this, it is no longer clear why this normative discussion should not form a part of the substantive theories.

> Suppose that we were to accept that normative statements cannot be rationally discussed. How should we consider a claim such as that positive economics should be judged by its predictive success or that economists should make positive statements, or that if, as economists, we do not try to test our theories empirically, 'we should cease right now giving policy advice' (Lipsey 1975 p. xx)? We would have to say that these claims cannot be rationally discussed and are rationally no better or no worse than the claims that positive economics should not be judged by its predictive success, and that economists should not make positive statements, and that whether or not we try to test our theories, we should not cease giving policy advice. To be consistent, we would have to say that any pronouncements we made about the methodology of economics were either descriptions of how economists do or might actually proceed or else not intended to be considered as rational claims at all but simply as expressions of personal whim. If this is the case, much methodological discussion seems to us to be pointless, and any, even implicit, methodological prescription not prefaced by a clear statement that such prescriptions cannot be rationally defended is misleading.
>
> (McLachlan and Swales 1978 pp. 15–16)

Yet it would seem strange to suggest that no dialogue on methodology is possible

> We can see no reason a priori for discounting the possibility that normative statements can be rationally discussed in the sense that reasons for and against their acceptance can be offered.
>
> (ibid. p. 16)

But this suggests that we should attempt to incorporate analysis of the normative into our theory. 'If normative statements can be rationally discussed, the failure to develop a normative economics is regrettable' (ibid. pp. 17–18).

Our claim here is that a normative metatheoretical position must contain an implicit normative theoretical position. If, in the case of positivism, we are to consider a convention for the demarcation of science, the convention adopted will be justified according to a normative evaluation of the 'science' it would yield. We would adopt the positivist criteria for science only if we value the contents of the science which would result. That is to say, the discussion is no longer what is 'correct' or 'incorrect' science, but what is useful science.

The problem for a positivist formulation is, of course, that it claims to be value-free. We have already seen how the normative justification of control of the social environment created insuperable problems for the observational and limited explanation aspects of positivism. Our criticism here is that, in addition, the need for a normative metatheory must result in a positive science contradicting its own criterion of value-neutrality, and that 'with regard to social science, there is ... an implied political theory as an element in its account of what it means to understand social life' (Fay 1975 p. 15).

The political theory of positivism Fay calls the concept of 'policy science', which consists of a 'set of procedures which enable one to determine the technically best course of action to adopt in order to implement a decision or achieve a goal'. However, the policy scientist is more than an adviser.

> Here the policy scientist doesn't merely *clarify* the possible outcomes of certain courses of action, he actually *chooses* the most efficient course of action in terms of the available scientific information. In this regard, the policy scientist really is a type of social engineer who makes instrumental decisions on the basis of the various laws of science – in this instance, social science – which are relevant to the problem at hand.
>
> (Fay 1975 p. 14; emphasis in original)

This view of policy science obviously has considerable implications for political practice, for to the extent that policy can be analysed impersonally and objectively without subjective argument, political debate would be removed from these areas. Furthermore, Fay argues, participation in the political process would be limited to those with requisite technical competence, and also the accountability of the policy-scientist is internal to the peer group.

Fay also outlines the inevitable direction that politics would take. The employment of the policy scientists would create a movement towards centralised government concerned with the planning of the social and the political (Fay 1975 pp. 26–7).[24] The sum total of these changes is, for Fay, 'the sublimation of politics ... an attempt to eliminate politics as we know it' (ibid. p. 27). It would be replaced by a 'social engineering view of politics, which is that there is a *correct* way of proceeding in human affairs and that it is the responsibility of the decision-maker to discover what this way is' (ibid. p. 28; emphasis in original).

This result, Fay maintains, is caused by positive social science because of the combined effect of the presumed value-neutrality and the connection between the concept of explanation and prediction. It will be recalled that the positivist conception of explanation was in terms of regularities, and that this was regarded as the same as a possible prediction. That is, understanding an event consists of knowing what produces or can prevent it, but this is exactly what is required for control. Positive science 'constitutes, [the] world from the viewpoint of how one can gain control over it' (Fay 1975 p. 40). Nothing else apart from control is to be regarded as scientific. It is not so much that scientific knowledge enables social manipulation, but that only this is regarded as scientific. 'Technical control is a defining element in the scientific enterprise itself' (ibid. p. 41). It is not a question of how science is to be applied. Given the form that knowledge takes, there is no other way it can be usefully applied (ibid. p. 39).

This brings us back to the argument that scientific rationality is political. Recall the claim of Habermas that the programme of modern society, namely 'modernity', has involved domination of knowledge of social norms, obtained through cultural sciences using intersubjective communication, by instrumental knowledge obtained by empirical science. Instrumental rationality has encroached upon our 'life-world', so that the political process is negated, and power is *de facto* exercised by a technocracy.

> The dependence of the professional on the politician appears to have reversed itself. The latter becomes the mere agent of a scientific intelligentsia, which, in concrete circumstances, elaborates the objective implications and requirements of available techniques and resources as well as of optimal strategies and rules of control . . . the politician in the technical state is left with nothing but a fictitious decision-making power. The politician would then be at best something like a stopgap in a still imperfect rationalization of power, in which the initiative has in any case passed to scientific analysis and technical planning.
>
> (Habermas 1969 pp. 63–4)

In this sense the method of science, and especially positivistic social science, serves a political end. Politics is 'scientised', and decisions which should be part of a political process are removed from the polity and decided upon by a technocracy or bureaucracy. Social theory is used to legitimate the society (ibid. p. 68). To the extent that positive economics attempts to scientise politics, it also should be viewed as implying a social and political theory. But while the orthodox economics scheme does attempt to exclude the political, it has in addition to justify *laissez-faire*. It was this additional burden that led to the analytic analysis of 'rational economic human'. We shall return to this shortly.

The political theory implied by the positivist analysis could be described as an end-state conception, the only concern is the efficacy of the means at obtaining the independently derived ends. Under this scheme, we make no other judgement as to which means should be used. Myrdal maintains this is an error. He believes that 'In any human valuation' means have independent values as well as instrumental values (Myrdal 1933 p. 49) and that 'means are not ethically neutral'. The alternative courses are compared through value judgements. But this causes the collapse of the whole construction – we now have to hypothesise each stage in the argument, not merely the final stage

33

MURDOCK LEARNING RESOURCE CENTER

(Myrdal 1933 p. 211). The means/end construction was supposed to allow the objective derivation of policy.

> But as soon as we admit that value can be attached to means independently, every single link in the chain of the argument is opened. It follows, first, that the problem can no longer be solved unequivocally even if the end is given.
>
> (Myrdal 1933 p. 212)

In addition, we no longer have any guiding principle for eliminating any possible alternative from consideration. We cannot limit our field of enquiry (Myrdal 1933 p. 212). Generalising becomes complex and difficult (ibid. 1953 p. 50), because 'the value premise which has to be introduced in order to allow policy conclusions from factual analysis has therefore to be a valuation of means as well as ends' (1953 p. 49)

The 'engineering' approach of matching means to ends must therefore be rejected, because the means must themselves be evaluated. That is to say that in place of the Newtonian conception of policy science, we should consider policy in Einsteinian relativist terms as it were. Ends and means are not fixed, but are relative. What we regard as a means is also an end which is to be achieved by a previous means (Fay 1975 p. 51). Similarly the end we are striving for can itself be a means to a further end. This implies that 'any given course of action may be either a means or an end depending upon the point of view which one adopts' (ibid.).

So the various means we have at our disposal will themselves have been arrived at as normative ends. 'And, upon reflection' Fay believes

> this seems an obvious point. For all political decisions, even those which are seen as means to an end, are social policies, and as such they embody a notion of what people ought to be required or permitted to do to others. No social policy's worth can be solely instrumental because any such policy will require that people interact with one another in certain definite ways, and for this reason it must have a moral value *in itself*.

Fay believes this can be easily shown through caricature of purely technical policy recommendations.

> What if it were concluded that the most efficient (i.e. the cheapest fastest, most simple etc.) way to deal with the population problem were simply to exterminate large numbers of some special class of people? The point is that such a proposal could be objected to not simply on the grounds of technical efficiency, but also on the basis on an antipathy to the moral values inherent in it.
>
> (Fay 1975 p. 52; emphasis in original)

Fay concludes that all political proposals – even those of which means to adopt for a given end – are moral in nature (ibid.).

Because we are unable to separate out objective means from subjective ends, we are unable to abstract 'economic human' from 'social human'. Since we cannot limit our field of enquiry, in this respect the act of abstraction is in point of fact, normative (Streeten 1958 p. xx). Our choice of question determines the answers (ibid. p. xxi). Myrdal outlines one method of abstraction which is sometimes proposed by economists. While admitting the subjectivity of valuations, the problem is split in two. One part is political, and is taken as exogenous, the other is economic, and is endogenous and value-free. 'The division usually runs along the old classical line drawn between income distribution and production. They say, for example, that they disregard the effects on income distribution, or that they presume a just distribution, etc.' He adds that 'such a separation of a political problem into a political and a purely economic section is, however, impossible' (Myrdal 1933 p. 218). In particular, we shall see that the distributional criteria cannot simply be 'imported' into the theory as an exogenous variable, because the price theories themselves have distributional implications. This means that at best the theory can only be static, since the distributional pattern can change with each time period. In addition, we will see that the development of a value theory as opposed to simply a price theory will necessarily involve dealing with distributional issues.

The neoclassical scheme was different from the classics though, in that it required a method of deriving social value. Its value theory could not be identified with a price theory: their congruence had to be shown. And because under positivism the abstraction of *homo oeconomicus* was non-arbitrary, the separation of distribution from value could not be achieved. These questions will be considered in the next chapter, where we look at the attempt to put the positivist philosophy into operation: the chapter will focus on the orthodox *laissez-faire* economic theories. However, as we saw, the positivist philosophy actually tends towards a process of economic planning. Chapter 3 will outline the market socialist approach to positivist economic planning, and will show that the positivist approach to social science cannot be maintained.

In summary form the argument being put forward is as follows. In order for positive economists to justify *laissez-faire*, they have to substantiate three arguments:

- That economic data are only available at the individual level;
- That these data are capable of aggregation;
- That only then can the best aggregate outcome be realised.

Orthodox, positive economists attempt to establish all three propositions but, as we shall see in the next chapter, are unable to do so. In Chapter 3 we will consider the debate in the 1930s between the market socialists, who believed that the latter two propositions could be sustained and who denied the first proposition; and the Austrian economists, who attempted to show that propositions one and three could be sustained and disagreed with proposition two. The Austrians also disagreed with the idea of positive science however.

If the positivist means/end scheme is abandoned, then both the conception of 'rational economic human' and the abstraction of economic from social and political action must also be abandoned. Chapter 4 will look at the American institutionalist critique of orthodox economics, and their attempts to include psychological and social elements in their economic theories. Chapter 5 will consider the response of the new institutionalists who attempt to square this critique with *laissez-faire* .

To explain the contents of Chapter 6 it will be necessary to return briefly to our analysis of positivism. If the political theory implied by the positivist analysis is an end-state conception of politics, the alternative could be described as a process conception of politics. We should concern ourselves not solely with the end product of the decision-making process, but with the organisation of the process itself. Since we reject the idea of policy being decided by the policy-scientist, we must hold a conception of a participatory process, and given that we cannot separate out the various elements of human action, we must also consider a theory of political as well as economic human:

> according to this theory 'politics' refers to men's deliberate efforts to order, direct, and control their collective affairs and activities, to establish ends for their society, and to implement and evaluate these ends. From this perspective, what is fundamental about politics is the interaction and participation of men according to mutually defined and accepted rules as they engage in this process of creating and administering the laws of their community, which is to say that what is most significant is the involvement of the citizens in the process of determining their own collective identity.
>
> (Fay 1975 p. 54)

It is this process of determining a collective identity that will be the subject of Chapter 6.

Our task then is to show that a positivist conception of economic science cannot deliver on its promise of value-free control over the environment. We will begin this task by showing how the orthodox economists from the nineteenth century to the present day were unable to put the philosophy into practice.

2

FROM UTILITY TO WELFARE
The trajectory of orthodox economics

We saw in the previous chapter that the Achilles heel of the positivist approach to social science was the need for a justification for the metatheory. The only cogent justification lay in the claim that positive science leads to an ability to understand and thereby control our social environment. This, though, necessarily involved a causal explanation of the social world, and explanations solely in terms of observable regularities were insufficient for this. Causal explanations invariably involved recourse to theories.

Positive economics faced extra difficulties, particularly in justifying *laissez-faire*. The idea of a positive economics would seem to lead to some notion of economic planning. *Laissez-faire* therefore has to be justified by showing both why social planning cannot succeed and how individuals acting in ignorance of an unknown social optimum nevertheless can collectively obtain the best social outcome.

This left the positivists two tasks in order to justify *laissez-faire*. The first task is to explain activity in terms of individual actions. They then had to show how the aggregate of these actions not only arrived at but actually revealed the optimum social outcome. That is to say, the theory must be based on individuals, must be capable of aggregating the individual actions, and must show that only then can the best social outcome be found. What we will see in this chapter is that it is impossible for the positivists to keep all three skittles in the air at once.

In order to put the positivist philosophy into operation the economic theory would require three elements. It would require a psychology from which causal explanation can be derived in order to explain why actions occurred. To aggregate these actions a second element – the theory of price – is needed. But to show that this aggregate is optimal a third element – a value theory – is also required, and it is this last that causes the tension in what is supposed to be a value-free positive science, because in order to support *laissez-faire* the values must be subjective, whereas positivism stresses objectivity.[1]

This chapter will trace the trajectory of orthodox economics as it tries out different ways of dealing with the dilemma of attempting to obtain objective results from subjective analysis. Our focus will be on value theory, which we can now identify as being the foundation of economic theory. It is value theory that enables the creation of a policy science. First we will look at the utilitarian marginalists, who claimed to be able to reconcile value and price through their knowledge of 'ultimate causes'. We will see that the hedonist psychology which this involved cannot be sustained, and the philosophy cannot be put into operation. The utilitarian philosophy gave way to a more orthodox conception of positivism, and in economics the marginalist school was succeeded by the neo-classics. The neo-classics used an objective value theory, but could not then defend *laissez-faire*, at least not without incorporating unsubstantiated psychological assumptions. The later ordinalist theories attempted to dispense with psychology, but in so doing had also to dispense with value theory, which meant that they could not show how the best social outcome can be arrived at. But without this ability to arrive at policy conclusions the positive approach seems pointless, and we shall see that orthodox economics arrives at an essentially vacuous theory.

UTILITARIANISM

Bentham

One method of deriving an objective social science from a subjective theory is to moot a theoretical approach based on human psychology. This then makes it seem possible to draw policy recommendations from 'evidence' because the ultimate facts of behaviour are (claimed to be) known. This is the approach of Benthamist utilitarianism, which Hollis and Nell refer to as 'the triumph of positivism' (Hollis and Nell 1975 p. 48). The avowed aim of the utilitarian philosophy of the eighteenth and nineteenth centuries was precisely to extend the principles of rational calculation to all aspects of human activity. Morality could be calculated in the same manner as the quantities of physical sciences. Utility was a guide both to what is and what ought to be. According to Bentham

> Nature has placed mankind under the governance of two sovereign masters, *pain* and *pleasure*. It is for them alone to point out what we ought to do, as well as what we shall do. On the one hand the standard of right and wrong, on the other the chain of causes and effects are fastened to their throne.
>
> (Bentham 1789 p. 11; emphasis in original)

There is therefore no distinction between ethical and technical considerations. Left alone, what we want to do is what we will do, and this is indeed what we ought to do. Ethics are therefore objective.

The consistency of the utilitarian moral philosophy will not be discussed here. Our interest is in the operationalisation of utilitarianism – the transition from social theory to social science. The ability to operationalise the philosophy is of vital importance to utilitarianism because of the claim for objective morality and measurement. Unless the philosophy can be put into operation, it will not be able to 'point out what we ought to do'. To show that morality is objective, it is important to show how it can be discovered. The technical cannot be separated from the ethical.

Following on from our analysis of positivism in the previous chapter, we can see that the key element in what we could term the utilitarian methodology is the perceived demarcation between that which is scientific and the non-scientific. We saw that J.S. Mill distinguished means from ends, and that this distinction was used later by Robbins as a defining feature of economic science. Mill's usage differed from that of Robbins, though. For the utilitarians there was no distinction between the scientific and the non-scientific. 'The quintessence of utilitarian moral philosophy, which at that time constituted the basis of economic thought', Myrdal maintains, 'was the conviction that the will both can and should be rational even with respect to the end towards which it is directed' (Myrdal 1953 p. 8).

The question for the utilitarians was not how human values could be examined scientifically, since all values were scientific. Because of the identification of science and morality, the problem appeared to be technical: how to arrive at a social 'maximum' of morality. Bentham's desire was to become 'the Newton of the Moral World', and he hoped to develop a method for calculating morals, a 'felicific calculus' (Mitchell 1918 p. 170). However, the problem is not straightforward. The calculation of a social maximum of utility would require the summation of the net utility of each individual (ibid. p. 171). This implies a universal cardinal measure of utility. It is far from clear how such a measurement could be derived. Even though Bentham did not appear to view the principle of measurement as problematic, in practice he could only measure on a nominal scale (ibid. p. 173).

Bentham actually began to move towards the notion of pecuniary measurement of utility and towards the concept of indifference analysis to find his way out of this difficulty:

> If of two pleasures a man, knowing what they are, would as lief enjoy the one as the other, they must be reputed equal ... If of two pains a man had as lief escape the one as the other, such two pains must be reputed equal. If of two sensations, a pain and a pleasure, a man had lief enjoy the pleasure and suffer the pain, as not enjoy the first and not suffer the pain must be reputed *equal*, or, as we may say in this case, *equivalent*

This equality then suggests the use of pecuniary measure:

> If then between two pleasures the one produced by the possession of money, the other not, a man had as lief enjoy the one as the other, such

pleasures are to be reputed equal. But the pleasure produced by the possession of money, is *as* the quantity of money that produces it: money is therefore the measure of this pleasure . . .

 If then, speaking of the respective quantities of various pains and pleasures . . . we would understand one another, we must make use of some common measure. The only common measure the nature of things affords is money . . . Money is the instrument for measuring the quantity of pain or pleasure. Those who are not satisfied with the accuracy of this instrument must find out some other that shall be more accurate or bid adieu to Politics and Morals.

(Bentham, in Halévy 1901 pp. 410–14 cited Mitchell 1918; emphasis in Mitchell)

It can be seen how in attempting to derive a method of measurement for utility Bentham began to move away from his original idea of the calculation of morality, for by utilising money as a measurement we immediately begin to place a boundary around those human activities which are to be deemed capable of 'scientific' examination. But the whole point of utilitarianism was precisely to get round this problem of demarcation. In the utilitarian political economy there was no real sense in which one could separate non-economic ends from economic means: both were governed by utility:

 In other words, the distinction was not one of principle. It was dictated entirely by expediency. That this was the sole motivation was, indeed, sometimes explicitly stated.

 It was thus regarded as both natural and desirable that political economists should venture beyond the frontier line.

(Myrdal 1953 p. 8)

Indeed, the later classics had little option but to deal with utilitarianism in this way, because they simply did not have the tools to deal with money measurements of utility. Myrdal believed that 'the hedonistic trimmings of classical theory show merely a desire to conform to the utilitarian philosophy' (Myrdal 1953 p. 80). The actual analysis of the later classics remained much as before. 'Not until later did utilitarianism exert its full influence upon economic theory' (ibid.).

Jevons

What the classics lacked in their attempt to obtain money measures of utility was the mathematical tools of the differential calculus. It was only with the work of the marginalists in the late nineteenth century that the method of 'measuring' utility was fully developed. Jevons' *Theory of Political Economy* was an explicit attempt to create the felicific calculus of Bentham (Jevons 1871 p. xxvi).

The marginalists linked price[2] with utility by distinguishing between the total utility of the entire quantity of a commodity consumed and the 'final degree' of utility: roughly speaking the increment in total utility caused by consumption of the last unit.[3] But in order to provide the connection with price a further concept was needed: the notion of diminishing marginal utility. This is, as Daly and Cobb put it, 'the commonsense idea that sensible people satisfy their most pressing wants first, so that each additional unit of income added is used to satisfy a less pressing want' (Daly and Cobb 1990 p. 48). That is to say that the additional 'want' – in technical jargon the marginal utility – for each commodity diminishes as more of it is consumed.

This concept enabled the link between utility and price to be made. Given diminishing marginal utility, an individual would maximise utility by switching expenditure until the utility gained from the last unit of each commodity purchased is equal. If the marginal utilities are unequal, so that the marginal utility of one commodity is higher than that of another, such that for example the marginal utility of bread is higher than that of brandy, the consumer would obtain more utility by consuming bread rather than brandy. Of course bread, as with all commodities, is subject to diminishing marginal utility, so the increased bread consumption would lower the marginal utility of bread. There will therefore be one consumption pattern where all marginal utilities are equal, and this is how aggregate utility will be maximised. Note that when this occurs there will be no incentive to change the consumption pattern; the position is said to be in equilibrium, and there is no incentive to move from it.

This treatment of the marginalists made it appear possible to find a social optimum. However, the new approach to utilitarianism was more than just an improvement in technique – Jevons' professional pique against Mill was in this respect somewhat misplaced. There had been earlier critiques of the labour theory of value, and several anticipators of the marginal utility technique used by Jevons. It would seem that the reason that the time for this idea came in the late nineteenth century was more as a response to the advent of socialist political economy than any notion of scientific progress (Dasgupta 1985 p. 95). Blaug does point out that Marx's work was probably unknown to Jevons and the other marginalists (Blaug 1962 p. 282), but he also writes that the utility theory itself was not accepted for many years. It could be suggested that the acceptance of marginal utility at the turn of the century – rather than earlier when it was first mooted – was due to the ideological content (Gramm 1988 p. 232). Recall that the utilitarian philosophy was itself a response to the natural law philosophy of Adam Smith. That the utility theory should provide a philosophical challenge to labour value theory should come as no surprise, but the treatment of utility theory itself shows clearly a conservative bias. We will be tracing these developments in due course.

The utilitarian theory of human nature focused theory on individual behaviour. The problem that Bentham was struggling to solve was in essence to derive from this an operational social theory. The significance of marginalism was that it made the calculation of this utilitarian social theory appear possible. The resultant theory enabled the marginalists to arrive at the same *laissez-faire* conclusions as the classics, but without employing any notion of objective value. Utility was subjective – it was located within the individual actor: 'The utility theory of value is primarily an attempt to explain price determination in psychological terms' (Viner 1925 p. 123). However, there is a difference in this approach, reflecting the problems of positive social science. The psychological 'explanation' remains an hypothesis – unlike production, utility cannot be objectively known: 'One does not proceed from a knowledge of relative utility to prices of commodities. The procedure seems to be the other way about; when one knows relative prices, one hypothesizes that they represent the relative marginal utilities of commodities' (Dasgupta 1985 p. 85).

If the methodological impact of utility theory was the movement towards individualism, the theoretical effect was to switch the focus of economics from production to demand (Gramm 1988 p. 232). The problem is how to move from a (subjective) utility to an (objective) market demand. Some of the marginalists (including Jevons) tended to move directly from utility to demand: the former was expressed in money terms, thereby identifying it with the latter (Viner 1925 p. 125). Actually, Jevons never really arrived at a fully fledged price theory. He does equate purchasing power with the ratio of exchange (Jevons 1871 p. 81), but he tends to move directly to this from price without showing how the ratio of exchange has been arrived at. In fact, all Jevons' examples involve barter (cf. Mitchell 1969 pp. 61 ff.). Price theory proper was only developed after Jevons. Furthermore, his treatment of the derivation of maximum aggregate utility is incomplete in other respects also. His analysis has no time factor present at all (Hutchison 1953 p. 44). Also, because Jevons limits his examples to barter, he is necessarily restricted to a two-person, two-commodity analysis, and it is unclear whether this can be generalised. Jevons therefore developed his rather ambiguous concept of the 'Trading Body'. This was defined simply as 'any body either of buyers or sellers' (Jevons 1871 p. 88). Jevons did not distinguish between individual traders and groups of traders: 'The trading body may be a single individual in one case; it may be the whole inhabitants of a continent in another; it may be the individuals of a trade diffused throughout a country in a third.' (ibid. p. 88) The actual size of the trading bodies was not a relevant factor in the theory, since 'the principles of exchange are the same in nature, however wide or narrow may be the market considered'(ibid. p. 89).

Jevons' use of the concept of the Trading Body is significant for the operationalisation of utilitarianism in two respects. Utilitarianism involved the derivation of a social maximum from the maximisation of individual utility. Subsequent analysis demonstrated that this social maximum would not necessarily occur when just two traders were involved; to ensure this maximum there is a minimum requirement of a large number of traders, notwithstanding the other requisites of perfect competition. Game Theory analysis was later to show that the maximum aggregate utility is often not arrived at in bilateral negotiation.[4] Jevons mentioned some of the conditions of competition in his 'law of indifference' (which gives a simplistic explanation of why a single price accrues for each commodity in a market), but dismisses these as 'extraneous circumstances', and also applies them to his two-trader models, where they are not sufficient.

In addition, the concept of the Trading Body tends to beg the entire question of aggregation. Jevons admits that explanations based on an aggregate Trading Body must be derived from individuals (Jevons 1871 p. 89). He also admits that the differential calculus is difficult to apply to individual behaviour, since the functions are not continuous (ibid. p. 15). The calculus is only applicable to averages of large groups: these show continuous functions, and the effect of small price changes is negligible (ibid.). Jevons terms this average the 'Fictitious Mean': the average does not correspond to any individual. Yet Jevons does not show us how this aggregate function is derived. Again, he switches from utility to demand in a rather disconcerting fashion. If we are only concerned with demand functions then the use of an aggregate function may have some legitimacy, but Jevons was concerned with utilities. In order to be able to derive an aggregate utility function, we have to assume that utility is comparable between people. Yet this Jevons denied (Myrdal 1953 p. 101, cf. Stigler 1950 p. 72). He states that

> The reader will find, again, that there is never, in any single instance, an attempt made to compare the amount of feeling in one mind with that in another. I see no means by which such comparison can be accomplished ... Every mind is thus inscrutable to every other mind, and no common denominator of feeling seems to be possible.
>
> (Jevons 1871 p. 14)

This problem actually has its roots in the positivist/policy dilemma we have already encountered. The dilemma is that the admission of interpersonal comparisons leads straight back to the sort of egalitarian conclusions that the labour theory of value led to. The problem is that the concept of diminishing marginal utility could also be applied to money, income or wealth. This would suggest that maximum aggregate utility would be achieved when these were equal, which implies a redistribution of wealth along egalitarian lines.

This points to egalitarian principles, justifies trade unions, progressive taxation, and the welfare state, if not more radical means to interfere with an economic system that allows so much of the good juice of *utility* to evaporate out of commodities by distributing them unequally.

But on the other hand the whole point of *utility* was to justify *laisser faire*.

(Robinson 1962 p. 53; emphasis in original)

Again, the dilemma of price and value emerges. If Jevons is to arrive at a theory of price based on the hedonist psychology, and move from utility to demand, he has to accept the interpersonal comparison of utility. This interpersonal comparison would, of course, result in an egalitarian value theory.

By denying that utility can be compared between different people, Jevons appears to have avoided this conclusion, but at a cost. As Myrdal points out: 'the concepts of utility and disutility which the marginalists took over from the utilitarians were intended for interpersonal comparisons' (Myrdal 1953 p. 90). The abandonment of interpersonal comparisons necessarily involves abandoning 'utilitarian comparisons and the social calculus. At this point economic theory parts company with utilitarian philosophy. It aims at a positive psychological analysis, and does not as such intend to be a rationalistic political metaphysics' (ibid. p. 87). The price of denying interpersonal comparisons is the failure to operationalise utilitarianism. We can no longer equate 'what we shall do' with 'what we ought to do', because we cannot compare the results of our actions between people. The social optimum becomes indeterminate.

In fact the question of distribution shows up well the limits that Jevons put upon his exposition of Bentham's theory. If we are not to have interpersonal comparisons of utility, along with the consequent egalitarian distribution, we may ask what distribution theory Jevons has to offer in its place. Here we find the limitation of the theory. Jevons' calculus was only really concerned with commodities and exchange (see Mitchell 1967 p. 43). Bentham was concerned with the entire range of human activities, especially with penal legislation and the legal system (Warnock 1962 p. 12). Of course, as we saw, the whole problem with the Bentham scheme was the measurement of utility. Jevons appears to have somewhat abandoned this general ethical calculus, and limits his analysis to market exchange. He evokes the notion of a hierarchy of pleasures to separate the higher (moral) pleasures from the lower (economic) feelings, and suggested that 'It is the lowest rank of feelings which we here treat. The calculus of utility aims at supplying the ordinary wants of man at the least cost of labour' (Jevons 1871 p. 27). Yet Jevons appears to believe in the moral calculus, and seemed to believe that distribution was a part of it:

Each labourer, in the absence of other motives, is supposed to devote his energy to the accumulation of wealth. A higher calculus of moral right and wrong would be needed to show how he may best employ that wealth for the good of others as well as himself. But when that higher calculus gives no prohibition, we need the lower calculus to gain us the utmost good in matters of moral indifference.

(Jevons 1871 p. 27)

Basically Jevons is passing the buck. He is simply asserting that somehow distribution and ethics can be calculated, but that this is not his concern.

Given that no indication is provided as to how a 'higher calculus' of morals is to work, we are left with something of a vacuum. The whole point of utilitarianism was that all human activity was determinate. Jevons is now saying that only part of this activity is determinate, and also that this part cannot be measured interpersonally while the rest can (since if we cannot make interpersonal comparisons of utility even in the moral calculus it is hard to see how any utilitarian policy conclusions can be arrived at at all). Jevons needs to maintain two different notions of utility: the ethical one which is comparable between people, and the political economy/exchange utility which is not. Jevons makes no attempt to distinguish between these: we have no boundary line between the one and the other. We are asked to distinguish between 'political economy' and 'ethical' aspects of behaviour without being given any distinguishing feature.

Without any distinction between the political economy and ethics, it would seem to be impossible to derive any policy prescriptions along Jevonian lines. In fact, Jevons himself originally expressed doubts as to the usefulness of his theory (Jevons 1871 p. 25), but in later editions of the *Theory of Political Economy* he expunged these passages. But separated from its utilitarian roots the theory had very little to offer in the way of practical advice, and a return to the utilitarian philosophy involved accepting interpersonal comparisons, along with the distributional consequences. This was the path chosen by Edgeworth.

Edgeworth

Edgeworth was in some ways far more utilitarian than even Jevons (Mitchell 1969 p. 95). His book *New and Old Methods of Ethics* was part of his attempt to derive a clear mathematical conception of exact utilitarianism (Hutchison 1953 p. 109). He believed that this was implied in the greatest happiness principle (ibid.), and he thought that the 'Economical Calculus' as he termed it, was an extension of this. His 1881 essay *Mathematical Psychics* was subtitled 'An Essay on the Application of Mathematics to the Moral Sciences', and was an attempt to formulate this economical calculus. The main title of the essay is of significance. Edgeworth believed that hedonism represented an accurate psychological analysis. Furthermore, the methods of both physical science and 'moral science' were identical: 'The central conception of Dynamics' according to Edgeworth 'is other-sidedly identical with the central conception of Ethics', and he believed that

> '*Mechanique sociale*' may one day take her place along with '*mechanique celeste*', throned each upon the double-sided height of one maximum principle, the supreme pinnacle of moral as of physical science.
>
> (Edgeworth 1881 p. 12; emphasis in original)

45

For Edgeworth utility was a measurable, observable fact. It was, to use Samuelson's phrase, 'as real as his morning jam'. Like Jevons, Edgeworth's felicific calculus was divided between the economic and the ethical calculus, but Edgeworth's arrangement was not hierarchical. The ethical calculus was in no sense a 'higher' calculus, as it was for Jevons, but is parallel with economics, and it is through the ethical calculus that Edgeworth derives his social value solution. 'The Economical Calculus' was to explain 'the equilibrium of a system of hedonic forces each tending to maximum individual utility', whereas the utilitarian calculus considered 'the equilibrium of a system in which each and all tend to maximum universal utility' (ibid. p. 15). The question of social value and distribution was therefore part of the moral calculus, but this calculus Edgeworth believed to be fully capable of operationalisation. Putting the moral calculus into operation did, however, require the use of inter-personal comparisons of utility, according to Edgeworth:

> For moral calculations, a further dimension is required; to compare the happiness of one person with the happiness of another, and generally the happiness of groups of different members and different average happiness.
>
> Such comparison can no longer be shirked, if there is to be any systematic morality at all. It is postulated by distributive justice. It is postulated by the population question.
>
> (Edgeworth 1881 p. 18)

Boundary questions were not of the same importance for Edgeworth as for Jevons, since the dual calculus were 'other-sidedly identical'. It will be recalled though, that the need for a moral calculus in Jevons' theory arose out of distributional considerations. We may ask if Edgeworth, who claims to be able to consider the moral question of distribution, accepts the egalitarian conclusion implied by diminishing marginal utility. Edgeworth avoids this conclusion by positing differing 'capacities' for the enjoyment of pleasure: the savage societies, the labouring classes and women may well, according to Edgeworth, have 'inferior capacities' for pleasure (ibid. pp. 77 ff.).

This artificial and arbitrary supposition of Edgeworth shows up well the problems the marginalists had in squaring the radical element of utilitarianism with the conservatism inherited from the natural law philosophy of the early classics. We will see this reconciliation emerge in the works of Marshall, which we will examine shortly, but there were several strands in Edgeworth's works which foreshadowed later developments. One of the problems we observed with the Jevonian treatment was that his examples of bilateral trading were not sufficient to derive a social maximum,[5] and that his device of the trading body involved an inadmissible additive utility function. Edgeworth dealt with the former problem by attempting to specify the requirements for perfect competition.[6] He also moved from an additive utility function to what Stigler terms a 'generalized utility' function (Stigler 1950

p. 77). For Jevons the utility of a commodity was independent of other commodities. For Edgeworth, the utilities were linked (Hutchison 1953 p. 114). It was in this way that he could address the problem of bilateral trading, which he did through the now familiar device of indifference curve analysis[7] (he was attempting to show the indeterminacy of this trade, and derived his well-known contract-curve). As Hutchison remarked, it was ironical that the most utilitarian of the marginalists should have developed the concepts that led to the eventual exclusion of utilitarianism from economic thought.

Edgeworth's formulation was dependent upon the moral calculus being operative: it was formulated directly upon hedonism. Later in his life he began to doubt the hedonist psychology in the light of advances in psychology and other sciences (Mitchell 1969 p. 94). Hedonism was no longer in keeping with the spirit of positivism.

> From the period of the later classics onwards, economic theory has been out of step with the general advance of ideas. Marginal utility theory attempted to give a hedonistic interpretation of value at a time when psychologists were abandoning hedonism in favour of a more realistic analysis.
>
> (Myrdal 1953 p. 81)

The early marginalists accepted utility analysis as a fact of common sense (Jevons 1871 p. 52, Edgeworth 1877 p. 35). They attempted to operationalise utilitarianism by narrowing the focus of political economy from that of the later classics, but were never really able to derive a distributional theory that was separate from an inoperative moral calculus. They also never properly developed a theory of social value, both of which were essential elements of the classicists' theories.

NEO-CLASSICS

Marshall

It was with Marshall that the reconciliation of the classics and the marginal approach was established, and it is Marshall's work that marks the beginning of 'neo-classical' economics proper. This coincided with the fall of utilitarianism as a moral science. It is notable how the most mathematically inclined of the economists (Edgeworth's background was in Law and English) was also the most sceptical of the usefulness of mathematical analysis.

> Though a skilled mathematician, he (Marshall) used mathematics sparingly. He saw that excessive reliance on this instrument might lead us astray in pursuit of intellectual toys, imaginary problems not conforming to the conditions of real life: and, further, might distort our

sense of proportion by causing us to neglect factors that could not easily be worked up in the mathematical machine.

(Pigou 1925, cited Coase 1975 p. 30)

Although he was perfectly able to use mathematical reasoning if and when desired, Marshall was very sensitive to the limits of mathematics. For Marshall, mathematics was simply a useful language; he advised one of his students to

1 use mathematics as a shorthand language, rather than as an engine of enquiry;
2 keep to them till you are done;
3 translate into English;
4 then illustrate by examples that are important in real life;
5 burn the mathematics;
6 If you cannot succeed in (4), burn (3). This last I did often.

(Coase 1975 p. 30)

It was important to Marshall that economics should be reflected in practical examples of everyday living. He was not concerned with developing ethical systems of interest mainly to initiates, although his work did have ethical motivation. For Marshall the idea of measuring ethics, or indeed any social phenomenon, was simply nonsensical. One of his marginal notes in the *Principles* reads 'Even common pleasures and pains can be compared only through the strength of the incentives which they supply to action' (Marshall 1890 [1920] p. 15)[8] – a clear indication of Marshall's break with utilitarianism. Marshall was not concerned with Bentham's 'springs of action', he was concerned with effect not cause. 'It is essential to note', Marshall writes, 'that the economist does not claim to measure any affection of the mind in itself, or directly, but only through its effect' (ibid.). He is also explicit in his rejection of utilitarianism (Marshall 1920 p. 17 n. 1). Typically, the reason for Marshall's rejection of the utilitarian ethic stemmed not so much from abstract methodological considerations as from simple practicalities: utilitarianism did not work. There was no way that Marshall could see of reconciling what is with what ought to be:

Lastly it is sometimes erroneously supposed that normal action in economics is that which is right morally. But that is to be understood only when the context implies that the action is being judged from the ethical point of view. When we are considering the facts of the world, as they are, and not as they ought to be, we shall have to regard as 'normal' to the circumstance in view, much action which we should use our utmost effort to stop.

One of the main problems of utilitarianism for Marshall was the undesirable side-effects of the *laissez-faire* policy latent in the orthodox implementation of utilitarianism. He continues:

> For instance, the normal condition of many of the very poorest inhabitants of a large town is to be devoid of enterprise, and unwilling to avail themselves of the opportunities that may offer for a healthier and less squalid life elsewhere; they have not the strength, physical, mental and moral, required for working their way out of their miserable surroundings. The existence of a considerable supply of labour ready to make match-boxes at a very low rate is normal in the same way that a contortion of the limbs is a normal result of taking strychnine.
>
> (Marshall 1920 p. 35)

The simple description of social events was not the point of Marshall's work. He justified economic science in the manner that we discussed earlier – it was to improve our lot in life. Marshall refused to accept that the squalor of the poor in Victorian Britain could be squared with the notion that *laissez-faire* led to the best possible social outcome. One of his major concerns in the *Principles* and elsewhere was the abject poverty which the Industrial Revolution left in its wake:

> Thus free competition, or rather, freedom of industry and enterprise, was set loose to run, like a huge untrained monster, its wayward course. The abuse of their new power by able but uncultured business men led to evils on every side; it unfitted mothers for their duties, it weighed down children with overwork and disease.

Furthermore the economists were also to blame:

> And yet the time at which free enterprise was showing itself in an unnaturally harsh form, was the very time in which economists were most lavish in their praises of it.
>
> (Marshall 1920 p. 9)

What Marshall seemed to find objectionable was not ethics, but ethics masquerading as science. He also seemed to disregard the idea of a purely descriptive social science. Marshall's aim was to study how to improve the lot of humankind, and this could be best done, he believed, by improving humans themselves. He believed that economic science could show ways in which human nature could be modified for the better (ibid. p. 35). This was part of Marshall's concern for the plight of the poor.[9]

It was for this reason that Marshall was unconcerned with deriving exact theories of transcendental economic 'laws' based on theories of human nature: 'Science may suggest a moral or practical precept to modify that nature and thus modify the action of the laws of nature' (ibid. p. 36). Theory was therefore of little value in itself, but had constantly to show application, indeed Marshall once wrote that 'in economics there is "no theory" to speak of' (Coase 1975 p. 28). Later he wrote to Edgeworth

> In my view 'Theory' is essential. No one gets any real grip of economic problems unless he will work on it. But I conceive no more calamitous notion than that abstract, or general, or 'theoretical' economics was economics proper. It seems to me a very small part of economics proper: and by itself even – well, not a very good occupation of time . . . general reasoning is essential, but a wide and thorough study of facts is equally essential . . . a combination of the two sides of the work is *alone* economics *proper*. Economic theory is, in my opinion, as mischievous an impostor when it claims to be economics proper as is mere crude unanalysed history.
>
> (cited Coase 1975 p. 29; emphasis is in Coase)[10]

Marshall was unconcerned with questions of pure theory and with philosophical and methodological disputes. He regarded himself as 'midway between Keynes + Sidgwick + Cairnes and Schmoller + Ashley' (cited Coase 1975 p. 28). He simply had no appetite for the debate. He wanted to 'obtain guidance in the practical conduct of life', and he required economics to generate pragmatic council as to the best policy.

For Marshall, the notion of measuring the effects of utility, and his approach to studying mental states through their manifestations (Marshall 1920 p. 14), was as much a matter of common-sense as utility was for the early marginalists: he uses such phrases as 'in ordinary life' and 'ordinary usage' several times in the early chapters of his *Principles*. It did not, for him, require extensive justification. Neither, Marshall believed, did the definition of economics, although he did move away from the 'wealth' definition of the classics. In the earlier *Economics of Industry* he had been happy to include the idea of wealth:

> Those portions of human conduct which are directed towards the acquirement of material wealth, and those conditions of human well-being which directly depend on material wealth, are called *Economic*. The *science of Economics* collects, examines, arranges and reasons about the facts which are connected with the economic habits and conditions of well-being in various countries at various times.
>
> (Marshall 1879 p. 5; emphasis in original)

Later on he placed more emphasis on the notion of action, and less on wealth. He also emphasised the 'common-sense' element more. He began the first three editions of the *Principles* by writing

> Political economy or Economics, is a study of man's actions in the ordinary business of life; it inquires how he gets his income and how he uses it

But by the fourth edition Marshall's concern with the idea of social welfare caused him to revise this definition. By then economics was

a study of mankind in the ordinary business of life; it examines that part of individual and social actions which is most clearly connected with the use of the material requisites of well-being.[11]

Marshall's interest was not in material wealth *per se*, but with the material aspects of 'well-being' – it was only for this reason that wealth was of importance, and it was this implicit ethic of the 'well-being' of society that was at the back of Marshall's endeavours.

The study of 'material requisites of well-being' required, for Marshall, a fusion of both the psychological approach of the early marginalists and the wealth delineation of the classics. He believed economics 'is on the one side a study of wealth; and on the other, and more important side, a part of the study of man' (Marshall 1920 p. 1). What was needed was the analysis of both subjective and objective elements. Writing to N.G. Pierson, Marshall says

The book [*Principles*] was written to express one idea & one idea only. That idea is that whereas Ricardo & co. maintain that value is determined by cost of production, & Jevons & (in a measure) the Austrians that it is determined by utility, each was right in what he affirmed but wrong in what he denied.

(Dasgupta 1985 p. 104).

We will consider Marshall's value theory in more detail shortly. What is also striking about Marshall's definition compared to that of the earlier marginalists is the lack of abstraction. We are not dealing with an abstract *homo oeconomicus* which later economists were to use, nor are we splitting human action into ethical and economic dimensions. We deal 'with man as he is: not with an abstract or "economic" man; but a man of flesh and blood' (Marshall 1920 pp. 26–7). For Marshall, the point was that it is economic forces which mould the character of humans. 'For Man's character has been moulded by his everyday work, and the material resources which he thereby procures, more than any other influence unless it be that of his religious ideals' (ibid. p. 1). It was not that humans are naturally rational, but that in regard to business conduct humans are at their most rational (ibid. p. 20). Habits and customs are followed, but have themselves arisen from calculation (ibid.).[12] However the only generalisable measure of motives, Marshall maintained, was that afforded by money, hence this 'is the centre around which economic science clusters.'(ibid. p. 22) Mitchell maintains that for Marshall money measures the 'force of motives that control human behaviour', and suggests that modern society 'is organised about the process of making and spending money incomes', a process which 'moulds the minds of people' and

makes them as economic characters substantially different from the denizens of another type of economy. If the theorist could take away the effect of the money economy from the modern civilised nations, he would find that their inhabitants would be very different creatures from what they are.

(Mitchell 1969 p. 158)[13]

Marshall's theory is therefore objective in the sense that he is concerned with an objective element: that of the material aspects of well-being. Furthermore, these material aspects have come to centre around money. Although he uses the differential calculus, he is not attempting to measure the same things as his marginalist predecessors. In addition, Marshall is far more cautious about the use of money measures than his predecessors: it is only with 'careful precautions' that money can be used as a measure of the 'moving forces' of human lives. We will see here that Marshall only provides scant exposition of the precautions we must take when using money measures of behavioural forces, and provides next to no institutional analysis of the predominance of money as the focus for modern behaviour. The reason for this is that Marshall was not as concerned with market equilibrium as the orthodox economists have tended to be, either before Marshall or since.[14] Part of Marshall's synthesis of the marginal and classical approach was that he drew no distinction between value and growth (Loasby 1978 p. 1). He wanted to incorporate the element of time that was so central to the classics. It was this that led him to insist upon the use of costs as well as demand in value theory: hence his famous dictum about the scissors. Marshall added the concept of diminishing returns to that of diminishing marginal utility to explain how market price was derived. An increase in one factor of production would yield a progressively smaller increase in product. Each extra hour that the labour force worked would result in a smaller and smaller increase in output, the other factors of production (especially plant) being fixed. This meant that while demand price fell with quantity, supply costs rose. At one particular price supply would equal demand: the market would clear.

However this is not the complete story. Costs were, for Marshall, determined differently from demand: the central element in the analysis of supply was time. There were three time periods, which represented different positions in the variability of output. He outlines the period of 'temporary equilibrium', where there is a fixed stock of a commodity for sale. This is Marshall's 'day'. The equilibrium price will be determined by the 'higgling and bargaining' of the market, and will represent a market clearing price – assuming that sellers and buyers are equally matched (Marshall 1920 p. 333).

Marshall's main concern though was not with this market equilibrium, but rather where output could vary: supply as a flow (cf. Dasgupta 1985 p. 104). One of his marginal notes reads 'In a stationary state the doctrine of value would be simple' (Marshall 1920 p. 367). It was the effect of changes over time that interested Marshall. His analysis can be divided into two such time periods where supply can be treated as a flow: the short period and the long period. During the short period a change in demand will cause a corresponding adjustment in supply and a change in price: an increase in demand will cause price to rise and supply to increase (Marshall 1920 book V sec. 5). However, this need not be an equilibrium price. Marshall did not subscribe to any notion of 'perfect competition' – as Loasby points out, the word does not appear in his index (Loasby 1978 p. 5). Marshall does suppose 'free play' of the forces of supply and demand, meaning an absence of combination, and he also supposed 'free competition' among buyers and also among sellers (Marshall 1920 p. 342). Although Marshall envisaged a large number of buyers and sellers, he did not rule out some imperfections in the market. He realised that firms have regular customers and regular suppliers and might not react to short-run changes in market price. Marshall uses an 'oligopolistic' information system (Loasby 1978 p. 6). It is this which brings about a competitive solution – but one which is neither perfectly competitive nor oligopolistic. Marshall believed that the realities of the industrial world would themselves lead to price maintenance. He believed that depressions were caused by a lack of confidence (Marshall 1920 pp. 710–11).

Marshall's analysis of the short run tried to show that the 'higgling' of the market should not affect 'normal' price greatly. It was his long-run analysis that formed the link with the classics, for in the long run it was costs which were the main variable: firms could adjust their plant to alter output. For Marshall the important element in this adjustment was the notion of returns to scale. Although diminishing returns held for the short run because size of plant was constant, in the long run increasing returns could accrue. For Marshall, this was what led to economic growth: technical changes and also changes in industrial organisation caused by increasing scale. It was this prevalence of increasing long-run returns that Marshall believed was the main justification for contemporary industrial organisation.

This is further underlined by Marshall's treatment of oligopoly. Marshall's conception of the effect of increasing returns upon industrial organisation is that of the industrial 'life cycle'. In the long run many firms presently trading would go out of business: only a few survive to dominate the market. However, these firms will in their turn stagnate to be replaced by newer 'younger' undertakings. By the 1910s Marshall acknowledged that this life-cycle analogy was looking somewhat dated, but he did not develop an oligopolistic theory. There is no place for market power in Marshall's analysis once poverty is removed.

In the long run, the industry will therefore be in equilibrium. It is worth stressing that this is an equilibrium of the industry: the firms themselves could come and go – there was no sense in which one could discuss the long run equilibrium position of the firm. Again, this is much more like the classics than a purely marginalist analysis.

Marshall's treatment of value and growth is of significance to our thesis for several reasons. Methodologically, the need for consideration of long-run effects mitigated against the partial equilibrium approach. *Ceteris* were not likely to remain *paribus* in the long run. This is possibly why Marshall believed his analysis to be realistic: this was not an abstraction but 'flesh and blood'.

We will recall the other aspect of Marshall's work, which was his concern to study real humans rather than abstract 'economic human'. This enabled Marshall to justify moving directly from utility to money. All his examples in the *Principles* are of market demand schedules, and he frequently uses the concepts interchangeably (e.g. Marshall 1920 pp. 92–4). There is nowhere an equation of utilities in terms of price. We therefore require an explanation of how maximum social value is coincidental with equilibrium in cash terms. Marshall uses the device of the surplus

Since marginal utility of a commodity diminished with quantity, the demand price for all units except the last will exceed the equilibrium price. Market price, of course, does not vary – the same price is charged for the first unit as for the last. Marshall therefore maintained that consumers gained a surplus by trade: they paid less for the first units of a commodity than they were prepared to pay.[15] By the same token, producers also gained a surplus: they would have been prepared to supply the first few units at a lower price than the equilibrium price, since the supplier is subject to diminishing returns. The total surplus is maximised when supply surplus equals demand surplus – at the equilibrium price. Note that this measure has currency as its unit – it is a direct money measure of satisfaction obtained through trade. Also note that, as such, it implies both interpersonal comparisons and a cardinal measurement of utility. Of course, as soon as we allow for cardinal utility, we run into the diminishing marginal utility of money and all the egalitarian implications that this holds. By contrast, the measurement of consumer surplus adopted by Marshall is only unambiguous if the marginal utility of money is constant (Dasgupta 1985 p. 113), and Marshall maintained that it was only in extreme cases that the marginal utility of money was not constant. This may explain why Marshall had misgivings about always using the competitive equilibrium position as an optimum (ibid.).[16]

> The exceptions (to a constant marginal utility of money) are rare and unimportant in markets for commodities; but in markets for labour they are frequent and important.

> When a workman is in fear of hunger, his need of money (its marginal utility to him) is very great . . . and he may go on selling his labour at a low rate.
>
> (Marshall 1920 p. 335)

Marshall's *social* value theory depended for the most part on an unrealistic psychological assertion concerning the marginal utility of money. This assumption enabled him to avoid the distributional implications of marginalism.

Marshall did, though, suggest a technical reason for particularly requiring the amelioration of poverty. He fully realised that the vast inequalities of wealth would mean that it would be most unlikely that the marginal utility of money would remain equal. Furthermore, the mathematical training of Marshall did not allow him to ignore the problems caused by the use of the differential calculus. The concept of diminishing marginal utility and diminishing marginal product rested upon a notion of a small incremental change. It was this that enabled the derivative to be obtained: if the changes are large, the margin becomes indeterminate. Marshall realised that one market where changes are likely to be far from incremental is the labour market. Changes in prices here may well have large effects on 'well-being'. The labour market is for this reason exceptional, and disadvantages in bargaining tend to be cumulative.

It was these reasons (as well as the common-sense observation of distributional problems), that led Marshall to question the marginal productivity theory of distribution proposed by J.B. Clark and later by Wicksteed. This was in fact the formal closure of the system: wages were determined by the value of the marginal product made by the labourer. Marshall never fully accepted the Marginal Productivity Theory.[17] One of the essential elements is that it only holds for constant returns to scale, whereas the entire thrust of Marshall's work stressed increasing returns. Both J.B. Clark's and Wicksteed's analyses were essentially static – they did not consider long-run supply costs as did Marshall. Indeed, Wicksteed believed that the supply schedule was simply an inverted demand schedule:

> But what about the 'supply curve' that usually figures as a determinant of price co-ordinate with the demand curve? I say it boldly and baldly: there is no such thing. What usually figures as such is merely a disguised and therefore unrecognisable portion of the 'demand curve'.
>
> (Wicksteed 1913 p. 261)

Of course, this was far from the case for Marshall: the whole point was that costs were the dominant feature in the long run. This also explains why his advocacy of redistribution did not extend beyond the amelioration of extreme poverty. The essential principle for Marshall was that although the analysis of value may show up imperfections, it leads to growth in production in the long run. Even monopolies could be justified in this way (Dasgupta 1985 p. 119). By increasing the quantity of production – with the worst evils of poverty eliminated – the competitive economy could create a *post hoc* maximum solution, even though there may be *ex ante* inequalities.

Marshall's growth theory was therefore an essential element of distribution also. It was growth that justified inequality (if not extreme poverty). Unfortunately, Marshall's emphasis on long-run growth impales him on the other horn of the positivist dilemma, because as we mentioned at the outset of this chapter a *laissez-faire* value theory must be subjective. The utilitarian theory was subjective, but only at the expense of a realistic psychology. Marshall has rejected the psychology of hedonism, but his emphasis on growth involved, as with the classics, a corresponding emphasis on costs. However, under Marshall's scheme costs are objective, and since they are objective it is not clear why production cannot be planned. If Marshall's analysis revolves around increasing returns to scale and if, furthermore, he only considers the equilibrium of the industry, then there appears to be little justification for *laissez-faire*: increasing returns to the industry could be easily served by large state enterprises. Marshall was forced to resort to casual psychological assertions to back up his position, claiming that planning undermined 'self-reliant and inventive faculties' and so on.

In addition, we can see that Marshall often resorts to unsubstantiated claims, most notably for the growth element of his theory. He does not explain exactly how the possibility of returns to scale will affect technical and industrial change, and conversely why only the market mechanism can achieve this. We are not told why oligopolistic markets would maintain price and not lead to depressions.[18] We are not told exactly why there should be a rotating elite of dominant firms or even why Marshall's limited concept of free competition should hold – or what would happen when it does not. Neither is there any but the most casual institutional analysis of our 'men of flesh and blood' – and no analysis of any other forces not measured by money. Furthermore, if 'Man's character' is malleable, as Marshall made out, then it can be manipulated, and utility and market demand are no longer guides to material well-being.

By the time of Marshall's death the sort of psychological assertions he invoked would no longer wash as science. Furthermore, Marshall's lack of oligopolistic theory was beginning to show as a major weakness in his theory, as the life-cycle analogy was called into question by dynasties of joint stock companies. His concept of increasing returns was coming under fire from within the profession. And in America his casual institutional analysis was being challenged by the American institutional school.

Pigou

The Marshallian analysis therefore foundered on the same problems that we considered in a methodological guise in the last chapter. If we attempt an objective, refutable analysis à la Hutchison, then we must either accept the viability of economic planning or provide proof as to why planning is not viable. In his attempt to move from static value analysis to dynamic growth – in order to escape the distributional consequences of the surplus – Marshall necessarily invokes the objective cost analysis of the classics, and is therefore not able to sustain the political theory implied in his position. Marshall is unable to escape the value implications of his price theory.

The critiques of the Marshallian approach had very little immediate impact upon orthodox economics. Indeed, Marshall's successor at Cambridge – his pupil Arthur Pigou – was to continue employing the same value theory as his teacher. Pigou was not as concerned with individual behaviour as Marshall was, however. His aim was to examine the aggregate results of marginal analysis. Aggregate individual utilities were known as welfare, and the analysis of this Pigou called welfare economics.

One of Marshall's early definitions of economics, it will be recalled, concerned how man 'gets his income and how he spends it.' Pigou's concern is the national income, or as he terms it, the 'national dividend'. Like Marshall, Pigou only considers 'that part of social welfare that can be brought directly or indirectly into relation with the measuring-rod of money' (Pigou 1920 p. 11). Unlike Marshall though, Pigou does not defend this choice of boundary by institutional analysis, however casual. He simply states that 'The one obvious instrument of measurement available in social life is money' (ibid.), and then proceeds without further ado. This lack of caution was to create problems for the analysis. In fact, even Pigou admits that this 'economic welfare' cannot be separated 'in any rigid way from other parts', and that 'The outline of our territory is, therefore, necessarily vague', but he still asserts that 'the test of accessibility to a money measure serves well enough to set up a rough distinction' (ibid.). Indeed, Pigou believed that effects on economic welfare were ' *probably* equivalent in direction ... to the effect on total welfare' and that 'in all circumstances the burden of proof lies upon those who hold that the presumption should be overruled' (Pigou 1920 p. 20; emphasis in original).

Although Pigou adopted the Marshallian value analysis, he did not adopt the concept of consumers' surplus. Instead he went directly to a marginal approach (Blackhouse 1985 p. 166). The marginal analysis itself is fairly standard once the initial concepts are established.[19] Pigou takes the concept of marginal product developed by Marshall and J.B. Clark: this he refers to as marginal private product. The contribution to the aggregate whole of a marginal act of production is the marginal social product. In a competitive economy, the national dividend is maximised when these two products are equal.

The aim of policy would therefore be to ensure that this is the case. There were several reasons for divergence, one of the most important of which were increasing returns to scale. It will be recalled that these formed a major plank of Marshall's value theory. Marshall suggested that a subsidy to industries subject to increasing returns may optimise welfare. Pigou believed that this should form part of policy. However, this notion came in for sharp criticism, most notably from Clapham's jibe that the concepts of constant, increasing and diminishing returns were 'empty economic boxes'. Clapham did not believe that the concepts were capable of being operationalised: he maintained that it was impossible to tell which industries were subject to falling costs and which were not (Clapham 1922). Indeed, for the purposes of fiscal policy which Pigou and Marshall proposed, it appears to be necessary to make an almost entrepreneurial *ex ante* judgement as to long-term costs.

Indeed, the whole Marshallian value/growth theory, upon which Pigou also based his work, was now being questioned. Unfortunately, it will be recalled that the prospect of growth was used to justify inequalities. Once the idea of growth is removed, inegalitarian *laissez-faire* policies lose their justification. And such a justification was indeed necessary under the neo-classical scheme, because of the egalitarian implications of diminishing marginal utility of money. Pigou's treatment is slightly more forthright than Marshall's:

> The old 'law of diminishing utility' thus leads securely to the proposition: Any cause which increases the absolute share of real income in the hands of the poor, *provided that it does not lead to a contraction in the size of the national dividend from any point of view*, will, in general, increase economic welfare.
>
> (Pigou 1920 p. 91; emphasis added)

There is even less analysis of the limitations of redistribution and intervention here than in Marshall's work, however. Presumably we are to take Marshall's qualifications and casual psychology *en bloc*. It was through assertions concerning psychology and technical progress that Marshall defended *laissez-faire*, and these problems have been imported straight into the Pigouvian scheme.

The other problem[20] both Marshall and Pigou fail to deal with concerns aspects of material well-being which cannot be judged by the measuring-rod of money. Marshall devotes considerable space to discussing external economies to scale of the industry, but he makes no mention of general external economies and diseconomies, especially as concern the individual. The problem of what economists now call externalities – where the supplier of goods or services renders a cost or benefit to other (third) parties who do not, or cannot, receive compensation for loss or submit payment for benefit – was more crucial for Pigou, who was directly concerned with the divergence between individual and social maxima. If the costs of production are not internalised but rather passed on to the community, then the private product; will be higher than the social product, similarly, if it is not possible to collect payments for goods which give universal benefit, these goods may not be provided: the marginal social product is higher than the private product. In these instances the marginal social product will obviously vary from the marginal private product. Sidgwick's example of the latter is that of a lighthouse: this would bring substantial benefits to shipping, but it is not possible in many cases to collect payment from them (Pigou 1920 p. 186). Pigou gives various other examples, such as pollution and loss of amenity.

The problem with externalities is that often it is far from clear that these are measurable by money – in fact Pigou himself observes that few real-life examples are capable of monetary measurement:

> If we were to be pedantically loyal to the definition of the national dividend ... it would be necessary to distinguish further between industries in which the uncompensated benefit or burden respectively is and is not one that can be readily brought into relation with the measuring rod of money. This distinction, however, would be of formal rather than real importance, and would obscure rather than illuminate the main issues. I shall therefore, in the examples I am about to give, deliberately pass it over.
>
> (Pigou 1920 p. 185)

Pigou's position is somewhat unclear: if there is a problem here he should attempt to deal with it. His tone ('pedantically loyal ... ') seems to suggest that he regards the non-pecuniary externalities as either exceptional or unimportant. He believed that, in spite of the non-pecuniary nature of many externalities, fiscal measures should prove sufficient to deal with the problem. It was not until much later that the possibility that the 'measuring-rod of money' may be faulty became widely debated. Hutchison remarked that the acceptance of externalities put the concept of marginal social net product in a rather dubious position:

> Any summation even of the more strictly economic 'products' into the single 'social product' of an economic act is bound to be more or less arbitrary, but would have nothing 'illegitimate' about it if the result emerging from this use of 'the measuring rod of money' was significant for a particular purpose. But under the one relevant heading where a wider range of clear practical examples is given, the introduction of the 'measuring rod of money' ... is held to obscure rather than illuminate the main issues.
>
> (Hutchison 1953 p. 293)

At any event, the imposition of taxes or subsidies on 'externalities' itself has distributional implications: fiscal policy itself presumes a net equitable level of distribution. Pigou disregards these distributional implications because he seems to regard the matter as trivial, but subsequent events have suggested this is far from being the case, and it has become a matter of importance where the incidence of taxation or subsidy for externalities should lie. Again, the distributional aspects of value theory cannot be ignored, as indeed the limitations of the neo-classical value theory cannot.

It had become clear that it would not be possible to separate out the marginal utility from its distributional implications. Jevons and Edgeworth tried to do so, but were forced to rely on an unoperational 'scientific' utilitarianism. Marshall and Pigou tried to deflect concern with distribution by incorporating growth into their value theory, but this was no more operational than before, and was looking less and less plausible as the 1930s approached. This decade was to herald a movement away from the analysis of material well-being towards a purely subjective analysis and the complete separation of distribution from value. The price of these changes was to propel economic theory further and further into an analytic shell.

ORDINALISTS

Pareto

The movement towards this state of affairs actually began contemporary with Marshall in the works of Vilfredo Pareto. Pareto discarded the utilitarian philosophy in favour of positivism. He also refused to adopt the marginalist partial equilibrium approach, preferring instead Walrasian general equilibrium. He says of Marshall that 'Marshall has not yet managed to grasp the idea of economic equilibrium ... He adds nothing remarkable to our knowledge' (cited Cirillo 1979 p. 15). He believed that the study of economic units in isolation from each other caused the imputation of incorrect causal relationships. One had to consider equilibrium in terms of the economy as a whole (Tarascio 1966 p. 109). We noted earlier how Edgeworth was moving towards the notion of interdependent utilities. Pareto, following Walras, extended this into a concept of equilibrium simultaneous throughout all exchanges. Pareto also used Edgeworth's device of indifference analysis. However, the indifference curves had a completely different meaning for the two theorists. Edgeworth, it will be recalled, believed very strongly in the utilitarian philosophy and cardinal utility. Pareto, on the other hand, rejected all notions of utility. The indifference curves for him were factual data (Mitchell 1967 p. 412). Pareto believed that it was necessary to go beyond hedonism:

> Subsequently it seemed to me that one could go one step further. I was worried about that *pleasure* and that *pain* which had to be measured, because in reality, nobody is capable of measuring pleasure.
> (cited Tarascio 1966 p. 410; emphasis in original)

Although Pareto still had some notion of utility in his *Cours* (1896), in the *Manuel* the use of indifference analysis enabled him to break away from utility altogether (Cirillo 1979 p. 21). In fact, by the turn of the century Pareto had broken with the idea of value entirely. The whole notion of value, he believed, was metaphysical:[21]

there are people who think that the new economic theories have been

produced to explain value. Far from it! I am looking for something very different from the metaphysical reason of value
(Pareto 1901, cited Tarascio 1967 p. 410)

Pareto's theory was one of price, not value – it was objective and positive: 'I look for a theory which may include and present economic facts' (ibid.). For Pareto, the economist should focus only on the objective data of choice (Tarascio 1967 pp. 411 ff.).

This would appear to be naive empiricism, but Pareto's concern is limited to what he called 'pure' economic theory. His objective is

> only to search for the uniformities that phenomena present, that is to say their laws, without having any direct practical usefulness in mind, without concerning himself in any way with giving recipes or precepts, without seeking the happiness, the benefit or the well-being of humanity or of any part of it.
>
> (Pareto 1909 p. 2)

We have seen that Pareto has eschewed both utility and value, and that he is not concerned to investigate 'well-being'. His sole stated concern is with uniformities. We may wonder, therefore, if he has any time for questions of distribution. Without a notion of value it would not seem possible to consider distribution, and indeed Pareto excludes distribution from his economic analysis. He believes that distribution is a question of social ethics (Cirillo 1979 p. 43). The 'ophelimities' of two people cannot be compared: they consist of heterogeneous quantities (Pareto 1916 sec. 2130). This has the corollary that it is not realistic to talk of a unique optimum for a commodity. Pareto distinguishes between a maximum *of* the community and a maximum *for* the community (ibid. sec. 2129). There may be many such maxima; we cannot compare one with another without considering distribution.

In fact, there is a severe restriction on the movements to general equilibrium which can be considered. Since the economist cannot consider distribution or redistribution, only movements that are not to the detriment of any individual are permissible; even if the social gain overall is positive, a loss to any individual would involve a redistribution. This condition leads to what is now called a 'Pareto-optimum' position. The originator of the condition did not view the ensuing optimum with anything like the contemporary enthusiasm, however. For Pareto, this condition simply represented the boundary between economics and sociology:

> Movements of a first type, P, are such that, beneficial to certain individuals, they are necessarily harmful to others. Movements of a second type, Q, are such that they are to the advantage, or to the detriment, of all individuals without exception . . .
>
> Consideration of the two types of points, P and Q, is of great importance in political economy. When the community stands at a

61

point, Q, that it can leave with resulting benefits to all individuals, procuring greater enjoyments for all of them, it is obvious that from the economic standpoint it is advisable ... to move on from it as far as the movement away from it is advantageous to all. When, then, the point P, where that is no longer possible, is reached, it is necessary, as regards the advisability of stopping there or going on, to resort to other considerations foreign to economics – to decide on grounds of ethics, social utility, or something else, which individuals it is advisable to benefit, which to sacrifice. From the strictly economic standpoint, as soon as the community has reached a point P it has to stop.

(Pareto 1916 vol. 4 sec 2129)

The condition for 'Pareto-optimum' is therefore in no wise an exclusive decision-rule for a society, and it is not really used in this manner. It is simply a statement of the limitations of pure economic theory, given the conditions which Pareto placed on economic theory.

We might hold that this limitation places extraordinary restrictions on policy formation. It would be well-nigh impossible only to promote policies which affected nobody for the worse. Of course, as we saw, Pareto was not concerned with economic policy. Pareto's exclusive concern as an economist was with pure economics, precisely what Marshall believed was a waste of time. The point was that in Pareto's view the economist, *qua* economist, could not give 'guidance in the practical conduct of life', to use Marshall's phrase. The practical conduct of life involved sociological elements as well as economic, and concerned, according to Pareto, non-logical as well as logical actions. The economist only considered logical actions (and also all logical actions were economic in nature), and viewed non-logical actions as beyond her brief (Parsons 1937 pp. 185 ff.). In order to derive a realistic policy science, the non-rational must also be analysed. In fact, Pareto makes explicit the analytic nature of 'rational economic human'. Economics, he maintained, abstracted from real 'flesh and blood' humans entirely, so that 'the individual may disappear; we do not need him any longer to determine economic equilibrium' (Tarascio 1967 p. 415). Unlike the later welfare economists, who ironically made such extensive use of the concept of 'Pareto optimum', Pareto himself 'removed the facade to expose so-called "economic man" for what he was – neither economic nor man' (ibid.). What Pareto wanted was a complete social science: a science of all human behaviour. He therefore attempted to construct a sociological supplement to his pure economic theory (cf. Tarascio 1967 *passim*, Samuels 1974 p. 8).

This sociology was to consider the non-logical aspects of action which Pareto believed pervaded human life. He realised that the economy as well as the polity is affected by systems of power (Samuels 1974 p. 88). Economic policy analysis therefore had to go beyond the market (ibid. p. 198). Market choice was only part of economic policy (ibid. p. 185). What Pareto hoped to do was to put sociology on the same footing as economics, and thereby derive a complete policy science.

Unfortunately Pareto's positive sociology never really gets off the ground. He attempts to use the same notion of maximisation and equilibrium simply transported into the social sphere, where they are not operative.[22] In retrospect, Pareto's work can be seen as another attempt to square the circle of objective social value, based on a notion of transcendental human nature. For the early marginalists, this theory of human nature could be found by a science of 'utility'. For Pareto, an invariable positive science of society is posited. Neither can be put into practice.

In spite of Pareto's strictures of the need for a sociological supplement to economic theory, the use of indifference analysis and the Paretian conditions for equilibrium were eagerly taken up by the later 'welfare economists' of the inter-war period, as was the idea that distribution is an ethical, not an economic, consideration. However, as we have seen throughout, ethical elements are essential in a value theory, and this theory cannot be separated from its distributional implications. The effect of replacing the neo-classical value theory was to move towards a behavioural – and therefore analytic – definition.

Robbins

This movement towards behaviouralism began with the new definition of economics developed by Lionel Robbins (Robbins 1935 [1932]). This change in definition, which has become common currency throughout the discipline since the 1930s, was couched in positivist terms. All traces of the discipline's utilitarian past were discarded; legitimacy now lay in the claim to 'scientific' truth in positivist terms. Economics was no longer to look at wealth, as the classical economists did, or material welfare, as did the neo-classics. Robbins' definition concerned itself with behaviour, with 'rational choice'. In fact, Robbins considers not Marshall's 'men of flesh and blood', but rather an abstract, 'rational' human. All that is necessary for a science of behaviour, Robbins asserts, is for actors to be able to choose between given alternatives. As long as these choices are transitive (and it would be strange for an individual to hold intransitive preferences), then it is possible to show (by the same indifference analysis as used by Pareto) that an equilibrium can occur at which each individual's utility is maximised. Robbins replaced a cardinally measurable utility with an ordinal utility, based on the idea of rational choice.

Robbins's definition (and, as we shall see, much of his substantive analysis) reflects his Austrian background, and is a curious mixture of positivism and Austrian praxeology. Although his theory is couched in behavioural terms, Robbins explicitly denies that economic theory can be based solely on observational concepts (Robbins 1935 p. 87). He believes that

After all, our business is to explain certain aspects of conduct. And it is very questionable whether this can be done in terms which involve no psychical element. It is quite certain that whether it be pleasing or no to the desire for the maximum austerity, we do in fact *understand* terms such as choice, indifference, preference and the like in terms of inner experience.

(Robbins 1935 p. 87; emphasis in original)

Robbins also specifically denied interpersonal comparisons of utility. Again, this affected the discipline boundary, in that it effectively excluded statements concerning redistribution (Cooter and Rappoport 1984 p. 521). The move to ordinalism therefore appears neatly to sidestep the distributional conclusions of the diminishing marginal utility of money. However, the cost of this move was high.

Ordinal utility theory gives the appearance of allowing us to reach similar conclusions to Marshall, but without the distributional implications attached to the theory.[23] It also laid the foundation for a positivist, behavioural economics.

Robbins assembled the elements of a new conceptual framework by joining together the scarcity definition of economics, the positivist conception of method, and the ordinalist view of utility. The only piece missing from the modern view was a behaviourist interpretation of ordinal utility, and that was supplied by others (Cooter and Rappoport 1984 p. 523).

Hicks

Hicks and Allen (1934) attempted to redefine Marshall in terms of ordinal utility and behavioural concepts. Hicks denied the legitimacy of any notion of quantitative utility (Hicks 1946 [1939] p. 42, cf. Hicks 1975 p. 220). Although accepting the notion of utility, he denied this is a measurable phenomenon in the sense of cardinal measurement. Hicks believed that 'the facts of *observable conduct* make a scale of preferences capable of theoretical construction ... but they do not enable us to proceed from the scale of preferences to a particular utility function' (Hicks and Allen 1934 p. 6 emphasis added).

Hicks claims that ordinal utility can be derived from observed behaviour, whereas cardinal utility cannot. Hicks therefore proposes to 'undertake a purge, rejecting all concepts which are tainted by quantitative utility, and replacing them ... by concepts which have no such implication' (Hicks 1946 p. 19). Marginal utility was therefore replaced with marginal rate of substitution (between two goods), diminishing marginal utility replaced by diminishing marginal rate of substitution and so on. Note though that the justification for the move to rational choice was not the same for Hicks as for Robbins. For Robbins, choice was justified by appeal to introspection. For

Hicks the justification is that the ordinal ranking can be observed in behaviour.

The Hicksian methodology can be viewed as a move towards a more positivist justification of economic 'science', and away from the psychologism of earlier schools.[24] But, as we saw in Chapter 1, the appeal to introspection was not an optional extra. The use of an abstraction as a definition automatically precluded any empirical input into the science. The Hicksian formulation is no more observational than the old cardinal theory was, since observation is precluded almost by definition. Samuelson believed that the concepts could not be justified without recourse to psychologism: the law of diminishing substitution, for example, is not an observational term (Samuelson 1938, cited Wong 1978 p. 49). 'Indifference' is not an observational term either. The switch to ordinalism cannot be justified on positivist grounds and indeed, as Wong observes, Hicks rather changes tack in later writings:

In Hicks (1939) the rationale for revising Marshall's theory is changed. The revision is not defended on the grounds that an ordinal utility rather than a cardinal utility function can be constructed from the facts of observable conduct, but on the grounds that only an ordinal concept of utility is necessary for the explanation of consumer behaviour:

and he cites Hicks:

Pareto's discovery only opens a door, which we can enter *or* not as we feel inclined. But from the technical economic viewpoint there are strong reasons for supposing we ought to enter it. The quantitative concept of utility is *not necessary* in order to explain market phenomena. Therefore, on the principle of Occam's razor, it is better to do without it.

(Hicks 1939 p. 18 cited Wong 1978 p. 34; emphasis in Wong)

Hicks has therefore changed the justification for replacing cardinal with ordinal utility from his original claim that it provided a more realistic, observable concept to the weaker (and somewhat trivial) claim that it provides a scientifically neater theory.

Samuelson

The cudgels for observability were taken up by Samuelson. Samuelson's aim was to devise a new theory of consumer behaviour which succeeds in 'dropping off the last vestiges of utility analysis' (Samuelson 1938 p. 62). He believes that the ordinal utility theory does not go far enough in severing all links with the concept of utility. Samuelson wishes to move towards a stronger positivistic economics – he believes that the theory must be based on purely observational concepts. Samuelson therefore proposes to employ the behaviour of consumers as data. He purports to show how the same conclusions as in the ordinal utility approach could be reached by observation of the choices made by individuals. Given a price and a budget constraint, we could simply observe the choices made by individuals. Samuelson maintains that rational individuals given the same axioms of choice as in the ordinalist construction, can be observed as 'revealing' their preferences in their choices. Given relative prices and a budget constraint, we could simply observe that the consumer has a preference for those choices made over all other viable choices. No recourse to utility need be made.

Does this new construction solve the problem of a policy science? Firstly we would observe that prices and distribution are givens. To derive policy these would, it seems, have already to have been settled. One presumes that price would be explained in a manner similar to the Marshallian short-run analysis, with the curves drawn from observation. Distribution, however, is not clear.

Nor indeed is it clear that Samuelson is providing a new theory, since in order to derive the theory we still are required to accept both transitivity over time (otherwise we have a trivial answer – the consumer chose what s/he preferred) and the other aspects of rationality (Wong 1978 p. 58). As Sen observes, these axioms are in fact identical with those of ordinal utility

> Faith in the axioms of revealed preference arises, therefore, not from empirical verification but from the intuitive reasonableness of these axioms interpreted precisely in terms of preference . . . if the theory of revealed preference makes sense it does so not because no psychological assumptions are used but because the psychological assumptions used are sensibly chosen.
>
> (Sen 1973 pp. 3–4, cited Wong 1978 p. 59)

In fact, as Wong notes

> Samuelson seems to move towards a non-observational ordinal utility in his derivation of indifference curves. Being indifferent is the opposite to holding a preference. Indifference curve analysis therefore involves assumptions of individual preferences and a limitation of the means to obtaining these preferences. This is already presumed by the ordinal utility approach – Samuelson's theory does not differ substantially.
>
> (Wong 1978 p. 73)

Samuelson was correct in his belief that ordinal utility contained non-observational concepts, but wrong in his judgement that these could be avoided. Moreover, the notion of scientific explanation that Samuelson seems to be adopting is very much the strong, Humean conception of regularities. Certainly Samuelson excludes any possibility of causal explanation. It is 'not an explanation in the sense that it explains why one bundle (of goods) were bought and all other bundles were not' (ibid. p. 61). This is in accord with the stated methodological position held by Samuelson, that explanation is constituted by descriptions (Samuelson 1964 *passim*).

Samuelson does not provide a description though. Following the ordinal utility theorists, he actually provides a corollary of an abstraction from human behaviour. The concept of rationality is never defined in operational terms. Inconsistent behaviour is redefined in terms of changing tastes, the wish for variety or some such. In addition, as Sen showed in his well-known 1976 article, by redefining the boundaries of egoism, any individual can be made to appear self-seeking (Sen 1976 *passim*).

This leads on to a major criticism of the ordinalist school, which is shown up well in the Samuelson formulation. The whole point of utility theory was to derive a theory of value. Meek suggests that the elimination of cardinality in favour of ordinality also eliminates value theory (Meek 1956, cited Gramm 1988 p. 238). What we are given instead is a price theory. Preferences are just preferences which we can neither judge nor compare. The rationality assumptions have removed any vestige of a maximand. It is no longer clear what the objective of ordinal utility theory is. Myrdal had earlier criticised Fisher on the same point:

> When hedonism is abandoned, utility, subjective value, satisfaction, pleasure and pain, etc., must be defined in terms of observable choice *(Wahlhandeln)*. This is done by Irving Fisher. But he, unlike, for example, Cournot and Cassel, does not try to give up the subjective theory of value. He abstains from psychology and yet retains a purely formal, behaviourist utility and value theory.

> But why retain psychological concepts without psychological content? What is the purpose of an analysis which is intended to prop up the theory of price and which, apart from small improvements and terminological changes, is identical with the old theory? Marginal utility theory proper had at least an objective; it purported to be a psychological explanation of price formation. But what is the point of the new theory of choice which claims to be non-psychological?

Myrdal maintains that economic explanations must of necessity involve a psychological formulation:

> The comprehensive modern non-hedonistic value analysis seems to have been constructed in order to replace marginal utility theory. The latter was intended to provide a psychological explanation of price formation. When hedonism became discredited psychological explanation generally suffered a loss of reputation. But the flaw in the marginal utility theory was not that it endeavoured to explain economic phenomena psychologically, but that hedonism could not explain them. The new school tries to salvage the hedonistic model by stripping it of its psychological content. Its concepts are formal and 'purely eco-

nomic'. But its theoretical model is not likely to provide a very happy formulation of the specifically psychological problems of economics, for in so far as it formulates them at all, it does so hedonistically.

(Myrdal 1929 p. 99)

The ordinalists' use of rationality actually abstracts any psychological content from economics: 'Rational economic man is not an actual man. He is, rather, any actual man who conforms to the model to be tested' (Hollis and Nell 1975 p. 55).

The abstraction of psychology from the analysis also reinforces the sex bias which we saw in the cardinal utility analysis. If we are to consider only preferences 'revealed' in the marketplace, then we need to consider the family as an economic unit. This is now standard practice in economics texts. The preferences of individuals within the family are not revealed, and are in fact ignored. The utility of the family may be maximised, but it does not follow that all the individuals within the family obtain a maximum. The theory attempts to analyse a market process in which women are marginalised. By ignoring what we will later refer to as social institutions, in this case the institution of gender, the theory gives a biased account of economic valuation. We will return to this later.

Welfare economics

The positive economic science has come to the impasse that we discussed in the previous chapter. If positivists are to base their theories on conditional observational statements, then we must be able to test when the conditions have held. The ordinalists – and especially Samuelson – cannot do this. The concept of rationality is being used both as what Musgrave earlier referred to as an heuristic assumption and also as a domain assumption. All the behavioural elements have been assumed away in the strictures of rationality. Indeed the professed belief in the justification of theories through observation was completely at odds with the welfare economics movement post-1930. This – as Hutchison complained – saw a veritable plethora of abstractions and unrealistic assumptions.

These become compounded when we try to move from the individual to the social utility. The essential methodological problem of orthodox economics, it will be recalled, was to derive a social theory from an individualist basis, if it is to develop an alternative to planning. Marshall attempted this by the concept of consumers' surplus, measured in monetary units.[25] Since this was a cardinal measure, the social 'well-being' could be derived by simply aggregating the surpluses. Obviously, ordinal utility, by definition, could not be aggregated in this way. By the late 1930s most welfare economists were moving towards Pareto's scheme of general equilibrium, using the 'Pareto criterion' of optimality, but employing indifference analysis derived from

68

ordinal utility.[26] Welfare economics became a study of the conditions under which a Pareto-efficient allocation is possible.

What was originally mooted by Pareto as an example of the limitations of pure economics was now to be used as an objective of economic theory. The entire thrust of Pareto's thought was based on the idea that social policy could not be derived from purely economic analysis – Pareto believed a sociological supplement was required. It will be recalled that Pareto's economics was limited to the presentation of 'uniformities'. He explicitly eschewed explanation or practical usefulness – it was a purely synthetic exercise. Yet the ordinalists are embracing Pareto's exposition of the limit of economics as a major tool for positive economics. The discipline consequently became more and more abstract and unrealistic.

This can be immediately seen in the conclusions concerning social utility which were arrived at. Social utility is only maximised under conditions of what were called 'perfect competition'. This concept was considerably different to Marshall's 'free competition' in that the axioms were impossibly strong. Perfect competition involves first and foremost a very large number of buyers and sellers in the market, such that no one seller or buyer can influence price. All economic agents are therefore price-takers. Further to this, there must be free entry to the market for suppliers and perfect knowledge of all present and future market conditions. All commodities must be divisible, and the product of the market homogeneous. Furthermore, government interference with the market (tariffs, subsidies and so on) are presumed not to occur.[27] Clearly, these assumptions do not hold in any real-world market. The theory is synthetic and vacuous and, unlike the Marshallian analysis, totally static in nature:

> The analysis is about a stationary economy in which everything exactly repeats itself from one period to another. In such a society all decisions are made only once; once made they are relevant for all time because the things . . . decided upon . . . remain constant for all time. Everything is assumed to take place at a point in time – no time elapses between one event and another; hence there is no future to be uncertain about. In such a timeless world, though there is no uncertainty about the future, there might yet be imperfect knowledge about one another's actions at the present time; but this, too, is assumed away by supposing there is perfect knowledge.
>
> (Nath 1969 p. 11)

Furthermore, unlike the partial equilibrium approach of Marshall, the general equilibrium approach of Walras is not only static but instantaneous. The optimum conditions must obtain simultaneously for all markets. It is not the case that the optimal conditions are a goal towards which we may strive: the analysis of Lipsey and Lancaster showed that it is 'all or nothing', as it were. If there is a departure from the optimal conditions in one part of the economy, the next best ('second-best') situation may involve further departures else-where. For example, if we have a large monopoly in one industry, it would not be possible to attain a Pareto-optimum: it is possible to make everyone better off. The second-best situation may involve even further imperfections – say, for the sake of argument, a monopsonist trade union. The second-best situation is not attained by conditions as close as possible to the ideal:

> there is no *a priori* way to judge as between various situations in which some of the Paretian optimum conditions are fulfilled while others are not. Specifically, it is *not* true that a situation in which more, but not all, of the optimum conditions are fulfilled is necessarily, or even likely to be, superior to a situation in which fewer are fulfilled.
> (Lipsey and Lancaster 1956 p. 144; emphasis in original)

But even if we suspend disbelief and accept the assumptions of perfect competition, it is still not clear that we can derive social value conclusions from this analysis. Recall that the ordinalists are attempting to obtain a maximum social utility from individual utilities. Since these individual utilities are held to be non-comparable, and since distribution is not con-sidered, the best that the ordinal economists can achieve is to consider situations where unanimity occurs: where any change in the economy lessens someone's welfare. This is clearly a maximum: the position is clear-cut. It was soon realised that it would be impossibly restrictive to limit economic analysis to these cases – indeed, as we have seen, the conditions were never meant to be applied. Kaldor's solution for extending the scope of what became known as the 'new welfare economics', was based around the idea that it would always be possible for the gainers to overcompensate the losers in any situation where total welfare is increased (Kaldor 1939). Given this possibility of compensation, the economist need not be limited to changes where no-one is worse off. Kaldor did not believe it to be the task of the economist to suggest that compensation should actually take place. This is a question of distribu-tion, which economists were forbidden to answer. As long as compensation could be paid, an improvement could be said to exist. The question of who should actually obtain the fruits of this improvement is, it seems, to be left hanging in the air.

Let us briefly recap the argument, before showing how the position we have arrived at leads to a complete impasse. The use of ordinal utility, originally mooted as an improvement in 'scientific' method, was in actuality no more scientific that the old cardinal utility theory, although it was considerably more restrictive. The need for perfect competition to obtain maximum social welfare meant that economists could not incorporate any form of market power or state intervention into their scheme. The ideological backdrop to the adoption of ordinalism was the need to avoid questions of objective 'well-being' and of distribution. Yet as we have seen, the compensation principle upon which the new welfare economics relied could not entirely distance itself from the question of distribution. This anomaly was soon to be picked up by Scitovsky, although it appears, as usual, in a technical guise.

Scitovsky criticises the compensation principle for containing an implied distributional bias in favour of the *status quo* (Scitovsky 1941 p. 393). All that is being proposed by Kaldor, Scitovsky points out, is that the redistributive effects of a change should be corrected. Scitovsky then shows that this leads to a paradox. Consider a change (say, in the relative prices of various commodities) which leads to an improvement in some people's welfare but leaves others worse off. Let us call the old position A and the new one B. The compensation principle states that a change from A to B is only a social improvement if it is possible for gainers to compensate the losers and still gain. Let us assume this is the case. B is therefore better than A, in Kaldor's sense. So far so good.

Now, Scitovsky argues, consider reversing this change, moving from B back to A. If it is possible for the original losers to give compensation back to the original gainers to compensate them for 'loss' they are now incurring – so that we arrive back at the original starting point – then, following Kaldor, A is better than B! We have a contradictory result, because we cannot choose any 'starting point'. Moving from A to B is an improvement, and moving back from B to A is also an improvement, since we cannot make any judgement about the respective distributions.[28] We cannot say which way compensation should go – compensation to the losers from change or bribes to the would-be gainers to maintain the *status quo* – and recall that we are still only considering the possibility of compensation!

Scitovsky suggests that the economist must abandon the idea of deriving policy conclusions without considerations of social justice (Scitovsky 1941 p. 393). This appears also to be Little's position. Neither appears to be able to bring themselves to suggest the abandonment of the scheme. Scitovsky decides simply to add one more qualification to the already long list to obtain a social optimum from the market mechanism: we can only make welfare judgements if two-way compensation is impossible.[29] Quite how this is to be operationalised is unclear.

Given the problems of this analysis another method of proceeding was advocated. It was suggested by Samuelson and others that we should posit directly a social welfare function, which would include a variety of ethical judgements from outside economics (Samuelson 1950). It is for this reason that he is apparently happy to forego any notion of welfare in his economics – this notion is to be 'imported' into economics, as it were.

In a sense we have come full circle, for we began by looking at the idea of measuring ethics and of deriving social policy from them, and we have traced two centuries' worth of efforts to put this into effect. We should not therefore be surprised to find that the ethical judgements which can be so imported are, as it turns out, remarkably restrictive – in fact, they must amount to a dictatorship over economic choice in order for the social function to be constructed. Arrow (1951) showed that even if individual preferences are defined as transitive by definition of rationality, the resultant social preferences need not be – unless, of course these 'preferences' are imposed. The social utility function cannot be derived.

Sen suggests that it is the 'informational restrictions' of welfare economics that cause the impossibility of transivity. Sen argues that this 'can be seen as resulting from combining a version of welfarism ruling out the use of non-utility information with making the utility information remarkably poor (particularly in ruling out interpersonal utility functions)' (Sen 1979 p. 539).

We have seen, then, that the move to ordinal economics, even though it is unjustified and results in a synthetic theory, fails because it cannot derive a social value theory which is independent of social distribution. The game is simply not worth the candle. We have no theory of social welfare or even any realistic theory of individual value. We have lost any idea of 'well-being'. In fact, as Sen points out, it is impossible within the framework of welfare economics to even distinguish a rich person from a poor one!

> Can we identify the rich through the observation that they have more utility than the poor? Not in the Arrow framework, since interpersonal comparisons are not admitted. Perhaps as those with a lower marginal utility of income? No, of course not, since that will go against *both* noncomparability and ordinalism. Can we then distinguish the rich as those who happen to have more income, or more consumer goods (nothing about utility need be said), and bring this recognition to bear in social judgement? No, not that either, since this will go against welfarism ... since this discrimination has to be based on non-utility information.

Sen believes that this is connected with the Arrow impossibility theorem

> 'Social utility', in Leontief's characterisation, as 'a function of utility levels', without interpersonal comparisons robs us of our ability to 'tell' effectively the rich from the poor. It is this peculiarity of traditional welfare economics in insisting on both that social judgements be based on utility information *and* that the utility information be used in a particularly poor form, that can be seen as paving the way to inconsistency or incompleteness – and thus to impossibilities.
>
> (Sen 1979 p. 544; emphasis in original)

The move to ordinal utility and 'rational economic human' results in an abstract theory devoid of practical application. This militates against the very purpose of positive social science. We argued in Chapter 1 that a policy science is justified by the possibility that it will yield instrumental knowledge. Contemporary ordinal economics precludes precisely this knowledge.

We can now attempt a classification of the main schools which are outlined in the present book. At the beginning of this chapter we suggested that orthodox economics needed to maintain three propositions:

1 that economic knowledge is only known to individuals;
2 that this knowledge can be aggregated;
3 from this we can arrive at the best overall outcome.

Orthodox economics maintains that all three propositions can be supported, but we have seen that this is problematic. At least one of the propositions has to be dropped. Unless proposition (3) is sustained, we cannot arrive at any policy conclusions at all. Maintaining propositions (2) and (3) yields some form of market socialism, while maintaining (1) and (3) gives us a libertarian/Austrian model of political economy. It is to the debate between these two schools that we will shortly turn our attention.

The fundamental problem of orthodox economics has not been solved. In order to arrive at a positivist social policy either we must show some psychological knowledge of human desires, which was the aim of the utilitarians, or we must investigate objective, empirical activity, as with the neo-classics. The former was simply unoperational, but the latter led to the social policy of planning that is inherent in the positivist approach. Since the positivist approach is pointless unless policy can be derived, it appears that we must either surrender the policy of *laissez-faire* and embrace positivist planning, or ditch positivism if *laissez-faire* is to be maintained. We will consider both options in the next chapter.

3

1930s' MARKET SOCIALISM

The inability to obtain a positivist subjective economic theory leaves us with two choices. We can either remain true to the positivist philosophy and accept the possibility of economic planning, or we can maintain a subjective theory at the cost of abandoning our claim to positivist science. In this chapter we will look at the 'English debate' on market socialism which, although the protagonists did not always realise it at the time, was directly concerned with this question. The 1930s market socialists attempted to base a socialist theory on the models of welfare economics we outlined in the last chapter.[1] This position was criticised by the Austrian school, who dismissed not only the socialist models, but also their positivist, orthodox basis. While their critique appears cogent, the move from positivist to normative theory carries with it the condition that an account be made of the political elements in the theory, and the attempts of the Austrians to abstract from political and economic power renders their substantive theory no more plausible than that of the orthodox economists.

MARKET SOCIALISM

It will be recalled that the argument of the previous chapter was that the abstraction of distribution from microeconomic theory was a response to the distributional implications of the early marginalist and the neo-classical analyses. Of course the result of arguing for the removal of distributional questions from economics is that economists cannot evaluate the different distributional schemes put forward by different political persuasions. Furthermore, welfare economists appear to be reliant upon the polity to derive such a scheme, since they have no distributional theory of their own. This abstraction of distribution – which we suggested was behind the move to ordinalism – also led to the problem of deriving a maximum social welfare from individual ordinal functions. As we have seen, Samuelson suggested that we consider directly a social welfare function. Again, if we are dealing with this function directly, and it is not derived from individual behaviour, it is not clear why a market process is required for production and distribution.

In principle, it would be possible to meet directly the requirements of the social function. Even if we concede the marginalist school may have established that a social maximum can be derived from individual actions in the market, this does not in itself show that a similar feat cannot be achieved through planning. This demonstration was attempted by Pierson at the turn of the century. The main point of his 1902 article was that a planned economy would still require a monetary valuation of goods and services. Only if the state can supply everything in plenty will this need disappear.

> As long as the communist state can supply each person with what he wants, no trading will arise ... but when this is no longer the case trading is inevitable.
>
> (Pierson 1902 p. 75)

Trading will inevitably involve markets and pecuniary evaluation – Pierson's 'Problem of Value'. He also maintains that an income distribution which is independent of labour productivity is inconsistent with free choice of labour.

> If the state is to provide us with all our needs, then it must dispose of all labour at its own discretion, otherwise its task will be impossible. It must be in a position to place us where our work is required and it must not be so far influenced by our wishes that they interfere with its plans.
>
> (Pierson 1902 p. 48)

If, however, we are to distribute income according to productivity, then monetary calculation is, Pierson believed, essential (ibid. pp. 80 ff.). This analysis was reinforced in the orthodox literature by Barone.[2] Barone was a follower of Pareto, and his 1908 article was an investigation, on general equilibrium lines, of the possibility of calculating the various coefficients of production in a collectivist state. Barone concludes that such a valuation would be impossibly difficult, and would involve solving a vast number of simultaneous equations (qv. Hoff 1938 p. 222).

Both these articles remained relatively obscure until Hayek's reproduction of them in 1935. The author whose work did succeed in provoking a response was Von Mises, not least because of his polemical and mocking style:

> When Marxism solemnly forbids its adherents to concern themselves with economic problems beyond the expropriation of the expropriators, it adopts no new principle, since the Utopians throughout their descriptions have also neglected all economic considerations, and concentrated attention solely upon painting lurid pictures of existing conditions and glowing pictures of that golden age which is the natural consequence of the New Dispensation.
>
> (Mises 1920 p. 88)

We will deal more fully with the work of Von Mises shortly, but his critique of 'physical unit' or non-pecuniary planning, and his criticism of the lack of economic analysis in Marxism were taken seriously by many socialists, who attempted to respond. The 'English debate' centred around the possibility of retaining pecuniary measurement of goods and the use of money and market within a socialist state; the impossibility of non-market socialism was conceded. Indeed, even Lange's ironic praise of Mises ('a statue of Professor Mises ought to occupy an honourable place in the great hall of the ministry of socialization . . .') did contain the admission that 'it was his powerful challenge that forced the socialists to recognise the importance of an adequate system of economic accounting to guide the allocation of resources in a socialist economy' (Lange 1938 p. 57).

Lange believed that the Marxist theory to be insufficient by itself, although remaining a necessary component of political economy

> The Marxists claim to superiority for his economics is that 'bourgeois' economics has utterly failed to explain the fundamental tendencies of the development of the capitalist system

which are the increase in the scale of production leading to monopolies, intervention and economic imperialism, economic instability and a revolt against the economic system, and so on (Lange 1934 p. 190). However, Lange believed the Marxian theory was insufficient

> But this superiority of Marxian economics is only a partial one. There are some problems before which Marxian economics is quite powerless, while 'bourgeois' economics solves them easily. What can Marxian economics say about monopoly prices? What has it to say on the fundamental problems of monetary and credit theory? . . . And (irony of fate!) what can Marxian economics contribute to the problem of the optimum distribution of productive resources in a socialist economy.

The point for Lange is that the two theories are operative in complimentary 'spheres':

> Clearly the relative merits of Marxian economics and of 'bourgeois' economic theory belong to different 'ranges.' Marxian economics can work the economic evolution of capitalist society into a consistent theory from which its necessity is deduced, while 'bourgeois' economists get no further than mere historical descriptions. On the other hand, 'bourgeois' economics is able to grasp the phenomena of the everyday life of a capitalist economy in a manner far superior to anything the Marxists can produce.

> (Lange 1934 p. 191)

The two sciences are valid for different domains. Marxian theory provides an historical explanation of the development of the political economy, whereas 'bourgeois' economics provides a useful tool for everyday economic administration. There is, Lange suggests, a functional difference between the two theories:

This difference is connected, of course, with the respective social functions of 'bourgeois' and Marxian economics. The first has to provide a scientific basis for rational measures to be taken in the current administration of the capitalist economy . . . the social function of the latter has been to provide a scientific basis for long range anticipations guiding the rational activity of a revolutionary movement against the very institutional foundation of the capitalist system.

Lange believed that the concepts of neo-classical theory would be of great use in the socialist economy

But in providing a scientific basis for the current administration of the capitalist economy 'bourgeois' economics has developed a theory of equilibrium which can also serve as a basis for the current administration of a socialist economy. It is obvious that Marshallian economics offers more for the current administration of the economic system of Soviet Russia than Marxian economics does, though the latter is surely the more effective basis for anticipating the future of capitalism.

and in this respect

Modern economic theory, in spite of its undoubted 'bourgeois' origin, has a universal significance

(Lange 1934 p. 191)

One response to the critique of Mises is therefore to attempt to develop market-based socialist models along neo-classical/welfare economics lines.[3] Indeed, one of the first contributions to the debate over market socialism – Fred Taylor's American Economic Association presidential speech (Taylor 1929) – was concerned primarily with a justification of consumer's sovereignty. Following the methodological stance of the marginalists, Taylor abstracts the question of distribution from the domain of the economic. Taylor believes that distribution under private enterprise is entirely an institutional matter.

First, on the basis of a vast complex of institutions, customs and laws, the citizen adopts a line of conduct which provides him with a money income of greater or lesser volume.

(Taylor 1929 p. 42)

The income is then used to demand goods from the producers, who 'promptly submit to the dictation of the citizen in this matter' (ibid.)

Taylor proposes to mirror this system in a socialist state. He begins with the assumption that

the authorities of such a state would have honestly and earnestly endeavoured to fix incomes so that they represent that distribution . . .

which is called for in the interest of citizens generally and of the group as an organic whole.

This being the case, the state should submit to their claims in the market:

> This socially correct system of incomes being assumed, it necessarily follows that the judgements reached by citizens with respect to the relative importance of different commodities would be virtually social judgements, and the resulting commodity prices would be prices which expressed the social importances of commodities.
>
> (Taylor 1929 p. 44)

Taylor then goes on to establish the optimal pricing level. Recall that the state is required to follow the consumer's sovereignty. Taylor therefore suggests that 'A single consideration is decisive. That price which equals resource-cost is the only price which would be consistent with the income system supposed to have been already decided upon' (ibid. p. 49).

The key factor is therefore to determine the cost of resources. This involves a measurement of the value 'imputed' to factors. Taylor believed that this could be achieved by constructing factor-valuation tables based on initial estimates. The key point is the feedback mechanism offered by market pricing. If the estimate is in error, either surpluses or shortages of the factor will result (ibid. pp. 52–4). Taylor's article was to form the basis of many of the models of the early market socialists.[4]

Dickinson's 1933 scheme was similar in many respects. He also accepted that consumer goods would be priced on free markets, and proposed the use of marketing boards to distribute goods through markets. But Dickinson additionally maintained that it would be possible to derive the various pricing and output coefficients directly

> once the system has got going it will probably be unnecessary to create in this way within the framework of the socialist community a sort of working model of capitalist productions. It would be possible to deal with the problems mathematically, on the basis of the full statistical information that would be at the disposal of the supreme Economic council.
>
> (Dickinson 1933 p. 242)

The plausibility of this scheme was bolstered by Dickinson's belief that 'under capitalism, demand schedules are apt to exist in the realm of faith' (ibid. p. 240). It is possibly for this reason that Dickinson was content to tackle the same problem that Barone despaired of. He did have second thoughts on this mathematical solution though, and abandoned the idea in his 1939 book *The Economics of Socialism*. By then the debate had reverted to the 'trial and error' method outlined by Taylor.[5] Taylor's method was adopted by Lange when he rejoined the debate in 1936, in reply to Hayek's intervention (Hayek 1935a and 1935b).

Lange believed that the trial and error method overcame the problems of computation of equations raised by Hayek (1935b) and also by Robbins (1933).[6]

> Neither would the Central Planning Board have to solve ... millions ... of equations. The only 'equations' which would have to be 'solved' would be those of the consumers and the managers of production. These are exactly the same 'equations' which are 'solved' in the present economic system and the persons who do the 'solving' are the same also. Consumers 'solve' them by spending their income so as to get out of it the maximum total utility; and the managers of production 'solve' them by a method of trial and error, making (or imagining) small variations at the margin, as Marshall used to say, and watching what effect those variations have either on the total utility or on the cost of production.

> ... there is not the slightest reason why a trial and error procedure, similar to that in a competitive market, could not work in a socialist economy to determine the accounting prices of capital goods and of the productive resources in public ownership.

Lange maintained that the feedback mechanism was sufficient to enable equilibrium prices to be determined.

> Any mistake made by the Central Planning Board in fixing prices would announce itself in a very objective way – by a physical shortage or surplus of the quantity of the commodity or resources in question and would have to be corrected in order to keep production running smoothly. As there is generally only one set of prices which satisfies the objective equilibrium condition, both the prices of products and costs are uniquely determined.
>
> (Lange 1938 p. 82)

Furthermore, Lange asserted (citing Wicksteed) that price did not need a free market to be operative. All that was required was 'terms on which alternatives are offered'. Given a preference scale and a quantity of resources, the economic problem of choice was soluble. Lange also believed that this trial and error method is analogous to the functioning of the market under capitalism, that 'The Central Planning Board performs the functions of the market' (ibid. p. 87) and even claimed that the method is the same as that outlined by Walras (ibid. p. 70).

Lange attempted to construct a working model of pure competition by instigating managerial rules for productive plants. The first instruction was for the managers to produce at lowest average cost. The second was to alter output so that marginal cost equals price.[7] This last rule also applied to the industry as a whole (ibid. p. 76). This is only desirable, though, if the managers act as price-takers – in Lange's terms the 'parametric function of prices' must be retained. Only if prices are given would the managerial rules be sufficient, because only then would the perfectly competitive market results be imitated (ibid. p. 80–1).

Lange noted that producing at lowest average cost leads to the marginal productivity of factors – measured in money – being equal. On this basis Durbin suggested an alternative set of rules based on what he claimed was a blend of Marshallian and Pigovian analysis. He believed that the solution to production coefficients should be found by equating the marginal products of all factors (Durbin 1936 p. 141–62). Durbin was not satisfied with the exclusive use of this rule though, since the marginal productivities would only be estimates (ibid. 143). He therefore includes a managerial rule based on Marshallian analysis – that at the point of equilibrium, the average cost will be at its minimum. At this point marginal costs equal average costs. Durbin's rules were to equate marginal productivity and also minimal average cost with price (ibid. pp. 144 ff.).

Durbin's analysis was designed to provide a more realistic set of policy proposals than the equation-solving system of Dickinson (ibid. p. 140). However, the entire idea of providing managerial rules was questioned by Lerner, perhaps because of his familiarity with Austrian theory (Bradley 1981 p. 26). Lerner views it as a mistake to attempt to recreate perfect competition, but believes that instead we should provide an analysis of how to achieve the same results. He begins his 1937 article by stating

> This article is in the main a protest against the developing tradition, in approaching the problems of socialist economics, of starting from the consideration of competitive equilibrium, instead of going direct to the more fundamental principle of marginal opportunity cost. This approach is not only subject to methodological criticism as indirect and cumbersome, but it is a fertile source of actual error deriving from unrealised implications of the static nature of competitive equilibrium.
>
> (Lerner 1937 p. 253)

That is to say, we can arrive at a simple conclusion:

> Price must be equal to marginal cost. This is the contribution that pure economic theory has to make to the building up of a socialist economy.
>
> (Lerner 1937, p. 270)

The significance of Lerner's intervention is to attempt to include the notion of opportunity costs into the socialist models – the marginal costs were marginal opportunity costs (ibid. p. 254). The concept of opportunity cost is designed to introduce a dynamic element into the static model: his costs rule includes long-term costs. Lerner criticised the solutions of Lange and Durbin for focusing on short-term costs.

AUSTRIAN CRITIQUE

In fact it is far from clear that the neo-classical based market scheme presented by Lange *et al.* does indeed have an universal significance. Many socialists would deny that a society based upon private property, private capital or commodity production could be regarded as socialist.[8] Lange himself appears, as Cottrell and Cockshott point out, to be somewhat ambiguous as to his attitude on the question of the applicability of markets. While his 1945 article appeared unequivocal, by 1967 Lange claimed that the market exchange process was only necessary because of the lack of computational ability at that time. He believed this was close to being remedied, and that the advent of computing power would enable central planners to compute directly the necessary equilibrium prices for all goods (Lange 1967, cited Cottrell and Cockshott 1993). This appears to offer a different interpretation on the *raison d'être* for neo-classical theory. Price appears to be simply a unit of account, and not involve valuations at all.

This question of whether the Lange/Taylor schema is actually socialist cuts two ways. Mises was well aware of the possibility of models along the lines of Taylor's and Lange's, but he excluded these from his attack on socialism, simply because he thought, as Dobb and Mandel believed, that such a system would not be socialist (Kirzner 1988 p. 167).

Socialist or no, the question remains as to whether the schemes are workable. The claim of Dickinson, Taylor *et al.* was that if general equilibrium theory was accepted as an explanation of the way in which a market economy functioned, then their system, based around general equilibrium, had to be accepted as valid. It was only during the course of the debate that the Austrians themselves became aware of the extent to which Austrian theory was radically different, and indeed antithetical to the neo-classical framework.

It was for these reasons that the 'standard account' of the 1930s debate is incorrect. Mises' focus was upon centrally planned economies, since he thought that only these economies could be said to be socialist. Furthermore, while the market socialist models have validity within the orthodox framework, the rejection of this framework was only gradual (and was not really complete until the 1970s) (Keizer 1989 pp. 63 ff.). Austrian theory should now be viewed as radically different to the neo-classical framework within which the market socialists were working, and the Austrian critique should be regarded as relating as much to neo-classical theory as to the application of this theory by market socialists. The difference between the two approaches was certainly not grasped by the socialists and the two sides talked past each other, so to speak, as a result.

The confusion was not helped by some rather loose terminology on the part of the Austrians, in particular Mises' claim that 'as soon as one gives up the conception of a freely established monetary price for goods of a higher order, rational production becomes completely impossible' (Mises 1920 p. 104). Mises' point was not that production would be impossible under socialism, but rather that such production would not be – in Mises' terminology – rational. Nonetheless, Lange and others believed that they – and also the solutions of Pareto and Barone – had successfully refuted Mises' claim, and that Hayek's subsequent defence of Mises' argument signalled a 'retreat' from the claim that allocation under socialism is impossible to a position that such allocation is impractical (Lange 1938 p. 62). But the whole point of the Austrian critique was that the general equilibrium models of Pareto and the neo-classical works of Marshall and Pigou – while they may be logically valid – were an irrelevance to real-world economic activity. The market socialists were criticised for using an abstract model as a blueprint for an actual working economy (Vaughn 1980 p. 543).

In order to understand the Austrian critique of neo-classical and general equilibrium theory, it may be helpful to examine the differences in the use of economic concepts. It will be recalled from the last chapter that it was Lionel Robbins, described by Vaughn as 'at least partially in the Austrian tradition', who moved the definition of economics from an objective to a subjectivist basis with his 'choice' delimitation. Unfortunately, this definition only succeeded in grafting Austrian concepts into neo-classical analysis, resulting in bastardised versions of the Austrian concepts. Of particular importance to the present argument is the notion of costs. The point of the Austrian concept of opportunity cost is that it is entirely subjective and can only be known by the individuals concerned. It cannot be measured in terms of money outlays, or by any other objective measurement (Barry 1984, p. 37). The Austrians would be contemptuous of the assumption of 'perfect knowledge' used by general equilibrium economists as a condition for market equilibrium. The whole problem is understanding entrepreneurial behaviour with imperfect knowledge (cf. ibid. *passim*). Indeed, the Austrians were also critical of the orthodox concept of equilibrium. Mises maintained that equilibrium is a stationary condition, and that 'To assume stationary economic conditions is a theoretical expedient and not an attempt to describe reality' (Mises 1922 p. 163).

The Austrians were dismissive of the entire welfare economics/general equilibrium structure precisely because they viewed it as static and unreal. For the Austrians, the central problem for economics was the analysis of dynamic activity through time – the analysis of economic change (Lavoie 1985 p. 65). Mises stated that 'the problem of economic calculation is of economic dynamics: it is no problem of economic statics'. That is to say, 'The problem of economic calculation is a problem which arises in an economy which is perpetually subject to change, an economy which every day is confronted with new problems which have to be solved' (Mises 1922 p. 139). Under perfect competition there would not be any economic problem, since the assumption of perfect knowledge assumes complete efficiency (Bradley 1981

p. 27). In fact, for Hayek, the theory of perfect 'competition' presumes that no competition as such can ensue

> what the theory of perfect competition discusses has little claim to be called 'competition' at all and . . . its conclusions are of little use as guides to policy.

This occurs, Hayek believes, because the current theory begs the questions set by the older theories, as a result of which

> if the state of affairs assumed by the theory of perfect competition ever existed, it would not only deprive of their scope all the activities which the verb 'to compete' describes but would make them virtually impossible.
>
> (Hayek 1946 p. 92)

The key concepts of the Austrian theory were competition and entrepreneurship. The stationary equilibrium cannot consider these concepts, because it is precisely entrepreneurship and competition that cause economic change. The market is 'not merely an allocative device, by which factors are assigned to their most important uses, it is a discovery procedure through which economic agents try out new techniques, experiment with different uses of resources and exploit new opportunities' (Barry 1984 p. 42).

So, far from accepting general equilibrium as a normal condition, the Austrians believed such a situation to be impossible (Lavoie 1985 pp. 65–108). What they were concerned with was the tendency towards equilibrium – the 'equilibrating' process (Bradley 1981 p. 26). While Marshall's 'market clearing' price may be reached, the price set for general equilibrium will not be attained (Lavoie 1985 p. 109).

The Austrian critique was not that the market socialists employ general equilibrium theory incorrectly, but that this theory is itself redundant (Barry 1984 p. 54). Any model based on general equilibrium/welfare economics would be rejected by the Austrians. Although Mises' 1920 article dealt largely with a moneyless economy, his writings do contain enough to suggest a critical attitude.

Mises believed that a moneyless economy would only be possible under primitive exchange conditions (Lavoie 1985, p. 60). He thought that exchange and markets would soon begin to reappear for consumer goods, even if these were originally rationed:

> The beer-tippler will gladly dispose of non-alcoholic drinks allotted to him, if he can get more beer in exchange, whilst the teetotaller will be ready to give up his portion of drink if he can get other goods for it.

Furthermore money could even reappear:

> The principle of exchange can thus operate freely in a socialist state within the narrow limits permitted. It need not always develop in the

form of direct exchanges. The same grounds which have always existed for the building-up of indirect exchange will continue in a socialist state, to place advantages in the way of those who indulge in it. It follows that the socialist state will thus also afford room for the use of a universal medium of exchange – that is, of money

(Mises 1920 pp. 91–2)

Mises did not view this development as a particular problem for consumer goods. The real problem was in capital goods. Mises claimed that these would therefore be impossible to value, since they are not subject to exchange. That is to say, since the value of factors is unknown, costs cannot be calculated – at least not in any common unit of money (Vaughn 1980 p. 539). This would mean that 'any economic system of calculation would become absolutely impossible' (Mises 1920 p. 109).

The whole problem, for Mises, is that equilibrium values are unknown. This results in a constant flux of economic action, and in the necessity to anticipate events in an uncertain future. This interpretation of present data, and the anticipation of future events, is a function performed by the entrepreneur in Mises' theory. He believed that this function must be performed in all economies (Murrell 1983 p. 95). Of course, the static equilibrium model removes this function.

The entrepreneur 'anticipates what future conditions hold and is penalised or rewarded in his quest for profits'. It is the reward for 'alertness' to consumer requirements that is the relevant function for the Austrians and is the dynamic equivalent of the 'trial and error' process. It is this constant need to change and adjust production decisions that is at the heart of the Austrian dynamic theory (Bradley 1981 p. 30). It was from this that Mises' distributional theory is derived. Mises' believed that the entrepreneurial ability that was such a vital function of the economy was unevenly distributed among the population. What is important for Mises is that the best anticipators are brought to the fore. The market performs this task by the profit or loss obtained in production and exchange. There were two aspects to this. The first was that the selection process required an incentive, since the production process involved risk. But just as important was the fact that the incentives – the process of reward – placed capital resources with those who were best able to make use of them. The market acts as a filter for processing entrepreneurial ability, only allowing those with proven ability to retain access to capital funds. The point of the market mechanism is not to obtain the objective equilibrium conditions, for such objective knowledge is impossible, but rather to select those whose speculative abilities are most developed, and to provide incentive and resources to encourage their speculation (Murrell 1983 pp. 95–6).

Mises maintains that this lack of an incentive scheme under socialism is detrimental

84

In an economic system based upon private ownership of the means of production, the speculator is interested in the result of his speculations in the highest possible degree. If it succeeds ... it is *his* gain. If it fails, then, *he* is the first to feel the loss. The speculator works for the community, but he himself feels the success or failure of his action proportionately more than the community. As profit or loss, they appear much greater in proportion to his means than to the total resources of society

whereas

under socialism it is quite different. Here the leader of industry is interested in profit and loss only so far as he participates in them as a citizen – one among millions. On his actions depends the fate of all. He can lead the nation to riches. He can just as well lead it to poverty and want.

(Mises 1922 p. 206; emphasis in original)

There are two elements to this argument. The first is that the market system gives an incentive to follow the society's wishes. The second is that the risk – although magnified – is also localised. Only the entrepreneur's speculation stake is at risk. Under socialism, Mises believed, neither aspect held. The managers of the state enterprises had no incentive to follow the demands of the market, while at the same time the effects of their decision were universal.

There is another, subtler, argument raised by the Austrians concerning the state ownership of production. This concerns a possible socialist defence against the Austrian charge that the businessman must obtain an incentive to follow the market, and that this would necessarily involve personal risk. It could be suggested that the separation of ownership from management in most modern corporations tends to give this notion the lie – few of the decision-makers in modern companies are risking their own capital. If this is the case, it is not clear why the same managers could not simply be employed to manage state corporations. It is due to this separation that the Austrians place great emphasis on capital markets:

it is the capital markets which keep private managers in line ... the owners of private capital can shift resources from unprofitable to more profitable ventures and thus put poor managers out of a job. Where profit or loss no longer serves as an objective test of managerial success, as it likely would not under socialism, it becomes exceedingly difficult to weed out inefficient managers.

(Vaughn, 1980 p. 548)

Hayek drew on this analysis later.[9]

We can see therefore that Mises would certainly reject any model based on static equilibrium, since this precludes the consideration of economic change. As Lavoie remarks

> Neoclassical equilibrium models, of which the perfect competition model is one variety, are attempts to include all alternatives in a given framework – that is, they presuppose a world of Robbinsian optimisers who have preset adjustment ready to meet any change that is anticipated under a given framework. There are no genuinely new ideas, no alertness to unimagined alternatives – in short, no genuine changes.
>
> (Lavoie 1985 p. 107)

Yet this is precisely the model that Lange *et al.* are proposing (Murrell 1983 p. 97). There are never any changes considered in these models:

> When Lange explains the 'trial and error' technique, one is immediately impressed with the banishment of change in his system. Such statements as 'so the process goes on until the objective equilibrium is satisfied and equilibrium finally reached' remind one more of natural scientists in the laboratory than applied economists checking inventory.
>
> (Bradley 1981 p. 28)

All these elements of Austrian economics were misinterpreted in the 1930s' debate. The interpretation of the claim by Mises that socialism was 'impossible' was misunderstood by a market socialist school derived from a general equilibrium tradition. In fact, it seemed to Lange that Mises was almost advocating an institutional view of economic action (Lange 1938 p. 62), presumably since it appeared that the general equilibrium logic only applied under capitalism and not under socialism. Of course, Mises' claim was that the logic of general equilibrium was inapplicable to any economy.

The confusion was probably not helped by the inclusion in Hayek's collection of critical articles (Hayek 1935) of the essay by Enrico Barone, 'The Ministry of Production in the collectivist state' (Barone 1908). This essay, it will be recalled, was in the Paretian mould, and showed that a calculation of the coefficients of production in a socialist state would require the calculation of a vast number of simultaneous equations. The point of its inclusion was presumably to substantiate the claim that the operation of the Dickinson/ Taylor models was wildly impractical. The decision to include the essay was unfortunate in two respects. Firstly, far from accepting the impossibility of a planned economy, the market socialists actually cited the Barone article as a proof of the possibility of the functioning of a socialist economy. Related to this, the article also caused attention to be diverted into what Lavoie calls the 'computation' debate, a debate over the possibility of computing the vast quantity of data (Lavoie 1985 p. 90). This was only a minor part of the problem, Lavoie suggests. The main point of both Mises and Hayek was the 'calculation' argument – that the data to be input into the equations is not available (Vaughn 1980 p. 545). That is, to at least Mises and Hayek, if not also Robbins, the problem was *formulating* the equations – not solving them. In a world of complexity and continuous change, the central planners would lack the knowledge of the coefficients that go into the equations.

(Lavoie 1985 p. 91; emphasis in original)

Hayek views the economic problem as 'not merely a problem of how to allocate "given" resources' but thought that

It is rather a problem of how to secure the best use of resources known to any of the members of society, for ends whose relative importance only these individuals know. Or, to put it briefly, it is a problem of the utilization of knowledge which is not given to anyone in its totality.

(Hayek 1945 p. 78)

The economic problem, for Hayek, was how to co-ordinate the information about economic variables which was dispersed among individuals. He regarded the price system as 'a mechanism for communicating information' between individuals, which therefore enables social co-ordination: 'in a system in which the knowledge of the relevant points is dispersed among many people, prices can act to co-ordinate the separate actions of different people in the same way as subjective values help the individual to co-ordinate the parts of his plan' (Hayek 1945 p. 85).

The reason that the socialist planners cannot draw up their equations is that the economic data available to any individual is always incomplete. 'The peculiar character of the problem of a rational economic order', according to Hayek,

is determined precisely by the fact that the knowledge of the circumstances of which we must make use never exists in concentrated or integrated form but solely as the dispersed bits of incomplete and frequently contradictory knowledge which all the separate individuals possess.

(Hayek 1945 p. 77)

This information could only be revealed through the market.

Of particular relevance to an understanding of the assertion of decentralised and incomplete information is Hayek's view of the commodity. For Hayek, each commodity is only a 'type', and variations in quality, time and location and a myriad of other factors all contribute to differentiate the usefulness of ostensibly identical commodities, so that 'Two technically similar goods in different places or in different packages cannot possibly be treated as equal in usefulness for most purposes if even a minimum of efficient use is to be secured'. In fact we 'would have to treat the existing body of instrumental goods as being constituted of almost as many different types of goods as there are individual units' (Hayek 1935b p. 209).

Vaughn refers to this as the problem of product specification (Vaughn 1980, p. 546). Each 'product' is capable of an infinitely large number of minute variations in availability and quality. In a sense, each object is a different 'good'. The information as to which 'goods' are available and which goods are required is therefore never complete, but is the subject of continuous discovery (ibid. p. 545).

It was for this reason that the entrepreneur was required in a rational economic system, and why Hayek believed that a planning board could not act as a replacement. It was the constant effort to find out how goods could be altered that was, for Hayek, the relevant feature of business. The planning board could never differentiate goods in this way.

> That the price-fixing process will be confined to establishing uniform prices for classes of goods and that therefore distinctions based on the special circumstances of time, place and quality will find no expression in prices is probably obvious. Without some such simplification, the number of different commodities for which separate prices would have to be fixed would be practically infinite. This means, however, that the managers of production will have no inducement and even no real possibility, to make use of special opportunities, special bargains, and all the little advantages offered by their special local conditions, since all these things could not enter into their calculations.
>
> (Hayek 1940 p. 143)

It was this element of differentiation that was crucial, because it introduced changes in the economy. The reason there could be no equilibrium in the market was because there could never be a fully specified product. Consequently, Hayek was not concerned with studying economics in general equilibrium. His concern was to study disequilibrium and economic change. The static equilibrium models were therefore inadequate.

In fact, the market socialist models regarded the disequilibrium of capitalism as a disadvantage. It was this constant change that made the task of the Central Planning Board so difficult. As each unit of each commodity was in a sense unique, having different qualities, location, availability and other contingencies, the price of each unit would need to be treated separately. Since the knowledge of the units constantly changes, these prices would constantly alter. The CPB would have to monitor constantly an infinite number of prices.

The other consequence of the employment of static equilibrium models employing 'given' choices was that it was unable to consider the development of new products, and the other advantages of economies of scale (Bradley 1981 p. 28).[10]

In this respect the static equilibrium economy may well involve lower welfare and higher costs than the dynamic disequilibrium economy, which could develop new production methods to lower costs.

The point where these differences materialise in the market socialism debate is precisely in the concept of costs. The Austrian notion of cost was opportunity cost – the value of alternatives foregone. The point – as was mentioned earlier – was that these costs were subjective, and could be known only to the individual who bearing them. This is because evaluating the opportunity cost involves knowledge of the value of all possible alternatives, and these alternatives, as we have just seen, are infinite. The knowledge of alternatives is therefore always incomplete, and is always diffused throughout the population, all the members of which have incomplete localised information of the different 'goods' which are available and which may be wanted (Hayek 1945 p. 88). Only the individual knows the opportunity cost of their choice, because only they can judge the value of alternatives foregone. This cost, moreover, will instantly change as the knowledge of alternatives changes.

The concept of cost used in the equilibrium models from which the market socialist models were drawn was not subjective, and in fact is only nominally opportunity cost. The general equilibrium approach uses 'objective opportunities displaced by a course of action' rather than a subjective approach. The costs are indeed often measured in money terms, which again presumes an objective measurement: it would be possible for any individual – including the socialist state managers – to objectively measure alternatives foregone. This, for the Austrians, is an error. Costs cannot be measured objectively (Lavoie 1985 p. 16).

Of course, both welfare economics and the general equilibrium socialist models have as a central requirement the measurement and knowledge of costs (Barry 1984 p. 36). However, to the Austrians, costs are not measurable, and are known only to 'the man on the spot' (Bradley 1981 p. 33). The use of marginal costs as a pricing rule would therefore be regarded by Hayek as impossible – no planning or marketing board could possibly know the marginal costs, since only Hayek's 'man on the spot' is aware of all the possible alternatives. Knowing the relative money price of already existing alternatives is insufficient. It is also necessary to know other possible alternatives (which maybe a change in a pedantic detail, such as location or packaging) which do not yet exist, but which could be delivered (Lavoie 1985 p. 102). Although the socialist managers could make decisions between the 'given' alternatives – production is not impossible in this sense – there is no real way of knowing whether better alternatives exist. Hayek's contention is that the market mechanism offers the chance to see if this is so, since new alternatives are constantly generated. This is what Hayek means when he claims that socialist managers would lack the necessary information to derive production decisions.

The Lange/Taylor trial and error model and especially the Lerner (and Durbin) marginal-cost rule were therefore rejected by Hayek as inoperative. The rule would simply be unenforceable. 'What is forgotten is that the method which under given conditions is the cheapest is the thing which has to be discovered anew, sometimes almost from day to day, by the entrepreneur' (Hayek 1940 p. 196). It would be impossible to know whether each decision took advantage of a possible change or not. Whereas the socialist models assume that these costs can be objectively measured, the Austrians rejected objective costs. Even Lerner's 'opportunity cost' was an equilibrium concept, and therefore remains static (Bradley 1981 p. 26, cf. Lavoie 1985 p. 140), in spite of his criticism of Lange's model as 'reactionary and static' (cf. Hoff 1938 p. 218). Furthermore, all the models deal with standardised commodities, whereas in fact almost all commodities have infinite differentiation. This results in the need for constant price changes, which would be impossible for the market socialist models to deal with.

> If in the real world we had to deal with approximately constant data, that is, if the problem were to find a price system which then could be left more or less unchanged for long period, then the proposal under consideration would not be so entirely unreasonable. With given and constant data such a state of equilibrium could indeed be approached by the method of trial and error. But this is far from being the situation in the real world, where constant change is the rule.
>
> (Hayek 1940, p. 188)

Hayek also pointed out that the trial and error method was actually very similar to the mathematical model. The prices of goods were all interconnected, and no one price could be changed in isolation: 'Almost every change of any single price would make changes of hundreds of other prices necessary' (Hayek 1935b p. 214).[11] The method of trial and error, Hayek believed, would therefore soon break down. There would be an enormous number of errors caused by the same number of trials, and no way of knowing which trial caused which error. The trial and error method only applies to prices individually – it cannot be used to obtain the general equilibrium (we can see that this is actually a partial equilibrium approach to a general equilibrium problem). Indeed, the entire process depends upon the assumption that no other change occurs whilst the trial is proceeding – that *ceteris* remain *paribus*. That is, it involves a static economy. As Barry puts it 'the socialist model was, in effect, an experiment in comparative statics' (Barry 1984 p. 55).

There are also good managerial reasons for the market socialist systems to break down. Lange especially insisted that the socialist managers must treat the market clearing price as parametric: each producer must act as though they were unable to influence price (Lange 1938 p. 70). In practice, it is most unlikely that the managers would act in this way, particularly if it runs contrary to their personal interests (Vaughn 1980 p. 548). It is entirely possible that the managers will use what amounts to a monopoly position to raise prices and reduce output (and therefore, of course, reduce costs), particularly since Lange's rules were to apply to the managers of the entire industry as well as the individual producers. It would be possible for the state undertakings simply to exploit their monopoly position (Hoff 1938 p. 125). In fact, the marginal-cost/trial and error method is less a model for socialism than a device for state marketing. Indeed, Lange was aware of the general nature of marginal-cost pricing, and accepts that the Taylor model is not specific to socialism but can also be used in a totally centralised economy (Lange 1938 p. 90). He mitigates this by asserting that 'such a system would scarcely be tolerated by any civilised people' (ibid. p. 45). It is unclear whether Lange is here relying on a Marxian analysis of the development of a socialist state, such that some correct political 'form' is presumed to come into existence.[12] Certainly, no analysis of political structures is given, and without this, toleration seems rather beside the point. It is unclear how effective political action is supposed to be taken. Humphreys describes Lange's model as somewhat 'politically innocent', and points out that the political structures may be undesirable or unrealistic (Humphreys 1987 p. 109).

Furthermore, it is far from clear how the managerial decisions could be challenged. There is no real method of obtaining information about the responsiveness of managers to market demand. Bergson points out that

> Lange nowhere provided any criterion for judging and rewarding managerial success. The rules themselves, it is true, might be viewed as such a criterion, but in order to gauge and reward success on this basis the Central Planning Board would have to probe deeply into the cost and other internal records of individual production units. This would vastly increase the CPB's responsibilities, which it is a cardinal concern of the competitive solution to limit. The failure to establish any practical success criterion for managers, it was held previously (Bergson 1948 p. 220) represents a major deficiency of the competitive solution and one not easily repaired.
>
> (Bergson 1967 p. 657)

There is no real method of ensuring that the production rules have been applied. In addition, the industrial managers will have less profit incentive, and even greater monopoly power than most of their capitalist counterparts (ibid. p. 658).

This managerial critique is also raised by Kornai. He suggests that the Lange/Lerner general equilibrium-based models abstract from the institutional setting.

> The people at his Central Planning Board are reincarnations of Plato's philosophers, embodiments of unity, unselfishness and wisdom. They are satisfied with doing nothing else but strictly enforcing the 'rule', adjusting prices to excess demand.

Kornai, with his experience of the Hungarian economy, believes that this conception is desperately wide of the mark

> Such an unworldly bureaucracy never existed in the past and never will in the future. Political bureaucracies have inner conflicts reflecting the divisions of society and the diverse pressures of various social groups. They pursue their own individual and group interests, including the interests of the particular specialised agency to which they belong. Power creates an irresistible temptation to make use of it.
>
> (Kornai 1986 p. 1726)

It will be recalled that it was precisely because of the need for judgements on managerial decisions that Mises emphasised capital markets. Further to this, Hayek points out that since it is near impossible to judge the performance of managers, a central bank, which Hayek regarded as the minimum requirement for any semblance of a socialist economy, would have very little knowledge as to which industries and enterprises to commit funds to. There is no automatic allocation mechanism, which was the function that the Austrian believed the profit and loss of the market performed, nor was there any 'track record' to judge the success of the present going concerns (Hayek 1935a p. 20, pp. 232 ff.).

The failings of centrally planned systems are legion, and have been well documented by Alec Nove and others.[13] The system of the USSR in particular was doomed to failure, as the centrally controlled economy was planned in terms of physical units.[14] Without the use of some common denominator or unit of account, and without even the slightest hint of deference to consumer sovereignty, the entire enterprise was doomed from the start:

> Basically, the central plan gives exclusive emphasis to production targets in terms of single quantities. As a result, the individual enterprise is often ignorant of precise requirements. For example, plan-fulfillment targets in terms of square meters in the textile sector can lead to the production of an excessive amount of thin, fragile cloth. The firm tries to achieve the target in quantitative terms, knowing or not knowing that the cloth is too thin. If the target is expressed in terms of weight, the tendency will be to produce cloth that is too heavy.
>
> (Hodgson 1984 p. 102)

The central plan was invariably overwhelmed by the necessity of such detail:

> Thus when window-glass was planned in tons it was too thick and heavy; so they shifted the plan 'indicator' to square meters, whereupon it became too thin. Common sense tells us that glass should be thick or thin according to the circumstances of its use, but such detail is not and *can not* be within the cognisance of the central planning organs.

Aggregation is a 'must' if next year's plan is to be drafted before the end of the century.

(Nove 1980 p. 6, cited Hodgson 1984 p. 102)

Nove believed that democracy is not relevant to this problem, and that 'Such distortions could occur in the most democratic of centrally planned systems' (ibid.).

At no time do the producers in the economy take cognisance of the consumers. Furthermore, at no time are there any cross-valuations between different commodities: each quota is of necessity given in isolation. No adjustment of production or supply is possible. This is, as was suggested earlier, of particular significance in the production of capital goods. Stories of shipments of machine-parts with incorrect threads, or of goods being stranded in the wrong part of the country are commonplace. Because there is no exchange mechanism, the planners require an impossibly vast array of technical knowledge to make the plan workable.

NORMATIVE THEORY

The 1930s market socialist models were the first systematic attempts directly to apply the pure economic theory of the welfare economists to a hypothetical economy. The attempt failed because the welfare economics theory is an inadequate approach to the analysis of real-world economies. The Austrian critique was a critique of the unrealistic approach of the orthodox theory from which the market socialist models were derived (Barry 1984 p. 54, cf. Murrell 1983 p. 102). The models of welfare economics – of an unchanging world in which rational optimisers act instantaneously with perfect knowledge – was regarded as of no practical consequence by the Austrians. It was the orthodox theory itself, not the market socialist application of it, that was the main point of the 1930s' debate.

The Austrian critique was in essence a critique of the application of orthodox economic theory. The debate outlined in the previous chapter was methodological in nature, and concerned the validity and scope of the orthodox theory. We saw that in order to remain logically valid whilst satisfying various methodological imperatives – that the theory should be positive and yield a social conclusion from the analysis of individuals – the scope of the theory had to be drawn so narrow that in the end it was rendered virtually analytic. The market socialist blueprints of the 1930s lay firmly within the scope of this orthodoxy, and represented an attempt to apply the models of the welfare economists to achieve a particular politically inspired outcome. The Austrian claim was that this market socialist scheme was inoperative because it was derived from a largely analytic or unrealistic theory.

In fact, the Austrian economists readily conceded that once one accepted the welfare economics/general equilibrium theory, the market socialist position is not readily assailable. It was this that Mises meant when he said that there was no economic calculation in the static state. Under the static conditions presumed in the orthodox theory, the calculation problem posed by Mises and Hayek would simply not exist (Bradley 1981 p. 28). Indeed, one may well hold the view that Lange has adequately refuted the sceptical conclusions of Barone:

> it cannot be denied that as an answer to the computation argument, Lange's demonstration is an impressive accomplishment, and indeed it would seem that neoclassical economists who doubt the workability of socialism face a difficult task in responding to this demonstration. If the equilibrating process of real-world capitalism is explained by recourse to a Walrasian auctioneer, it is not clear why a planning bureau could not similarly function as a coordinating agent.
>
> (Lavoie 1985 p. 122)

Indeed, criticising the Lange/Lerner socialist models on the basis of the computation difficulties alone is insufficient. As Lavoie goes on to point out, the computation argument is dependent upon the calculation argument, which necessarily involves a rejection of general equilibrium theory:

> Some might argue here ... that Hayek is showing that Lange's answer was ineffective not only against the calculation argument but also against the computation argument. However, Hayek's objection holds only if one rejects (as I believe Hayek did, at least implicitly) the Walrasian explanation of how capitalism works. For any neoclassical theorist who takes his Walrasian auctioneer seriously, Lange's formal analogy argument shows quite plausibly that his central planning board can do as well at finding a general equilibrium configuration of prices as the auctioneer could. Thus no doubt Lange would have responded to Hayek that if the planning board could not find the right prices, then neither could capitalists. Within what I have called the 'neoclassical' perspective, this response would be unanswerable.
>
> (Lavoie 1985 p. 168 n. 12)

This general equilibrium function performed a methodological function in economic science though, as outlined in the previous chapter. The pure theory of choice enabled the orthodox economists to maintain a positivist, neutral science of society. The economic science was to show how the society was to be organised in order to accrue maximum benefit. The positive science was required in order to show how much (or how little) control over social affairs was necessary. The science was to be individualistic to show how centralised control was undesirable, and a 'rational economic human' was posited to show how economic value was subjective.

This entire scheme can now be seen to have fallen through. The essential the measurement of costs must be imputed from values. If value is subjective, then costs are also subjective (Bradley 1981 p. 33), and neither are capable of pecuniary objective measurement.[15] The choices facing the 'rational economic human' were infinite in number, and any talk of preference sets should be dismissed. The theory therefore does not show how social value could be derived. The orthodox theory was accordingly not able to make any comment upon how a society should obtain maximum benefit. The *raison d'être* for positive economic science has disappeared. It no longer provided instrumental knowledge of how to improve our lot. Moreover, as we noted in Chapter 1, the very notion of a policy science is not politically neutral. The resultant theory will inevitably result in a particular view of the political process. It was this dilemma of positivist policy that the orthodox economists were unable to solve.

If we are to abandon the idea of a positive economic science, then following the classification of Keat and Urry outlined in Chapter 1 we must turn to either a realist or a conventionalist metatheory. Conventionalist philosophies were associated with the institutional school, which we will discuss in the next chapter. The Austrian scheme could be said to be more along the lines of a realist approach to social science. Realism, according to Keat and Urry, involves the discovery of 'the relations of natural necessity that exist in the physical world' (Keat and Urry 1975 p. 27). This will involve attempting to uncover causal relations. Causal explanations require not only the discovery of regularities between phenomena, but also the discovery of a connecting mechanism. They require descriptions of the process of change, not simply a description of antecedent events. The process of explanation requires answers to 'why' questions, and these answers will also involve answers to 'how' and 'what' questions. This is the purpose of scientific theories. They describe the structures and mechanisms involved in the causal process (ibid. pp. 27–32).

Although the concept of realist philosophy was developed with Marxist and socialist philosophies in mind, it need not be restricted exclusively to these theories, and it is a moot point as to whether the Austrian theory fits within the realist mould; there are differences between the realist metatheory outlines by Keat and Urry *et al.*, and the Austrian view. In particular, realists for the most part are attempting to preserve methodological monism. Their claim is that positivism is inadequate for all sciences. The Austrians[16] usually defend methodological dualism. They claim that different methods should be employed in physical and social sciences (Shand 1990 pp. 7 ff.). They argue that the sort of objective economic science which the marginalists were hoping to achieve was impossible. They rejected the idea of prediction in the social sciences, claiming that the sort of regulations and laws which characterised positivist scientific activity did not exist in the social world (Barry 1984 p. 35). Hayek in particular denounced 'scientism': the use of physical science methods in social science (cf. Hayek 1955 pt one), precisely because he believed that it inevitably denied the social scientist the sort of individualist basis that he viewed as an essential element of political economy.

With the denial of positivist social science, the sort of hedonistic psychology which formed the basis of orthodox theory becomes redundant. The Austrian economic psychology – as put forward by Mises above – moved towards a Darwinian explanation of social structure. The capacities of individuals are deemed to be unequal: those 'best fitted' to handle economic decision-making would eventually obtain the necessary economic power to do so. Note that the evolutionary mode of explanation is different to its positivist predecessors. There is no longer an equivalence of prediction and explanation. The explanation of evolutionary theories is always retrospective. Furthermore, the denial of objective economic theory means that the boundary between economic and social/political action disappears.

The Austrian methodology can be described as hermeneutical or interpretive. They claim that social science, unlike physical science, requires a nonempirical interpretation of action and thought. They criticize the neo-classical scheme for treating the human mind as simply a mechanism, with the inputs to decision-making regarded as exogenous.

> Action is here confused with mere reaction. There is no choice of ends. Given a 'comprehensive preference field' for each agent, what is there to choose? The outcome of all acts of choice is here predetermined.
> (Lachmann 1990 p. 135)

In positivist economics, no 'real' choices are made, since in reality choices are uncertain. Austrian economics attempts to replace the mechanistic theory of action with a voluntaristic theory. The point is to understand the meaning ascribed to a series of actions, and hermeneutics is the study of the methods by which such interpretation can be carried out (ibid. pp. 136 ff.).

Although most interpretive social science has been influenced by Weber, the main developments in Austrian theory stem from Hayek, who developed Austrian political philosophy and philosophy of law, and from Mises' conception of human action. Mises believed in an 'essence' of humans which is 'known' a priori, that humans deliberately choose actions to achieve ends. The science of this Mises called praxeology; a general science of human action. Economics is a subset of this science (Shand 1990 p. 8).

Let us briefly return to the question of whether the Austrians should be regarded as realists. This is not a pedantic question, since the claims being made by the Austrians will have a bearing on our discussion of their theory. Shand believes that 'Mises' apriorism places him in some strange company', since according to Shand Marxian economists also retain an a priori notion of action. Although neither Marxism or indeed Austrian economics need necessarily be regarded as a priori in essence,[17] there would appear to be common ground in their approach to the philosophy of science. Keat and Urry suggest, for example, that a realist view of models is that they are 'an attempt to *describe* structures and mechanisms which are often unavailable to observation' (Keat and Urry 1975 p. 34 original emphasis). This appears entirely in keeping with Austrian philosophy.

Hutchison suggests that it appears impossible to make decisions between differing *a priori* claims (cf. Hutchison 1981 pp. 295–7). However this appears to be a slight misunderstanding of the realist project. The realist does not reject empirical evidence, but claims that the sort of bridge principles used to link these to theories ought usually to be regarded as causal explanations. They are used to devise indirect tests of theories (Keat and Urry 1975 p. 38).

Returning to the Austrian political economy, we are in fact able to offer empirical criticisms of their substantive theory. We may well maintain that this school is no more realistic than the orthodoxy. Again, we can derive our critique from the methodological roots, as we did with orthodox economics. Although the Austrians rejected many of the positivist tenets, they nonetheless retain a methodological individualist approach, and with it the concept of the 'invisible hand' explanation of the derivation of the optimal social outcome from the individual actions. This leads the Austrians to retain a psychology based on rationality, and also to retain the notion of causal explanation. We will see that these prove to be incompatible under Austrian theory.

The point of departure for the Austrians, it will be recalled, was their conception of entrepreneurial activity. This, broadly speaking, consisted of speculative action based on localised knowledge. Because the knowledge of production possibilities and opportunity cost was unavoidably localised, it was necessary to encourage and reward entrepreneurial activity. It will also be recalled that the Austrians placed great emphasis on capital markets. It was these that enabled entrepreneurs to run very large corporations 'by proxy' as it were: by employing managers.

Further to this, we also noted the accompanying psychological assumption made by the Austrians. In order to derive a distributional theory from this analysis, it is necessary to assume both that business success is largely a result of some sort of undefined entrepreneurial 'capacity' and that this capacity is inherent and unequally distributed among the population. Only then is it possible to show, as Mises attempted to do, that distribution will settle into an optimal pattern. Mises' analysis was that given this unequal entrepreneurial talent, it was indeed functional for assets to be channelled to those who were best able to employ them.

Unfortunately, no causal link is established between the cited cause – entrepreneurial talent – and the cited effect – business success. It is necessary for the theory to demonstrate that success in the market is due primarily to entrepreneurial talent, rather than market power or simply luck. This demonstration is markedly absent from the analysis and remains a presumption. Without this demonstration the theory moves away from an Adam Smith type 'invisible hand' theory and towards a Darwinian style of evolutionary theory which neither explains nor predicts. This can be seen most clearly in Mises' treatment of distribution. In essence, this is an evolutionary theory, which states that the market acts as a filter mechanism to move resources away from bad entrepreneurs towards good ones. The actual manner in which the market does this is not specified, as a result of which we are unable to show that distribution is indeed optimal. There remains simply an assumption that those in some way 'best fitted' to receive wealth did indeed receive it. In order to explain that the distribution is optimal, it has to be shown that markets do indeed respond mainly to entrepreneurial activity.

In fact, it is far from clear that this is the case. The possibility that market power may affect the optimal outcome is not considered by the Austrians – they simply presume that the market will filter out 'inefficient' monopolists. But their evolutionary system must have some sort of starting-point. Given the sort of vast inequality of wealth which has been in existence for hundreds of years, it is hard to see how the pecuniary evolutionary process envisaged by the Austrians is to be got going.[18] It would not be at all fanciful to suggest that the market is manipulated by the already powerful rather than the market being a mechanism to re-allocate wealth in a functional manner.

Much of the theory rests on the vaunted capital markets. The theory presumes free entry and exit of firms, and that entrepreneurs are able to obtain capital for speculation: the capital markets are 'open-ended'. It also presumes capital is mobile, and will pursue whichever areas will lead to greatest profit. In point of fact, present capital markets clearly reinforce market power, and access to funds for speculation will be denied to those who do not already have collateral. Indeed, the instability and constant crises of financial and capital markets gives an air of unreality to the Austrian theory.

The present state of the capital markets, dominated by multinationals and pension funds, does not seem to bode well for the sort of liquid capital which is required by the Austrian theory. It is also far from clear how many of the critiques of managerialism raised against the market socialist models outlined above will be solved by a completely *laissez-faire* economy. If it is impossible to give socialist managers incentives to manage efficiently (such as linked salaries or shares), then it is unclear why managers working under *laissez-faire* should differ, or why there would be insufficient data on the viability of socialist concerns, whereas entrepreneurs have sufficient data on concerns operating in a *laissez-faire* economy. Many of the problems will remain.

Apart from the evolutionary aspect of the Austrian psychology, we can see that it also retains a notion of rationality. All institutional influences are ignored. This, combined with the evolutionary/Darwinian psychology, results in the Austrian 'explanations' being *post hoc* in nature. The theory has ceased to explain why events have occurred, and as a result can never be proven wrong – the economist is always wise, but only after the event. The theory has, just like the orthodox economics, become closed. Should markets not work in the required manner, the Austrians assume it is due to institutional barriers, or because individuals are not being entrepreneurial or some such. The Austrian theory is therefore no more capable of application than the orthodox theory was. We will examine the Austrian endeavours to consider institutions in Chapter 5. In the next chapter we will look at the American institutionalist critique of positivism and rationalist psychology, and consider the employment of social psychology and the pragmatist conception of science in economic theory.

4

AMERICAN INSTITUTIONALISM

In the previous chapter we saw that orthodox economics could not derive the sort of social policy conclusions that were necessary in order to justify the positivist metatheory. The use of orthodox theory by the 1930s' market socialists, while legitimate, failed because the orthodox theory itself could not be sustained. In particular, the concept of rationality employed by the orthodox economists was static, and was therefore not able to consider questions of dynamic economy. The Austrian critique was that economic values – and therefore imputed costs – are totally subjective in nature and cannot be known to any planner. Furthermore, they believed, the interaction of rational individuals led to a distinct order which it would be unwise to attempt to alter.

We suggested that in fact it was near impossible for such an aggregate social order to evolve. In addition, the Austrians retained the concept of rationality. Both of these elements – rationality and aggregation – were attacked by the American institutionalists. They maintained that human action was not determinately rational, but was influenced by social culture and habit, and that individual action was insufficient to derive an optimum social order. They also attempted to revive the idea of economic planning by trying to base their value theory on objective technological/scientific criteria. We shall see in this chapter that although the critique of individualism and rationality is correct, the renewed calls for planning solutions cannot be sustained.

The American institutionalists, in so far as they can be called a distinctive school of thought, are certainly a much 'looser' school than any of the others we have looked at. In so far as the authors have a common thread, it is that they view the economy as a sub-system of an evolving socio-cultural system, and also that they believe that scientific and technological advance is a primary force in this evolution. They would not accept the rational self-seeking model of conventional economics. Instead, they would claim that the behaviour of humans in society is specific to each epoch (Gruchy 1987 pp. 2–3).

We can identify two main streams of thought in the disparate institutionalist school, representing two different interpretations of social institutions. We shall consider first of all the more deterministic wing of Veblen,

100

Mitchell and Ayres, who invoke the pragmatist philosopher's conception of institutions as habits of thought, followed by the 'purposive' theories of Commons, who interprets institutions as deliberate social control over individual actions whilst employing to a greater or lesser extent a similar rationalist conception of human action as the conventional economists. We shall argue that both interpretations are necessary. In this chapter and in the chapter following, we will suggest that while the rational economic conception of behaviour is inadequate, we must hold, and work towards, a non-deterministic model of self-expression. This model, we will suggest, will invariably involve non-market, deliberate social action.

DETERMINIST THEORIES

Veblen

We saw earlier how the utilitarian formulation of individual and social action had metamorphosed into rational choice explanation by the 1930s. This theory was also used by the market socialists as the basis of their models. Meanwhile in America, contemporary with Marshall and just preceding the English market socialism debate, Thorstein Veblen was developing a social psychological critique of orthodox economic theory. His critique led to many theoretical revisions which now form part of the orthodoxy, but his work was in itself heterodox and radical, and led to a distinct socio-economic theory.

The utilitarian hedonist psychology was individualist and transcendental. The utilitarians conceived human nature as given, and derived economic laws which they considered immutable. Veblen, by contrast, insisted on the historical relativity of all social science generalisations, because of the malleability of human nature. Furthermore, human nature was an endogenous variable, not a 'given'. It changed as a result of the normal functioning of the social system.

The basis of Veblen's critique was the employment of hedonistic psychology. Veblen joins together the classics and marginalists in this; he regarded the marginal utility school as a 'specialized variant' of the classics (Veblen 1909 p. 155).[1] They may have provided a 'sufficient reason' for human behaviour, but not an 'efficient cause';[2] they have not postulated a causal explanation. Economic explanations were given in teleological terms, not cause and effect (Veblen 1909 p. 158). The fact was that, for Veblen, 'each generation of economists had taken for granted the very things that most needed proving – the "preconceptions" they took over from the prevalent world outlook and the accepted institutions' (Lerner 1948 p. 20). The classics and marginalists ignored the social and cultural effects of society upon the humans who create that society.

A gang of Aleutian Islanders slushing about in the wrack and surf with rakes and magical incantations for the capture of shell-fish are held in point of taxonomic reality, to be engaged on a feast of hedonistic equilibration in rent, wages and interest.

(Veblen, cited Lerner 1948 p. 20)

Since human behaviour is regarded as a universal datum, all that is left for the social scientist to do is to classify this behaviour – taxonomy. All economic behaviour is 'hedonistic equilibration' in one form or another. Economics makes no allowance for the possibility of changing human nature. In the 'received formulations of economic theory', according to Veblen

the human material with which the inquiry is concerned is conceived in hedonistic terms; that is to say, in terms of a passive and substantially inert and immutably given human nature. The psychological and anthropological preconceptions of the economists have been those which were accepted by the psychological and social sciences some generations ago. The hedonistic conception of man is that of a lightning calculator of pleasure and pains, who oscillates like a homogeneous globule of desire of happiness under the impulse of stimuli that shift him about the area, but leave him intact. He has neither antecedent nor consequent. He is an isolated definitive human datum

(Veblen 1898 p. 73)

For Veblen, the psychological theory of the hedonists was outdated, as indeed was their conception of science. He rejected the scientific basis of teleological explanation. Modern science in Veblen's time was Darwinian. Veblen criticised the classics and marginalists for not positing a theory of the evolution of human nature. This would provide a causal explanation of human action. The acceptance of the present social norms by economists as 'intrinsic to the nature of things', Veblen suggests, 'limits their inquiry in a particular and decisive way. It shuts off the inquiry at the point where the modern scientific interest sets in' (Veblen 1909 p. 161). If Bentham wanted to be the 'Newton of the moral world', then Veblen wanted to be the Darwin of economics. Anthropology was to replace physics, and the concepts of equilibrium and calculus had no part in Veblen's scheme. Instead, he wanted to search for the reasons behind the presently existing social norms to explain what the orthodox economists took for granted.

Veblen believed that human nature underwent an evolutionary change along Darwinian lines (Copeland 1958 p. 50). In place of a human nature modelled on rational thought, Veblen posited thought as conditioned by habit, social conventions and social experience. Veblen replaced the hedonism of the utilitarians with the social psychology of the pragmatists. The term used by the pragmatists to describe habits of thought and social conventions was 'institutions'. It was with institutions that Veblen was primarily concerned. He was interested in cultural evolution rather than biology, and unlike the 'social Darwinists', he was unconcerned with biological attributes of individuals. He regarded biological traits as universal (McFarland 1985 p. 97, Lerner 1948 p. 210). The important element for Veblen was the effect of the institutions upon basic human nature.

Veblen held that although primary instincts were of importance as a determinant of human nature in the early stages of cultural evolution, by the later stages these were dominated by the institutional structures (Rutherford 1984 p. 332). The instincts were the fixed 'prime movers' of human action. Veblen mentions three such instincts: the drive towards the provision of welfare for both family and society (parental bent), a drive towards explanation of the world (idle curiosity), and a drive towards technological improvement (instinct of workmanship).[3] In Veblen's schemes, the social institutions acted and (to an extent) reacted upon these instincts.

The heart of Veblen's social theory is the 'bitter and unending struggles that go on in the cultural arena'. One such struggle is the conflict between animistic and matter of fact explanations, between superstition and science. Science weakens the cultural institutions, which will attempt to overcome or divert the results of inquiry (Lerner 1948 p. 24). Since the institutions are the result of habits of thought, they are antipathetical to matter of fact inquiries. And the members of the social order who gain from the institutional system would obviously have a vested interest in conserving the order: their class was called the 'vested interests'.

The conflict between superstition and science emerges in other forms. Of particular interest to Veblen, and the link between his social and economic theory, is the clash between the workmanship instinct and the pecuniary institutions. The emergence of modern civilisation had altered an instinct for well-being to one of a predatory culture (Veblen 1899 *passim*). When this leads to individual esteem being judged by reward, property is no longer possessed for use, but as a mark of status. Goods take on what later came to be called 'positional' attributes (cf. Hirsch 1977). Goods are only of value in so far as they are not possessed by others. This makes wealth, by definition, socially scarce:

> In the nature of the case, the desire for wealth can scarcely be satiated in any individual instance, and evidently a satiation of the average or general desire for wealth is out of the question. However widely, or equally, or 'fairly' it may be distributed, no general increase of the community's wealth can make any approach to satiating this need, the ground of which is the desire of every one to excel every one else in the accumulation of goods.
>
> (Veblen 1899 p. 32)

By changing human nature from a concern for welfare to positional wealth and predation, the vested interests can legitimise their position in the social order. By creating social scarcity they can then legitimise business activity. What is actually for Veblen the creation of waste is seen to people under the pecuniary institutions as a vital social function.

The creation of waste enables business to draw upon 'intangible assets', assets which have no relationship to material productive sources. They represent free income to the businessman. Industry, on the other hand, employs only tangible assets: 'mechanically productive capacity' (Veblen 1919b p. 69). This difference concerns one of the main areas of Veblen's framework.

The conflict between workmanship and the pecuniary institutions manifests itself in a conflict between business and industry. Business attempts to sabotage industry by providing a check upon the productive capacity of industry, and by keeping prices high. The main weapon of industry was technology. It was progress in technology – the 'industrial arts' – that provided the challenge to the old institutions. The owning groups respond to the challenge by reasserting the existing principles: the assertion of vested ideas by the vested interests (Lerner 1948 p. 25). There is therefore a 'lag' between the state of the industrial arts and business. The outcome of the cycle is uncertain, there is no suggestion of technological determinism (Rutherford 1984 p. 331).

The main aim of business, then, is to take an ever-expanding and productive industrial complex, and ensure that nonetheless a condition of scarcity exists. This is achieved through non-market means. We have mentioned one of these – the instigation of positional wealth. Following from this is the production of conspicuous waste. This is Veblen's concept of the 'leisure class': that conspicuous expenditure and leisure are taken as signs of well being. The leisure class – those whose wealth precludes the necessity of work – dominate the cultural norms of the society. Standards are judged against this norm: the 'standard of living' is judged against this cultural level which is set in relation to the leisure class. Patterns of consumption of the 'common man' are emulative of the leisure class – dress, entertainment, food, drink, housing and so on. The vested interests – business – utilise the productive capacity of industry for profit by producing articles of waste.

Veblen stressed that this wastefulness may well be invisible to the participants. 'Ordinarily', he believes,

> his motive is a wish to conform to established usage, to avoid unfavourable notice and comment, to live up to the accepted cannons of decency in the kind, amount, and grade of goods consumed, as well as in the decorous employment of his time and effort.
>
> (Veblen 1899 p. 155)

The tastes that the orthodox economists took for granted were, for Veblen, created by business and vested interests.

In contrast to the position taken by the Austrians, which we outlined in the previous chapter, Veblen believed that there was actually a drive in industry towards standardisation, which was advantageous. It was business which created the desire for individualised goods, because the uncertainty which this created enabled the businessman to extract profit (Veblen 1904 p. 28, cf. Nabers 1958 p. 88). Veblen believed that the uncertainty which according to the Austrians formed the entire problem of economics was in fact deliberately created by the business class. This uncertainty was heightened by periodic cyclical crises, caused by expansion of credit. This led to a rapid expansion of industrial capacity, and then to overproduction and glut (Veblen 1923 p. 91 ff.). The cyclical tendency was often curbed through the 'business-like sabotage' measures of restriction of output, and unemployment (Veblen 1923 p. 97).

There were other methods of diverting production into waste. One method that was to assume considerable significance in the coming years (and has maintained that significance up to the present) was the use of patriotism and militarism to serve business ends. Veblen was concerned not only with the Leninist analysis of imperialism. He also believed that the use of nationalism was an intrinsic part of the operation of the vested interests (Veblen 1917 *passim*). The use of militarisation was held to be a good illustration of the duality of business and industry. On the one hand the industrial arts were vital to the successful prosecution of warfare

> modern warfare not only makes use of, and indeed depends on the modern industrial technology at every turn ... but it draws on the ordinary industrial resources of the countries at war in a degree and with an urgency never equalled. No nation can hope to make a stand in modern warfare ... without the most thoroughgoing exploitation of the modern industrial arts.
>
> (Veblen 1917 p. 310)

Yet the business interests which the state was to represent were antithetical to the machine process of industry. There is a dilemma. The vested interests are reliant upon technological development, but this very development works against the vested interests. However, in the case of war, the change may sometimes be so sudden as not to allow the development of new institutions (ibid.).

Veblen seemed to regard the actual production and distribution of artefacts as unproblematic. It was only the business interests that create the need for a pecuniary valuation of goods (Veblen 1904 *passim*). Similarly, the 'laws of distribution' posited by the orthodox economists were simply reflections of the institutions of private property. The orthodox theory served to legitimise these institutions, indeed they formed part of the institutions themselves (see Nabers 1958 p. 88). The orthodox economists confuse value with price. The medieval notion of the 'just price' was replaced by a notion of competition. The 'natural order' was replaced by the 'invisible hand' which had the advantage of making the benefit to the community an irrelevance to the individual. All that the orthodox theory has achieved is to explain pecuniary exchange. Progress is implied, but cannot be shown. Waste is outside of the domain of the theory.

In summary, business exercised a cultural control over the common man which camouflaged the real nature of the social system. Orthodox economic theory was a part of this cultural control. Veblen's theory was, in this respect, somewhat similar to that of Marx. Indeed, in many ways Veblen's theory can be viewed as a supplement to Marx (Gruchy 1972 p. 27). In this light, we will consider Veblen's theory of the state and his class theory. Veblen was less concerned with the means of production than with the ends of production. His class cleavage was between those who benefited from the product set, the 'vested interests', and those who had no stake in affecting this set, the 'common man'. Veblen turns the separation of ownership and management into a critique: it is the absentee owners who create the requirement of pecuniary measurements of production. Business controlled industry. The division was

> not between those who have something and those who have nothing – as many socialists would be inclined to describe it – but between those who own wealth enough to make it count, and those who do not.

The key factor was those who were of the 'kept classes', who had a

> legitimate right to get something for nothing, usually a prescriptive right to an income which is secured by controlling the traffic at one point or another.
>
> (Veblen 1919b p. 161)

Veblen's concern was not so much the Marxian concept of 'one capitalist driving out many', but rather the idea of a dynastic class of vested interests, who manipulated culture and law to protect their vested interests.

Just outside of the vested interests are their 'agents', who will act for and protect the vested interests proper. Notable among these are the clergy, the state and the military. Also of interest is that Veblen puts the labour unions among the agents of the vested interests (cf. Pluta and Leathers 1978 p. 127).

It will be recalled that one of the cultural controls that Veblen believed was exercised upon the common man was that of nationalism. This was possible because, for Veblen, the state was one of the agents of the vested interests. The government was the institutionalised means of physical coercion in any society, and would protect the existing social order (Hunt 1979 p. 130). It would act on behalf of the business class, and would also attempt to preserve itself, hence Veblen's term 'dynastic' state. The state-run concerns would also invariably reflect the business interests, most notably the education system (hence his work *The Higher Learning in America*, subtitled 'A Memorandum on the Conduct of Universities by Business Men' (Veblen 1918)). Veblen did not regard it as particularly desirable that the state should increase its intervention in the economy, or undertake public expenditure, he regarded the latter as 'ceremonial'.

Let us return briefly to Veblen's view of orthodox economics. We discussed earlier his claim that the scientific methodology of orthodox economics was outdated. Veblen also claimed that the theory itself was outdated. It may have had empirical reference in the eighteenth century, but had no reference in the twentieth (Veblen 1909 p. 151, cf. Veblen 1919b p. 162). Veblen rejected the classical and marginalist concept of perfect competition. This was no longer applicable to modern business. The economic world of Veblen was one of monopoly, oligopoly and large corporate groupings. It should be reasonably obvious that this is a necessary prerequisite for the level of influence Veblen ascribes to the 'business class'. The completeness of Veblen's system may also explain why he did not attempt to formulate his own system of political economy. His outlook, unlike virtually all the other theorists we have considered, was one of pessimism. Even the hopes he did have were to be proven somewhat false. Veblen placed great store in the machine process, and in the engineers as a force for change. This has palpably failed to occur.

In spite of the fact that Veblen did not systematise his socio-economic system, we can gain some idea of his thought through his critique. The first step in analysing Veblen's theoretical scheme is probably to attempt a separation of his psychology from the social psychological theory. It has been noted that while Veblen attacks the psychology of the utilitarians, he tends to replace this with his own assertions of instincts. A far more consistent approach would be to reject psychologism altogether (Rutherford 1984 p. 333). The use of instincts is an obvious target for critics, and is generally regarded as the weakest element of Veblen's work (Pluta and Leathers 1978 p. 133, Ayres 1958 p. 25). Veblen's use of the pragmatists' theory of instincts is idiosyncratic (Mirowski 1990 p. 98) and can also lead to racism, which Veblen tended towards (ibid. p. 132, Hunt 1979 p. 118). The concept of instinct is not necessary to the social theory. 'One could abandon the psychologism in Veblen's work and still maintain a perfectly cogent non-psychological theory. Indeed, the social psychological concept of institution leads exactly to this point.' (Rutherford 1984 p. 345). The reason for the instinct concept was mainly because of Veblen's fascination with Darwin (cf. ibid. p. 333). Darwin was cautious about using evolutionary theory in the social sphere however. Veblen's use of Darwin gives no significant insights (Hunt 1979 p. 118).

Veblen appeared to regard a theory of value as unnecessary. Value was a question of scientific use, not of pecuniary measure. Pecuniary valuation was simply a business class institution, and was not required for serviceable production for the community. Veblen believed, to use Zingler's phrase, that there was a contest of 'vendability versus serviceability' (Zingler 1974 p. 227).

The value of commodities was measured in technical terms by the service to society it performed – by its contribution to the continuity of the life process (ibid. p. 224). The economic value was socially determined:

> Private utility may reflect only the whim or caprice of the individual, whereas social serviceability reflects what is fundamental to human survival. Social or brute serviceability is a matter of the 'mechanical' and 'chemical' qualities of goods that make them useful for enhancing 'human life on the whole'. In other words social serviceability is a matter of science and technology and the ultimate criterion of value is not subjective personal utility but science and technology.
>
> (Gruchy 1972 p. 23)

Veblen appears to maintain that if production was standardised then the industrial system would be able to produce adequate quantities of goods. This is especially the case if the emulative expenditures were not in existence. Indeed, Veblen viewed most human wants other than that for survival as largely social phenomena (Zingler 1974 p. 325). The whole concept of scarcity, central to the Robbins definition of economy, was for Veblen created by the vested interests (cf. Nabers 1958 pp. 96–8).

The entire question of consumer sovereignty, which was such an issue in the debate on market socialism, was regarded as trivial by Veblen. Nabers' analysis is interesting. In reply to Frank Knight's objection that a rejection of consumers sovereignty has dangerous political implications for a democracy (Knight 1920 pp. 518–20), Nabers suggests that

> Veblen would have replied (1) consumer sovereignty is a myth derived from an acceptance of the hedonistic calculus; (2) in any event the gains to be made from the application of the canons of serviceability for society as a whole would outweigh any other possible loss and (3) to the implied question of who is to make the decisions for individuals he would ask 'Who makes them now'?
>
> (Nabers 1958 p. 99)

On the production side, Veblen posited three sources of inputs the availability of which determined the limits of community production: the size of the population, the natural resources and the state of the industrial arts. The last is of primary importance. Veblen believed that the capacity of industry set the limits for population (Veblen 1919b pp. 293 ff.), and also that 'The state of the industrial arts determines what natural materials will be useful as well as how they will be made use of' (Veblen 1923 p. 63).

The major source of production was the industrial arts. These industrial arts were for Veblen a public domain factor – he referred to them as a 'joint stock of knowledge' which belongs to the community. It was impossible to factor out the level of productive efficiency of an individual unit, as the marginalists had suggested. Veblen viewed the factors of production as public goods (Nabers 1958 p. 103).

We would add that Veblen would also have rejected Knight's notion of a democratic political system, since the political is dominated by the business class. Consequently, Veblen did not undertake extensive analysis of the state, or of the political system. Since the cultural controls affected the behaviour of the common man, the vested interests would not be simply demolished. Business would continue to control industry, even though industry had no need for business. Unlike Marx, Veblen did not believe the state would wither away.

Veblen believed – correctly or otherwise – that Marx had used an unscientific Hegelian philosophy in his belief in the inevitability of a socialist antithesis to capitalism. Veblen wanted to change or update Marxism into a 'neo-Darwinian' theory. Although Veblen saw the economic as in a state of constant flux, this was not due to any 'inner contradictions' of the social system. Neither was there any pre-ordained goal for history (cf. Pluta and Leathers 1978 p. 133, Lerner 1948 p. 35). There was no inevitability concerning the Veblenian analysis, indeed he was considerably pessimistic. In a way, Veblen was Marxism *sans* materialism and determinism. The cleavage between workmanship and predation is similar to the Marxian class analysis (Hunt 1979 p. 122). In practice, many radicals use a Veblenesque class scheme (Pluta and Leathers 1978 p. 128).[4] Furthermore, aside from the common belief in the centrality of the economic, we can see how the 'exploit' of Veblen's theory would only be possible in a class society, after technology and tools had made production efficient (Hunt 1979 p. 122). Veblen rejected the labour theory of value though; he considered it a leftover from the natural rights philosophy of the classics (Veblen 1906 p. 278). And although the conflict between the common man and the vested interests is very similar to the labour/capital clash, the two theorists did have different emphasis: Veblen on the social-psychological, Marx on the economic-legal (Hunt 1979 p. 126).[5]

Veblen's work gives a clear example of how the cultural critique of institutionalism took it beyond the realm of orthodox economics. By positing the manipulation of wants, Veblen undermines the entire rationality approach of individualist economics. Even if equilibrium is attained and markets cleared, and even if maximum 'satisfaction' is attained, this need not be construed as a social optimum, since these wants are created artificially.

At the level of critique, Veblen's work is powerful. It is when Veblen attempts to construct his closed, Darwinian theory that the project weakens. As we have seen, evolutionary theories tend towards determinism. Darwinian theory replaced teleological explanation with

> a fully materialistic explanation in terms of 'opaque cause and effect': evolution has no course, and no consciousness guides it – or even affects it. Veblen clearly wants to translate this idea into economics. Taken to its logical conclusion, of course, that would mean eliminating all

consciousness from economic explanation, creating an economic ana-
logue of Skinnerian behaviouralism.

(Langlois 1989 p. 273)

Veblen is in effect positing a deterministic theory, in which all behaviour is
socially determined. This may be the reason that Veblen reached such
pessimistic conclusions. He has left no room in his theory for conscious
action. All behaviour is controlled – there is no way of breaking out of the
vicious circle. We should reject such a fatalistic theory, not least because
Veblen does not consistently employ a strictly materialist approach (Langlois
1989 p. 275). He frequently employs conscious actions on behalf of the vested
interests – such as the employment of nationalism and war, for example. His
critique is as much concerned with the conscious use of power as with the
inevitable consequences of structure, which is in contrast to a structuralist,
deterministic theory along Darwinian lines.

Methodological questions arise within substantive economic theories in the
theory of value, where they take on a technical guise. Veblen views value as
entirely a technical problem: value consists in the technical uses to which a
commodity can be put, and is measurable by physical science. Unfortunately,
this value theory is inadequate. Without a common unit of account, there is
no way to compare the values of different commodities. We cannot say
whether, for example, land should be used for industry or agriculture, or any
other comparison of different commodities. Such comparisons require at least
a unit of account to balance production across the board. This was the scheme
put forward by Clarence Ayres, whom we will discuss shortly. We will
maintain that some notion of subjective valuation is still necessary unless the
accounting prices are to be arbitrary.

Veblen's scheme replaces the money-based conception of objective value
used by the 1930s market socialists with an objective value theory based on
the material properties of commodities. As such, it is open to many of the
criticisms of the socialists we outlined in the previous chapter: in particular
that no change in circumstances could be accounted for. Veblen's value theory
is actually as static as that of orthodox economics, and the engineers whom
Veblen believed could plan the economy would run into exactly the same
problems as the socialist Central Planning Board.

Mitchell

If Ayres can be considered to be attempting to develop Veblen's objective
value theory, Mitchell can be viewed as attempting to reconcile subjective and
objective values. He thought that it would be possible to objectively
'understand' the subjective basis of price. The link between Veblen and
Mitchell has often been misunderstood, possibly since Mitchell's main work
was ostensibly on business cycles and his books were highly quantitative in

content – indeed he was one of the first economists to use statistical data extensively. This has led to his work being dismissed as empiricist (cf. Starr 1983), especially by book reviewers (e.g. Koopmans 1947). There is a structure to Mitchell's work, but it is implicit and not codified. His acceptance of Veblen 'has been more complete than those are aware who have read his books but not his essays' (Tugwell 1937 p. 234).

Tugwell believes that the orientation of Mitchell's work was provided by Veblen; 'If he has been an observer, he has always known what to observe' (Wolfe 1939 p. 212).[6] The criteria for deciding what to observe are seldom stated though, and have to be pulled together from a variety of sources.

One such source, which although not directly concerned with methodology strongly suggests non-empiricist sympathies, is Mitchell's *Types of Economic Theory*, his seminal work on the history of economic thought. Mitchell lectured at Columbia in this subject for 24 years,[7] which suggests more than a passing interest. It rather suggests a concern for questions of methodology. We shall see that this is indeed the case.

Mitchell did not reject all theory *per se*. Few academics would spend 24 years analysing something they reject outright. What Mitchell was concerned to attack was certain types of theory. Mitchell realised that theory is necessary for the generation of working hypotheses and for effective thinking (Wolfe 1939 p. 212). What were not useful, Mitchell believed, were deductive systems based upon untested and unsound assumptions, and 'pure' theories which were completely synthetic. The confusion arises because historically orthodox economic theory evolved as hedonistic, and Mitchell implicitly associated deductive theory with hedonism (ibid.). It was hedonism which Mitchell was opposed to, and it was this which led to his interest in the history of thought. He was against the 'conscious use of assumptions contrary to fact', especially when economists use them 'not in the purely logical development of their untrue assumptions' but rather attempt the 'use of these assumptions to facilitate comprehension of the complex conditions of reality' (Mitchell 1910 p. 109). Hedonism was such a false assumption, although the hedonism was not always explicit: Mitchell believed Fisher's work to be 'Bentham's ideas under new labels' (ibid. n. 28), and he viewed Marshall's work as an attempt to move away from hedonistic concepts (Mitchell 1916 p. 145). For Mitchell, the whole idea of an economics based on 'the mechanics of self-interest' is misconceived.

Nonetheless, he believed that the development of economic thought consisted precisely of theories of this nature. Marshall, Mitchell believed, simply qualified his use of hedonism in an essentially hedonistic theory, 'reserving an air of reality by sagacious qualifications of the conclusions' (Mitchell 1910 p. 910). Marshall's theory remains based on the pleasure/pain continuum, expressed as differentiable functions. 'Marshall based his whole system upon a theory of value. He thought of economic conduct as governed by two opposing sets of motives the force of which can be measured in money' (Mitchell 1944 p. 213).

For Mitchell, this form of unrealistic postulate could never lead to realistic conclusions. The views of Mitchell and Marshall on the relationship between theory and data differed. Marshall had also called for quantitative work, but he believed the kinds of market forces were already marked out. Quantitative analysis was supposed to give an objective account of these forces – indeed Mitchell thought they formed the entire scope of Marshall's economics. However, Mitchell believed that Marshall's model of two opposing motives was obsolete, and Mitchell did not search for a statistical measurement of these forces (Homan 1928 p. 139). Rather, he wanted economics to turn to psychology for an explanation of motivation. He believed psychology would give no credence to hedonism. Indeed, the point of his 1912 article 'The Backwards Art of Spending Money' was precisely that observed consumer behaviour, and especially economic behaviour within the family unit, was clearly not governed by rational self-interest (Mitchell 1912 *passim*).

For his analysis of human motivation Mitchell turned to the institutional psychology of James and – especially – McDougall. It was socialised habits which evolved from repeated usage which Mitchell believed lay at back of social behaviour.[8] If economic rationality did exist, it was this rationality which had to be explained and this by explaining human nature. Rational actions were only a limited part of human activity (Homan 1928 p. 182). For Mitchell 'human nature is conceived, not as a ready-made something taken over at the outset, not as a *postulate* whose consequences must be developed, but as itself the chief subject of investigation' (Mitchell 1910 p. 111).

The major institution which governed economic rationality was money. It was 'the use of money' which was one of the main rationalising institutions.

It gives society the technical machinery of exchange, the opportunity to combine personal freedom with orderly cooperation on a grand scale, and the basis of that system of accountancy which Sombart appropriately calls 'economic rationalism'. It is the foundation of that complex system of prices to which the individual must adjust his behaviour in getting a living. Since it moulds his objective behaviour, it becomes part of his subjective life ... Because it thus rationalises economic life itself, the use of money lays the foundation for a rational theory of that life. Money may not be the root of *all* evil, but it is the root of economic science.

(Mitchell 1916 p. 157; emphasis in original)

Far from the neo-classical notion of money being used to measure motivation, money becomes the motivation in Mitchell's view. It is precisely because the individual is socialised into the use of pecuniary rationality that this is applicable to economic activity. It is not the case that money gives the economist a guide to satisfactions. It gives little guidance to anything at all except current institutional practice. By the same token, if we wish to study this institutional set, then the study of the money economy is, he believed, the only objective way of so doing (cf. Vining 1951 p. 114).

It was the concept of money which is one of the links between the history of economic thought and Mitchell's work on business cycles. Although the work appears to be positivist and even empiricist, there is a definite framework for his investigations, which was institutional and Veblenian in nature. We have already seen that Mitchell had criticised the use of false assumptions in orthodox theory. We have also seen that he criticised the avoidance of the institutional role of money. Of course, the combination of these two aspects was necessary for the equilibrium model of orthodox economics to hold.

Mitchell therefore considered data pertinent to cyclical fluctuations, as an antithesis to equilibrium. The data were part of a quantitative study which he believed to be objective, but he did have a 'framework of preliminary ideas' which he employed to guide his search for data. We can view this as his theory.

> However objective we might wish to make such a study, it was nevertheless essential to have some framework of ideas into which to fit the data. In short, there must be some test of relevancy. In setting up this test, Mitchell displays an implicit theoretical position. For he prefaces his investigation by a brief statement of his view of the operation of the economic system. And in this statement, negatively or by neglect, he may be said to discard adherence to any orthodox view of economic process, while, positively, his descriptive analysis rests upon the distinction, taken explicitly from Veblen, of the distinction between business and industry.
>
> (Homan 1928 p. 166)

The main aspect of this dichotomy of industry and business which Mitchell believed was the main institution of contemporary activity was the use of money, 'not the use of money as a medium of exchange, but the fact that economic activity takes the form of making and spending money incomes' (Mitchell 1913 p. 21). This meant that there was no direct connection between the well-being of the community, which was determined by the production of useful goods, and the pecuniary-motivated behaviour of the individual units – the family and the firm.[9] Useful production functioned according to the dictates of businesses which were connected by an 'endless chain of interlocking indebtedness' (Homan 1928 p. 167), which determined business action. It is what Mitchell termed the 'pecuniary aspect of economic activity' which must be dealt with, and fluctuations are problems of the fluctuating prospects of profits (ibid.).

The price system is the means whereby the pecuniary behaviour is co-ordinated. Mitchell viewed it as an endless and continuous chain, without any logical beginning or end (Mitchell 1913 p. 31). Because of this inter-connectedness of business, the outlines of the system remained stable, even if the individual units changed (Vining 1951 p. 116). But because each unit was only motivated by profit, Mitchell did not believe any overall co-ordination would be achieved. 'In detail, then, economic activity is planned and directed with skill, but in the large there is neither general plan nor central direction.' (Mitchell 1913 p. 38). The money economy gives no assurance of a desirable distribution nor of smooth functioning; this may be upset by uncertainty.

This, then, is the theoretical framework which Mitchell moved in. Having established that the postulates of rationality and motivation used in orthodox economics were wrong, he then went on to consider the question of equilibrium. 'The whole bearing of his study, in fact, tended to discredit the notions of normality and of an equilibrium of forces' (Homan 1928 p. 174). Mitchell believed that his review of business behaviour belied any notion of normal or static conditions.

> But a review of business annals never discloses . . . a 'static' or 'normal' state . . . On the contrary, in the real world of business, affairs are always undergoing a cumulative change, always passing through some phase of a business cycle into some other phase . . . In fact, if not in theory, a state of change in business conditions is the only 'normal' state.
>
> (Mitchell 1913 p. 86)

Using his Veblenian framework, Mitchell disproved the logical consequents of the orthodox model. This was the relationship between the master Veblen and his pupil Mitchell.

> Veblen's method of demolishing systematic theory is to cast doubt upon its postulates. Mitchell appeals to his mass of facts and distils them into a convincing picture of economic process which lends no support to the conclusions of systematic theory. He thus appears, not as a parrot of Veblen, but rather as his complement, proceeding from a different angle and with a wholly different technique, to complete the discrediting of the scheme of thought in which economic theorists have framed their systems.
>
> (Homan 1928 p. 176)

Veblen's theoretical framework could be ignored or dismissed by orthodox economists. Mitchell's factual examination of the conclusions was harder to avoid. However, the fact that the link between the two was often not made facilitated this avoidance as did the fact that Mitchell did not offer any ultimate 'cause' of business fluctuations. They were simply a function of the actions of business in the money economy. His was a 'static' study in the sense that his concern was not to trace the evolution of institutions, but rather to describe cyclical fluctuations within the domain of the present institutional set. Institutions are fixed rather than variable (Homan 1928 p. 173).

The other way in which economic theory could avoid analysing money as an institution was simply to take preferences as data, and not to seek to instil any valuation theory into this data. This was the line of Pareto, and later of Samuelson. Mitchell classifies this as pure theory. He wrote in 1916 that

> It is clear, at once, that this type of theory eliminates the problem of valuation from economics. That is, it does not concern itself with the way in which men find out what relative importance different goods have for their purpose. Instead, it assumes that this process of valuation has been completed before they come to market.
>
> (Mitchell 1916 p. 150)

Later, Mitchell became more critical of this pure theory. 'First and most obvious, it meant that economic theory moves on a more superficial level than in its more confident days. The theorist works with data he does not profess to explain' (Mitchell 1944 p. 215). Mitchell also believed that price theory was insufficient for an explanation of economic behaviour. The Benthamite value theories may have been incorrect, 'But the policy of dispensing with a theory of value seems to me unhappy and unnecessary. When economists deal realistically with human behaviour, they find themselves needing ... to understand how people evaluate goods' (Mitchell 1944 p. 216).

Mitchell believed that economics should be able to give guidance as to future conduct. Pure economics was a futile indoor sport (Wolfe 1939 p. 214). He would not accept the notion of the economist as 'disinterested observer'. Economics has the moral purpose of obtaining rational control for societal welfare. This was never explicitly discussed, however (Wolfe 1939 p. 219).[10] Defining welfare is of course the central problem of economics. Mitchell leaves welfare undefined. Nonetheless, the task of considering social welfare, however hazy the concept may be, determines the nature of economics.

> The motive is now not idle curiosity but the 'instinct of workmanship'. And from this point of view, understanding is something more than hindsight or knowing the genetic causation of things. It now takes on the complexion of foresight or a certain teleological character.

> The issue, therefore, involves no questioning of our need of factual knowledge. It lies in the significance or meaning of the knowledge we have or can get. And in this frame of reference meaning has an instrumental or value complexion. For all welfare economists ... the meaning of meaning must lie in the sphere of values.
>
> (Wolfe 1939 p. 225)

Wolfe criticised Mitchell for not bringing out the significance of the means – end relation (ibid.). The criticism is valid, but much of the relation is implied in Mitchell's articles. Mitchell also believed that only factual work could further the science.

Much of the critique of Mitchell comes from the fact that he did not propose a system to replace the orthodoxy he criticised. He appeared to favour economic planning, which he saw as an inevitability (Wolfe 1939 p. 210). His main concern was to gain objective data from psychologists as to the actual motivation of humans. However, he is not very clear as to what exactly we would do with these data. It is unclear how motives would relate to welfare (ibid.). Mitchell seems to cling to the Veblenian notion of instincts and believes these could be uncovered. Veblen believed that institutions functioned to raise the desire for consumption and thereby artificially create shortage. No economics would be necessary if industry could run unhindered. Mitchell is ambiguous as to how far along this road he is willing to travel. Without a definition of value or welfare, it is not possible, as we have seen throughout, to derive policy recommendations.

> it is a little difficult to see how welfare economics, which assuredly is without frame of reference unless it discovers or posits some human aims, can be much advanced by generalisations, no matter how illuminating otherwise, which have no reference to the purpose of the human behaviour on which they are made.
>
> (Wolfe 1939 p. 217)

Mitchell has provided us with an objective critique of equilibrium theory. He isolated the question of equilibrium by reference to Veblenian social theory. However, he then wished to derive an objective replacement theory which would enable the economist to prescribe policy. As we have seen throughout, the search for an objective basis for value remains doomed to failure. Even if Mitchell were to uncover the institutional basis of market demand, it is far from clear how we are then to proceed. To say that market value is not objective may be correct, but does not in itself give an objective account of value which is required for non-arbitrary economic planning.

Ayres

This objective foundation for planning is precisely the basis for Ayres' theory. Ayres believed he could go 'beyond' the values given by price to some notion of 'real' value given by science and technology. Ayres' scheme was that prices could be adjusted to account for these real, social values.

Ayres began his system with a critique and rejection of classical and neo-classical price theory. He drew a distinction between value, price and capital, which he believed were the essential components of the 'classical tradition'. Although these three concepts were irretrievably interconnected they were nonetheless distinct. Price itself was only the guise in which economic problems emerge (Rostow 1976 p. 76). While price has no significance in itself, in the classical scheme it is used as a catalyst 'by the action of which capital and value were combined' (Ayres 1944 p. 37). The key element of orthodox theory for Ayres was the way in which a concentration on price theory enabled the neo-classics to derive a value for capital (and labour). The neo-classics confused capital funds with capital goods (Walker 1980 p. 651). By equating these two distinct elements, neo-classical theory was able to explain the growth of capital goods by the accumulation of capital funds, which they suggested occurred through abstinence or saving (Ayres 1944 p. 50, cf. Walker 1980 p. 651). This also provided a moral justification for 'the great inequality of income which is one of the most conspicuous features of capitalism' (Ayres 1944 p. 52). (In fact Ayres interprets the classics as justifying inequality on the grounds that it leads to capital accumulation (ibid. p. 53)). Once we understand the real role of technology this justification will be abandoned (Ayres 1953 p. 284).

The confusion of capital funds and capital equipment made it appear that the growth of funds was required before industrial growth could occur, whereas for Ayres 'industrial growth is a consequence, not of non-consumption, but of technological development. No community has ever starved itself into prosperity' (Ayres 1953 p. 284). The level of economic wealth is determined not by the accumulation of funds, but by the level of technology (Ayres 1944 p. 283, cf. Walker 1980 p. 653). It was technological growth that, for Ayres, was the most important force in civilization (Walker 1979 p. 521). An understanding of economic growth required not an understanding of market mechanisms, but rather an understanding of technological development.

Since Ayres rejected the neo-classic notion of price as the focus of value, he must also reject the Robbins means/end dichotomy. Ayres follows Dewey in this, and bases his theory of value upon the concept of 'continuity'. Value is a synonym for continuity which is the human 'life process', the 'continuity of civilization' (Ayres 1944 p. 221 cf. Rutherford 1981 p. 658). The continuity of experience is the basic scientific postulate of both physical and social behaviour (Ayres 1944 p. 91), and it is technology which enables the continuity of civilisation to occur. Value is therefore instrumental, and located in technological knowledge (Chung 1978 p. 119). Whatever causes technological development is valuable (Rutherford 1981, p. 659). The criterion of every economic judgement is 'keeping the machines running' (Ayres 1944 p. 223). Value is objectified within technological instruments (Rutherford 1981 p. 658). 'True values are not a matter of individual taste or institutional conditioning, but a matter of demonstrable efficiency in the maintenance and production of the technical continuum and the life process' (ibid. p. 660). Questions of value are simply technical questions of choosing the right tools, as it were. Value is objective and transcendental.

Ayres is a technological optimist. Whereas for Veblen institutions can be either serviceable or disservicable, for Ayres all institutions are ceremonial in nature. They are formed as a mixture of conventions, myths and social mores (ibid. p. 660). These institutions serve to hide true value, and to assign 'rank through ritual', thereby maintaining the social order (Walker 1979 p. 524).

The aim of institutions is to convey the social order of the past into the future. They are therefore in opposition to technology, which is concerned with future development. Institutions constitute a cultural brake to technological change (Rostow 1976 p. 76). The processes of technological and economic development therefore required large changes to the institutions of society (ibid.).

Ayres dichotomised human behaviour. The main force for progress was technological-based behaviour. This was held back by institutional/ceremonial behaviour. The price economy was one of these ceremonial institutions, and Ayres held that price bore no relation to social value. Ayres, following Veblen, believes that the industrial economy is more fundamental than this price economy (Gruchy 1972 p. 97), in fact, the price economy is viewed as simply a power system. 'Real' value is determined technologically and, as for Veblen, is capable of measurement by physical science. Prices can then be adjusted to reflect these 'real' values, and the economy planned accordingly (ibid. pp. 97–109).

It was for these reasons that Ayres thought the level of finance capital to be an irrelevance. Progress occurred through technology, not through investment. The development of Western societies is due to the 'triumph' of technology and rational behaviour over ceremonial actions and institutions, Ayres believed (Ayres 1944 ch. ix). He considered that the key to progress was to cut away the institutions which dragged back the progress of technology. Ayres believed that 'the technological revolution is itself irresistible' (ibid. p. xxiv), and would lead to an improvement in the welfare of society.

In his interpretation of technological development, and his interpretation of value, Ayres could possibly be said to be extending institutional theory along Veblenian lines. With his analysis of institutions he begins a significant departure from the Veblenian position. Veblen considered that the vested interests held sway over scientific development. The institutional set was dynamic and evolutionary. In Ayres' work all institutions are imbecile. He replaces the Veblenian institutional lag with his concept of institutional drag, implying that technological progress is inexorable and drags all institutional behaviour behind it. This raises the possibility – or even probability – of the short-run triumph of technology over institutions, thereby completely changing the conclusions of the theory. Veblen believed that only wholesale replacement of the institutional set could achieve maximum social welfare. Ayres' theory makes it possible for reform to achieve this. In contrast to radicalism and pessimism, Ayres harbours liberalism and optimism (McFarland 1985 p. 100).

Indeed, Ayres' definition of the concept of 'institution' borders on the tautological. Veblen interpreted the concept somewhat loosely, using the term for ceremonial practice, customs, widespread social habits and culture, among other things. Of these, the usual usage was social habits, the first in the list is the least central (McFarland 1985 p. 100). Yet Ayres takes ceremonial practices as his exclusive meaning. The technology/institution dichotomy may then be tautological: all institutions are bad (McFarland 1985 p. 100).

> Anything that hinders economic development is by definition an institution in Ayres' work. If a habit of thought or behavioural pattern that we would call an institution contributes efficiently to the process of production, Ayres would call it a technological activity.
>
> (Walker 1979 p. 535)

Ayres's use of tautology is typical of deterministic theories, and Ayres' scheme is indeed deterministic. By his use of the concept of technological drag, his view of technology as a self-generating process and his view of institutions as ceremonial, Ayres creates a technological over-determinism (Walker 1979 p. 522). The tautological aspect of Ayres's definition of institutionalism is necessary to protect himself against a charge that some institutions may be beneficial to technological growth. If they are beneficial, they cease to be institutions.

There is another charge which can be raised against Ayres, which is harder to dodge. Deterministic theoretical systems must be functionalist in nature. If the determining element can be shown to be dysfunctional, then the determinist system begins to break down. Ayres was not really able to cope with the fact of the employment of technology for unarguably evil uses. Ayres argued that these uses were the result of institutional forces. Yet if this is the case, then institutional value judgements are apparently of major importance in the development of particular technologies (Rutherford 1981 p. 668).

> Clearly, however, the recognition that the evil consequences of some uses of technology result from institutions should entail the recognition that the machines are ethically and morally neutral in themselves with respect to all uses, and that what are considered to be their beneficial effects are also determined by institutions. Uses of technology that are judged harmful in some or all respects are the result of decision to employ technology in those ways. Beneficial consequences of technology result from value judgements about what is beneficial . . . The value judgements are the outcome of the social institutions that operate to select objectives and to define problems. Science and technology enable the achievement of the objectives, but do not select them, as can be inferred from the different uses to which science and technology are put in different societies. The conclusion must be that Ayres was not correct in supposing that there are universally true moral values which are objectively determined by technological operations, and that he was unable to demonstrate scientifically that culturally relative values are harmful. This rejection of his theory of value is a logical corollary of

119

the rejection of his theory of the antithetical roles of technology and institutions in the process of economic development.

(Walker 1979 p. 534)

The technological determinism of Ayres's theory is therefore in doubt. We can also see that his value theory is open to doubt. The essence of his value theory was that value can be identified with technological progress: the 'instrumental' theory of value. This was to replace the classical/neo-classical value theory (Chung 1978 p. 118). Since technology is a positive determinant of all human values, these values can be objective. Ayres does not allow for differences over values – all choices are the same as choices between tools (Ayres 1944 pp. 212–13). Science can give us objective analysis of value judgements. This is 'an example of the naturalistic fallacy that statements of obligation can be derived from statements of facts' (Rutherford 1981 p. 669). Without showing that science can make values objective, Ayres's theory falls.[11]

We arrive at the same place as we departed in 1789. Predetermined theory is held to be possible because values can be objectified. For Bentham this possibility existed because values were based upon calculation. For the marginalists values could be measured by price. For Ayres science equates with 'real' value. All attempt to show how what appear to be subjective valuations are in fact objectively measurable. None of them can be operationalised.

In fact, Ayres, far more than Veblen, appears to be heading down a parallel path to Bentham. This movement is accentuated by his conception of the 'unity of value'. He maintains that all values – not only commodity valuations – form part of value systems which can be compared.

True values are trans-cultural . . . because they are interrelated. All are manifestations of the same process, the life process of mankind. All knowledge is related to and conditioned by all other knowledge, and all skills are mutually contributory. Good health, freedom from disease and famine, is contributory to the acquisition of skill and knowledge; and the acquisition of knowledge and development of skill are contributory to good health.

All true values define and fortify each other.

(Ayres 1961 p. 167)

Ayres also extends this analysis to such values as freedom and equality, and even aesthetic 'excellence'. These were also capable of technological expression (ibid. p. 34 and relevant chapters). The parallels with Bentham are clear: everything is reducible to scientific measurement. Unfortunately, in actuality these elements are not measurable in this way, and any claim to the contrary remains faintly absurd. It seems worth pointing out that some of the 'growth of knowledge' has been distinctly unhealthy: although Ayres would no doubt claim that this was due to institutions, not technology. But such reasoning smacks of *post-hoc* rationalising. 'Bad' technology is imbued with ceremonial practices, 'good' technology is not. By contrast, *ex-ante* judgements of how disparate technologies are to be deployed is required if planning is to succeed.

The idea that technology is itself neutral should be rejected. It is never possible to separate social from technological change.[12] There is no sense in which technology can be objectively judged. Again, the idea of objective value cannot be realised.

PURPOSIVE THEORIES

Commons

The other wing of the institutional school concerned itself less with the replacement of orthodox rationality than with analysing the social outcome and offering policy proposals to supplement and reform the results of orthodox analysis.

Commons[13] responded to the prospect of radical overhaul by developing a reformist theory. We shall see that Commons did not attempt a reassertion of the neo-classical approach, but rather tried to alter this analysis to accommodate the boundary extensions that he believed the discipline badly needed, and which fitted in with his early twentieth-century Christian ethics (Starr 1983 p. 110).

Commons's avowed purpose was to cure the inadequacies of economics, both in theory and practice. He was 'trying to save capitalism by making it good' (Commons 1934 p. 143, cf. Dugger 1979 p. 369). This would be achieved not by a rejection of orthodox analysis, but by providing an institutional 'supplement' (Rutherford 1983 p. 722). 'The problem now', Commons believed, 'is not to create a different kind of economics – "institutional" economics – divorced from preceding schools, but how to give to collective action, is all its varieties, its due place throughout economic theory' (Commons 1934 p. 5). In Commons's view, orthodox economics was necessary but insufficient to provide an adequate analysis of behaviour (Commons 1936 p. 242, Starr 1983 p. 118).

Commons also did not dichotomise theory and practice. Rather, his approach was inductive: he attempted to generalise from his experience. Much of his writings are taken up with references to case studies and personal anecdotes as examples. He also believed in active reform, and his work should be viewed as bordered by the possibilities of what he viewed as possible reform within his stated ethical guidelines. Commons's reform method 'transcended the rather artificial normative/positive dichotomy', instead of which 'he was always practical, which means that he investigated what *could* be rather than what *should* be' (Dugger 1979 p. 370; emphasis in original).

This meant taking existing practice as his starting point, but he also believed that the ethical inputs to his analysis were that of the society under scrutiny. Reform must be based on the values of society (ibid.).

Commons's first major work was his *Legal Foundations of Capitalism*, completed in 1923. Most of his main concepts were developed by this time. However, Commons's writing style is, by common consensus, the most unintelligible of all Western economists. The 1934 work *Institutional Economics* was a restatement of his theory (Ramstad 1986 p. 1090), the earlier exposition of which many people had criticised 'to the effect that they could not understand my theories nor what I was driving at' (Commons 1934 p. 1). *Institutional Economics* did little to solve this problem, however, and *The Economics of Collective Action* (1950) was an 'attempt to explain in simple terms the essentials of a complex system of thought' (Parsons, preface to Commons 1950 p. v). The references below are taken in the main from *Institutional Economics*, which was his major work of exposition.

We saw previously how the attempt of orthodox economists to arrive at a social value function faltered when they attempted to aggregate the individual functions which they posited. For Commons to successfully supplement orthodox theory, he must either add a supplement or find an alternative to the orthodox methods of deriving a social value. Commons's response was to extend the boundaries of economics to embrace the political and the legal. These became necessary constraints upon individual activity. Commons defined an institution as 'collective action in control, liberation and expansion of individual action' (Commons 1931 p. 644). Social value was not derived from individual values, but rather formed the constraints within which individuals may act. These constraints were necessary, but were also interactive and dynamic, and the change in institutions was what caused the social evolution.

The initial point of departure from orthodoxy of Commons was the necessity for law in economic relations. In the orthodoxy law and ethics

> were necessarily excluded, because the relations on which the units were constructed were relations between man and nature, not between man and man. . . . Neither statute law, nor ethics, nor custom, nor judicial decision had anything to do with either of these relationships; or rather, all these might be eliminated by assuming that ownership was identical with the materials owned, in order to construct a theory of pure economics based solely on the physical exchange of materials and services.
>
> The latter was done. This identity of ownership and materials was accepted as a matter of custom, without investigation. It was assumed that all commodities were owned, but the ownership was assumed to be identical with the physical thing owned, and therefore was overlooked as something to be taken for granted. The theories were worked

out as physical materials, omitting anything of property rights, because
they were 'natural'.

(Commons 1934 pp. 56–7)

For Commons the crucial omission of orthodox economics was the concept
of the transfer of rights. 'Although we speak of the price of commodities',
Commons believed that 'what we actually value in the market is the legal
rights to these uses or services, namely property rights. Physical control
follows legal control; legal control is strategic and valued' (Commons 1950
p. 151). What was involved in exchange was not the exchange of materials,
but the exchange of property rights to economic goods:

> If the subject-matter of political economy is not only individuals and
> nature's forces, but is human beings getting their living out of each other
> by mutual transfers of property rights, then it is to law and ethics that
> we look for the critical turning points of this human activity.
>
> (Commons 1934, p. 57)

The distinctive feature of political economy is the exchange of property rights.
Commons maintains that ownership is the relevant question, and this involves
human interaction. It also involves social action, in the form of legislation and
judiciary. Ownership implies, in the modern world, law. This transfer of title
is different to the act of physical delivery, which is part of the labour process
of transportation. Property rights require the existence of a state. 'The
individual does not transfer ownership. Only the state ... by operation of
law as interpreted by the courts, transfers ownership by reading intentions
into the minds of participants in a transaction' (ibid. p. 60).

Commons distinguished between institutional economics and engineering
economics. The former was concerned with the transfer of property rights
and involved human-to-human relations. Engineering economics was the
relation of human to nature, and concerned only the 'physical attribute of use-
values' (ibid. p. 256). The engineer would go on producing indefinitely unless
restrained, producing even to the point where goods were oversupplied. The
production of use values – wealth – is distinguished from value, which is the
scarcity value of wealth. Wealth had a double meaning; the engineering
meaning of output (use value) and the business meaning of income (scarcity
value). Business is necessary to regulate the output, such regulation being a
feature of all societies (ibid. p. 256).

Orthodox economics confused efficiency with scarcity. Technical efficiency must be supplemented by collective action in order to maximise real
value. Efficiency and scarcity are complementary and, Commons maintained,
set limits to each other (ibid. p. 259).

Scarcity was the factor which Commons (following Hume) suggests
requires the institution of property rights. Abundance would mean that there
is no need for or possibility of title or ownership (ibid. p. 237, Commons

1925 p. 371). Commons does not reject the Robbins definition of economics, but suggests that it is insufficient. Scarcity was one of the requirements of economic analysis, since it explained the need for ownership, but the analysis of the legal and ethical institutions which enabled property rights to exist was also necessary.

The classics and neo-classics derived economic order from the 'invisible hand' mechanism. Commons, however, maintains that the scarcity mechanisms of the market are only partly causal of the economic order: there are intervening parameters of institutions. There is no presumption of Adam Smith's 'harmony of interests', in fact, the opposite is presumed. Commons believed that conflict would inevitably ensue, and that 'harmony is not a presumption of economics, it is a consequence of collective action designed to maintain rules that shall govern the conflicts'. Commons expressly denied the concept of the 'invisible hand': individuals' self-seeking would not lead automatically to the best social outcome. The imposition of collective order is required. Given that political economy involves transfer of legal title, it becomes a requirement for a sovereign state to exist, to enforce the legally binding contracts. The state monopolises sovereignty; the 'extraction of violence from private transactions' (Commons 1934 p. 684, Commons 1950 p. 74, cf. Rutherford 1973 p. 727). Other forms of power and other sovereign bodies also exist: both economic and moral power may be employed by other 'governments' than the state government. There is a hierarchy of governments in the political economy (Commons 1950 p. 75).

Law, ethics and custom also provide, for Commons, a necessary security of expectations. Because exchange involves exchange of title, this requires a legal duty concerning future behaviour, a concept Commons terms 'futurity'. Because of this, it is possible for legal title to be negotiated: credit, debt and goodwill become negotiable. Property need not be limited to tangible objects; intangible goods are also tradeable (ibid. 1950 p. 30).

To summarise, Commons designated five broad principles of economic action: efficiency, scarcity, sovereignty, futurity and one other not yet discussed: working rules or customs (Parsons 1942 p. 347). These rules were the mixture of ethics, custom and collective action which have evolved and which define the rights and duties of individuals. An organised form of collective action Commons termed a 'going concern' (Rutherford 1973 p. 723). The working rules of the going concerns may involve moral as well as physical or economic sanctions. Furthermore, the institutions were themselves changeable by individuals, although to what extent Commons believed this possible is a matter for conjecture. We will return to this.

Economic activity for Commons took the form of what he called 'Transactions'. These contained a bargain struck between parties of varying legal relationships concerning ownership rights. Commons identified three types of transaction. 'Bargaining transactions' are between legal equals. Either party has the ability to withhold from the bargain. This form of transaction is connected with scarcity. The form connected with efficiency is the 'manager-ial transaction': a transaction between manager and managed. This is a relation between legal superior and inferior: the worker has less right to withhold. There are no available alternatives to the bargain – the 'limits of coercion' are less (Rutherford 1973 p. 725). 'Rationing transactions' involve sovereignty: the imposition of transactions by superior authorities, such as taxation.

The working rules of the society may constrain the negotiations within the transaction. For Commons, the key rule upheld by the judiciary is that of 'reasonable value':

> The key word for Commons was 'reasonable', reasonable value, cost, price, wage, profit and so on, and he always viewed expectations of future economic activity (transactions) in terms of prevailing notions of equity and justice. The ultimate criterion of reasonableness with respect to bargaining and division of economic power, income and wealth was what the highest courts would accept in the final analysis. The specific manifestations of that social or collective criterion could be altered smoothly and continuously as the system evolved via a continuing re-interpretation of the law by the courts.
>
> (Zingler 1974 p. 335)

The use of legal or economic coercion which was unreasonable would be disallowed. It should be noted that Commons viewed his method of analysis as universal and applicable to any form of society. A communist or fascist society would simply have different proportions of the three types of transaction, different institutions and different working rules (Commons 1934 p. 7).

Changes in institutions would also come about through transactions of individuals with going concerns. In particular, political parties played a key part in the control of the sovereign power of the state in democracies. Commons distinguished between routine transactions and strategic trans-actions; the latter establish customs and working rules for the routine transactions. The system is therefore evolutionary (Commons 1934 p. 656).

This evolution is not, however, of the same nature as that posed by Veblen. Commons interpreted Darwin as positing a dichotomy of natural and artificial selection: of purposeless and purposeful selection (Commons 1950 p. 91, Commons 1934 p. 657). Commons believed that possible to engender 'moral selection', to direct the trajectory of social evolution. This he regarded as the distinctive feature vis à vis Veblen (Commons 1950 p. 91). The evolutionary theory of Veblen was expressly that of natural selection.

We saw above, though, that this aspect of Veblen's theory was in fact its weakest part, and was not necessary for his social psychological critique. Commons also believed that Veblen effectively abandoned natural selection, in that his workmanship instinct introduced a purposefulness into the theory (Commons 1934 p. 661). Commons's main point of contention was that

Veblen ignored scarcity and the need to regulate the efficient production of industry (ibid. p. 673 ff.). Veblen also misunderstood, Commons believed, the consequent relationship between managerial and bargaining transactions (ibid.). There is also a more trivial claim that Veblen considered the actions of the wrong 'going concern': Commons claimed that Veblen's experience at the 1901 Industrial Commission was too narrow, and that his own perusal of Supreme Court decisions since 1810 constituted superior data (ibid. p. 660).

To an extent the debate on scarcity, which is the main point of contention, is never joined. The question is whether the regulation of industry is a service to the community. Veblen believes that it is not, Commons that it is. The matter of the power of the Supreme Court relative to business is an important but secondary issue. Veblen's contention was that the business interests use cultural institutions to mould the 'needs' of socialised individuals: to create scarcity. If it were not for these institutions, no scarcity would exist. This argument was not met by Commons.

In a way, the question of sovereignty is not contradictory to Veblenian analysis. The concept is derived by Commons in an almost game-theory manner.[14] Sovereignty is required to solve the inevitable conflicts occurring from bargaining transactions, which themselves occur because of the transfer of legal title to scarce commodities. The sovereign state functions by working rules which enable it to decide upon reasonable behaviour. Given the institution as the fact of scarcity, the regulators of industry may well need regulation themselves. It may well be impossible or impractical to practise untrammelled *laissez-faire* . But all this is to say that it is in the best interests of business to organise a sovereign state. While the state may be sovereign to an individual going concern, it is far from clear that it is immune from control by the collective vested interests.

On the face of it, the idea of judicial control of the economy as a cure-all for market mechanisms appears naive. Raising a critique of Commons is quite problematic though, due to his obscure style. In particular, it is unclear whether Commons is proposing an analytical technique or a theory of political economy. The orthodox theory, at least in principle, purported to show how economic order is derived from individual self-seeking. It is far from clear whether Commons is offering a similar theory or whether he is offering typologies as to what to consider when investigating any given society. Zingler suggests the latter:

> Commons was not the theorist that Veblen was. Rather he was a conceptualist. He developed ways of viewing economic phenomena, not theoretical constructs that had predictive value.
>
> (Zingler 1974 p. 336)

At times he suggests that his own concepts could be supplemented or replaced by others (Parsons 1942 p. 347). It is also hard to apply the idea of political neutrality to Commons's theory in quite the same way as to orthodox economics, since the legislature and judiciary are expressly endogenous.

This is indeed the weakness of the system as a theory. It is by no means clear either why the courts should be primary or why they should adopt 'reasonable value' as a criterion – unless, that is, 'reasonable value' is identified as being congruent with judicial decisions. This would then amount simply to a revision of orthodox theory which points out the need for legal institutions to enforce contract or duty, which is precisely how the theory has subsequently been incorporated into conventional economics. We shall return to this in the next chapter.

Nonetheless, the critique raised by Commons remains powerful, and was rightly perceived as threatening by *laissez-faire* economists. If we remove the naive assumption of 'reasonable value' from the analysis, then we are left with a very convincing case for economic regulation. The analysis need not be limited to the reformism that Commons envisaged, but can be extended to form a powerful radical critique. Commons's focus on the legal basis of capitalism goes to the very heart of the concept of a 'free market'. Markets, it would seem, are never 'free' at all, since they are installed and maintained by the legislature and judiciary, and require the existence of 'going concerns' within the society. The question therefore becomes one of which laws should be passed and which forms of collective action need to be taken in order to enable markets to function well. In this sense the term *laissez-faire* becomes a misnomer, since markets would never exist if left alone.

A defence of *laissez-faire* will therefore entail showing that these institutions can evolve by themselves without requiring intervention from the state or the restraint of individual action by collective action that Commons suggested. It is this defence that we will examine in the next chapter.

5

NEW INSTITUTIONALISM

In methodological terms the American institutionalists raised two challenges to orthodox economic theory. The first, connected more with Veblen, was a psychological critique of hedonism. It was a denial of the entire notion that the objective welfare of individuals corresponds to their subjective wants. The question of how the subjective utility functions of individuals could be maximised was therefore an irrelevance, since these functions did not correspond to the objective well-being of the individual, whose wants were not exogeneous, but were manipulated by the major players in the political economy.

In this critique, maximising 'utilities' would not correspond to an optimal outcome even at the individual level. The other strand of criticism concerned itself with showing that even if individual utility functions were to be taken as given, an optimal social outcome would not result from individuals following their own self-interest. Mitchell believed that business cycles were caused by the social institution of money, Ayres that technology needed to be accounted for in the calculation of the social optimum, and Commons suggested that social institutions needed to be deliberately designed so as to restrain individual action, in particular by laws.

There was also by the 1960s a growing doubt amongst orthodox economists themselves concerning the structure and method of the discipline.[1] At about the same time a growing body of literature arose which attempted to reconcile the orthodox theory with an analysis of institutions, and it is these theorists, the 'new institutional economists',[2] that we shall look at here.

The acceptance of the concept of the institution marks the final abandonment of the traditional or 'classic' positive approach to economics. We shall see that the idea of the congruency of explanation and prediction, which was the hallmark of positivism, has necessarily to be abandoned in favour of a functional or evolutionary mode of explanation. Furthermore, the demarcation of the economic and the political, the hallmark of orthodox economics, must also be abandoned. If it is accepted that the institutional set can have a non-negligible effect on economic behaviour, then the *laissez-faire* economist has to establish the primacy of the economic, and cannot simply ignore the political. Given the existence of institutions, there can be no explanation of the economic without an explanation of the social and political. The value-neutrality of *laissez-faire* economics, it will be recalled, rested upon the idea that we could have a science of 'human nature', and also that individual actions would lead naturally to a social optimum without further interference. With the adoption of institutions, it is accepted that the social and the political do influence the economic actions of humans, and therefore a science of 'human nature' must account for the political and social institutions also.

A further consequence of the abandonment of classical positivism is that the debate on policy (the derivation of which was the whole point of a neutral social science)[3] has now shifted to a debate over the best institutions. We will divide the protagonists into two main schools, which we could call the new institutionalists and the new market socialists, although the latter would also include many authors from within the green movement. The new market socialists attempt to combine a measure of liberal principles into socialist arguments whilst rejecting the statism and the emphasis on production that was the hallmark of the older socialism and of the 1930s market socialist models. We will look at this school of thought in the next chapter. This chapter will consider the work of the new institutionalists. Although these authors accept the need to include institutional analysis in the liberal framework, we shall see that in the final analysis the original framework is retained. The new institutionalists accept the need for institutional analysis, but the main thrust of their argument is that these institutions themselves tend to evolve from individual action. They wish to retain methodological individualism, but feel that the orthodox analysis is inadequate.

Much of the work of the new institutional economists was derived from what Nelson and Winter call 'a sense of general malaise afflicting contemporary microeconomic theory'. They wish to move 'beyond the intellectual territory claimed by modern general equilibrium theory', which will as they put it 'require a theoretical accommodation with one or more of the major aspects of economic reality that are repressed in general equilibrium theory' (Nelson and Winter 1982 p. 5). The school attempts to deal with what Williamson calls the 'human factor' of economic organisation (Williamson 1975 p. 2). Schotter views his work as 'a first step in an attempt to liberate economics from its fixation on competitive markets as an all encompassing institutional framework' (Schotter 1981 p. 1).

In this respect the new institutional economics can be seen as a response to the old or American institutionalism, in that the orthodox account of rationality – of *homo oeconomicus* – was now perceived as inadequate. Nelson and Winter point to the assumptions of perfect knowledge:

As theoretical representations of the problems faced by economic actors increase in realistic complexity and recognition of uncertainty regarding values of the variables, there is a matching increase in the feats of anticipation and calculation and in the clarity of the stakes imputed to those actors. Never is such a theoretical actor confused about the situation or distracted by petty concerns; never is he trapped in a systematically erroneous view of the problem; never is a plain old mistake made. It is a central tenet of orthodoxy that this is the *only* sound way to proceed; recognition of greater complexity in the problem *obligates* the theorist to impute a subtler rationality to the actors.

(Nelson and Winter 1982 pp. 8–9; emphasis in original)

whereas Schotter raises a neo-Austrian critique of perfect competition

The neoclassical agents are bores who merely calculate optimal activities at fixed parametric prices. They are limited to one and only one type of behaviour – that of acting as automata in response to the auctioneer.

(Schotter 1981 p. 150)

Far from being concerned with 'choice', in the orthodox formulation no choices are ever made. The entire idea of choice and action is, the new institutionalists believe, removed from economics by the orthodox approach. For Lachmann, Austrian theory replaces a mechanistic theory of action with a voluntaristic theory (Lachmann 1990 p. 135). Langlois raises a similar criticism regarding competition. He believes that in orthodox theory

the discipline of the market consists entirely in limiting the discretion producers have in setting the prices they will charge. One competes not by taking action but, in a real sense, by being unable to take action.

(Langlois 1986 p. 8)

The new institutional critique was also influenced, as were the later American institutionalists, by the literature on imperfect competition and on monopoly. Firstly, as Langlois points out, the reasons why a monopoly (and by extension an oligopoly) should emerge are never explained (Langlois 1986 p. 9). Furthermore, the imperfect competition models require an understanding of the conduct of the firms in order to examine how close the market outcome is to the social optimum (ibid.).

If the new institutionalists were influenced by their American predecessors, this influence was somewhat selective. Their response largely ignored the Veblenian psychological critique and instead took up his (in our view discredited) employment of an evolutionary methodology. The other aspect of the old institutional critique which was accepted into the new models was Commons's definition of institutions as a deliberate restraint on individual activity, and his attempt to incorporate legal institutions into this concept. However, the new institutionalists, on the whole, did not follow Commons in attempting to investigate deliberate, intentional restraint. Their concern was more to show how unintentional institutions could evolve. That is to say, although the new institutionalism acknowledged the force of the old institutionalists' arguments, 'it is perhaps fair to say that this modern institutionalism reflects less the ideas of the early institutionalists than it does of their *opponents*' (Langlois 1986 p. 2; emphasis in original). The new institutionalism can best be viewed as complementary to orthodox microeconomics, rather than conflicting with it (see Williamson 1975 p. xi), and in this respect is antipathetic to the original American formulations.

GAME THEORY

We will not attempt an exhaustive survey of the wide-ranging literature in this field, but will instead try to give a general outline of the school, and will draw on illustrative texts to examine the inadequacy of the new institutional response. Their task was to reconcile institutions with orthodox microeconomics. As we mentioned, this consisted in essence of a denial of the need for institutions of the sort Commons specified: a need for intentional imposed restraints, for collective action in control of individual action. Rather, as illustrated by Schotter (1981), the new institutionalists attempted to show how institutions could emerge unintentionally or spontaneously, 'by human action but not by human design'. This form of institution Menger referred to as 'organic'. They were derived from the same maximising behaviour as other economic activity, and helped allocate resources in an optimal fashion. Organic institutions arose from 'the selfish interaction of a myriad of individual economic agents each pursuing his own self interest' (Schotter 1981 p. 4).[4] In fact, while Veblen's criticisms of orthodox economics' complete omission of institutional analysis had considerable force, Menger was a bad target for him to pick. Menger was actually greatly concerned with the questions of institutions (Langlois 1986 p. 4). Indeed, Menger believed that the 'most noteworthy problem of the social sciences' to be how 'institutions which serve the common welfare and are extremely significant for its development came into being without a *common will* directed towards establishing them', and that 'The solution of the most important problems of the theoretical social sciences in general, and of theoretical economics in particular is thus closely connected with the question of theoretically understanding the origin and change in "organically" created social institutions' (Menger 1883 p. 147, cited Schotter 1981 p. 4; emphasis in Schotter).

It is these 'organic' institutions, as opposed to the 'pragmatic', consciously designed institutions, that the new institutional school, following Menger, are attempting to derive. Thus Schotter, eschewing Robbins' definition of economics, defines economics as

the study of how individual agents pursuing their own selfish ends evolve institutions as a means to satisfy them.

(Schotter 1981 p. 5)

131

Schotter's work attempts to show how these organic institutions could evolve through the use of game theory. The game theory technique models the results of social interaction directly, by positive 'pay-offs' for each combination of decisions made by the economic actors.[5] Of particular note are those games where the pursuit of self-interest apparently does not lead to the social optimal.

Schotter identifies two main types of game. The most well-known type of game is the 'prisoner's dilemma'.[6] Although neither actor has an incentive to change from the sub-optimal scenario in equilibrium, since the pay-off if the other protagonist does not change is lowered, both would ideally like the other to change.

A 'coordination problem', on the other hand, is where some form of coordination will always increase *both* actors' pay-offs, although not always equally.[7] The actors have preferences, but there is also an incentive to forgo their preferences.

Both of these situations appear to lead to a solution which is sub-optimal. The prisoner's dilemma appears to lead to a sub-optimal equilibrium, whereas the coordination problem suggests that no unique equilibrium exists (Schotter 1981 p. 23).

What Schotter suggests is that economic actors repeatedly dealing with these problems – what he calls 'supergames' – will eventually evolve 'rules' which enable the optimal behaviour to occur. These may take the form of social conventions, which are self-policing, or the economic actors may agree to the convention being policed externally (ibid. p. 11).

Schotter calls the method of showing how institutions can arise the 'state of nature' approach. This technique considers a pre-institutional state of nature, and shows how institutions could have emerged without being imposed.[8] The institutions which could subsequently emerge would then be endogenous to the model rather than given (ibid. p. 21).

The institutions emerge without any form of external coordination, or any agreed cooperation (ibid. p. 28). The only information required for the economic actors is the alternative actions available and the possible payoffs. These are called the 'rules' of the game, which also define how much the player 'knows' about previous actions in the supergame (ibid. p. 110). The institutions arise as a solution to the game problem. They are not part of the behavioural rules of the game (ibid. p. 29).[9] The institutions are not imposed, but are unplanned agreements (ibid. p. 155). The institutions are needed to supplement the market.

> Social and economic institutions are informational devices that supplement the informational content of economic systems when competitive prices do not carry sufficient information to totally decentralise and coordinate economic activities.

That is, institutions help the coordination process as per Hayek.

social institutions convey information about the expected actions of other agents when these actions are not perfectly coordinated by prices and consequently create incentives for such coordinated activity.

(Schotter 1981 p. 109)

The inequality which persists under the present social institutions is not justified directly by Schotter, as with the other Austrians. Rather, he simply suggests that nothing could (or should) be done about it, since redistribution would involve a planned institutional change. His justification of inequality – why we should agree to inequality-preserving institutions – is Hobbesian. We should agree because unequal social institutions are nonetheless preferable to no institutions at all:

> The fact that the rights assignment may be arbitrary and preserving of an unequal distribution of income merely reflects the fact that the equilibrium achieved with property rights is preferred by all agents to the state of conflict that would result if all property rights were removed, but not necessarily preferred by all agents to the state that might result under another set of property rights.
>
> (Schotter 1981 p. 44)[10]

Schotter is dismissive of the idea that institutions may be planned, though. He suggests, following Hayek, it would be undesirable for these unequal social institutions to be replaced by planned, equal ones since such institutions only reflect the preferences of the planner (ibid. p. 21). Consequently, the only governmental intervention should occur when 'empirical study shows that the equilibrium institutions are sub-optimal, such as with some externalities' (ibid. 1981 p. 156).

Schotter, following the Austrian school, attempts to show how social and political institutions can evolve through a need to supplement the information system of the market when it is insufficient. The problems (games) which occur are the result of insufficient information being available to the actors to find an equilibrium solution. This is similar to the position that we saw Hayek take earlier.

TRANSACTION-COST ANALYSIS

The problem which Williamson (1975) raises is that, in his view, market prices are very frequently inadequate information for exchange, and he believes that institutions evolve less as a supplement than in order to bypass the market. He is somewhat more orthodox than Schotter though, in that the rationality problems with which he is concerned are not so much calculational as computational. Recalling the 1930s' socialism debate we looked at earlier, Williamson believes the problem is not so much that the market does not contain sufficient information (the calculational problem) as that the individual cannot process the information quickly enough. This is what H.A. Simon referred to as 'bounded rationality' (Simon 1959). Simon suggested that the computational ability of human actors was limited and could never be sufficient to successfully compute the optimal strategy in order to constantly maximise utility (or welfare or whatever). Simon distinguished in his later works (Simon 1976) between substantive rationality, which is precisely the sort of goal-oriented behaviour of the orthodoxy, and procedural rationality, which considers behaviour as a process of reasoning. The study of behaviour under procedural rationality is concerned not with the goals of action, but with the process by which decisions on the action are taken. Simon had earlier suggested that, given the impossibility of maximising utility, a more realistic analysis of human behaviour is that

> Economic man is a *satisficing* animal whose problem solving is based on search activity to meet certain aspiration levels rather than a *maximizing* animal whose problem solving involves finding the best alternatives in terms of specified criteria.
>
> (Simon 1959 p. 277; emphasis in original)

However this 'satisficing' aspect of bounded rationality has been largely ignored by the new institutionalists,[11] who have focused instead on the costs of acquiring information. It is in this sense that it is used by Williamson (1975). For Williamson, it is problems of bounded rationality caused through uncertainty that are of relevance, together with the belief that transactions are costly.

Williamson also differs from Schotter in that he explicitly evokes J.R. Commons and his concept of the transaction, and attempts to use it to explain the growth of large firms through vertical integration which bypasses the market, thereby (according to Williamson) economising on both bounded rationality and transaction costs.

Williamson, referring to the work of Coase on transaction costs (Coase 1937), maintains that the transaction – the passing of legal control – would occur either in the market or the firm depending on which was more efficient. The contracts involved in specifying transactions, he held, were complex and therefore costly to administer. These costs would vary both within the market and within the firm. The relative efficiency of the internal structure of the firm would effect the outcome of the internalisation of the transaction. The main thrust of the argument is that the cost of drawing up and executing complex contingent contracts is high, and as a result firms tends to adopt the most efficient internal organisation – which Williamson suggests is hierarchical – and to integrate vertically to bypass the market and cut costs (Williamson 1975 pp. 3–9, p. 254).

The reason for the high costs is not simply a function of the market, Williamson believes, but rather due to the factors in the business environment which are often left out of orthodox economics – uncertainty and what

Williamson calls 'small numbers exchange relations' (i.e. oligopsony and oligopoly). However, it is not these market conditions alone which cause the competition and enforcement of contracts to be costly, but rather their combination with the aspects of rationality that the orthodoxy ignores which explain the high cost of complex, contingent contracts. These aspects were bounded rationality and what Williamson calls 'opportunism' (ibid. p. 9), which he defines as 'self interest with guile' (i.e. lying) (ibid. p. 26). It is the combination of these which caused problems within market transactions. Lying during a market transaction would be self-defeating if there were a large number of bidders in the market (ibid. p. 27). By the same token bounded rationality would not be problematic unless there was uncertainty (ibid. p. 22).

Williamson, then, is attempting to explain market structure by reference to the very areas which orthodox analysis leaves out. Furthermore, Williamson does not even assume homogeneity of product, and he also points out that even if competitive markets for homogeneous products may have ensued at the initial contracts the renewal of contracts may be for an heterogeneous product supplied by a monopolist or oligopoly (ibid. pp. 27–8). But while these elements may show why markets fail, Williamson has also to show why internalising the transactions should be superior, and why such internalisation should necessarily involve hierarchy.

These factors occur because of what Williamson calls 'information impactness'. Because of the existence of opportunism, often the information required for a transaction is, according to Williamson, distributed unevenly between the parties, or alternatively the cost of acquiring the necessary information for a contingent contract is prohibitive (ibid. p. 32). The costs of such a transaction may then be lowered through vertical integration (ibid. p. 255). In addition, Williamson believes that bounded rationality can contain both computational and linguistic elements (ibid. p. 254): knowledge may be difficult to fully communicate. Both these elements, Williamson implies, are distributed unevenly among the population. It is for this reason that hierarchies emerge, since 'those whose rationality limits are less severely constrained than others are natural candidates to assume technical, administrative, or political leadership positions . . .' (ibid. p. 24).

The analysis of hierarchies is therefore taking on a distinct evolutionary aspect. The relevant abilities for leadership and management are unevenly distributed, and the most cost-efficient organisation is where these people 'rise to the top'. Indeed, this aspect is actually similar to the Mises account of entrepreneurial talent that we mentioned earlier. Williamson believes that egalitarian or democratic decision-making structures – what he calls 'peer-groups' – are inefficient compared to hierarchies. He first of all points to the inefficiency of a fully democratic decision-making structure where everyone is consulted about all decisions. Obviously, this process would be far too slow for use in business. But even if a 'centralised' decision-making structure was agreed (perhaps by rota), this would come under increasing strain through 'differentials of bounded rationality', that is, different ability levels (ibid. pp. 45–7). Given self-interest, it can be seen that a hierarchy will eventually evolve.[12]

Williamson is therefore critical of attempts by government to intentionally intervene in the functioning of the resulting integrated firms and large conglomerates since these represent the most efficient method of lowering transaction costs and ensuring sufficient management (ibid. pp. 159–60, cf. Dugger 1983 p. 106). Williamson's concern is to show, like Schotter, how a socially optimal solution can emerge even when markets fail to provide this, and how institutions are evolved to supplement the market mechanism. Williamson's model is also evolutionary, since it outlines the emergence of institutions and proposes a selection process (cost-efficiency) whereby the 'best-fitted' institutions are sifted out. In fact, generalising from these authors, we can see how the explanations of the new institutionalists must tend towards functional-evolutionary modes of explanation, precisely because with their rejection of the orthodox 'rational economic human', and with their insistence on explanations of social end-states which are unintentional (this being justified because insufficient information emerges for rational choices to be relevant), no predictive element is left in the theory. There is no hedonist-style 'theory of human nature' which can be employed as a predictable element within the theory. The marginalist theory could predict social optima because 'human nature' was known and human behaviour was known. This enabled the congruence of explanation and prediction, which we saw in chapter one to be the hallmark of positivism, to be maintained. Here prediction is denied – all explanations are *post hoc* .

By removing the predictive elements in economic theory, and thereby positing explanatory theories which have no predictive element (and therefore no possibility of enabling social control), the new institutionalists ensure *post hoc*, evolutionary/functional explanations.

EVOLUTIONARY THEORIES OF THE FIRM

We can see this in the work of Nelson and Winter (1982). These authors explicitly adopt an evolutionary model in their work.[13] Their theory 'emphasises the tendency for the most profitable firms to drive the less profitable ones out of business'. Their quibble is not with the concept of self-seeking, but rather with its application to individuals (ibid. p. 51), and with the idea of perfect knowledge and of automatic profit-maximising. Their operative concept is that of organisational profit-seeking (ibid. p. 31). They have a 'partial accord' with the ideas of competition and equilibrium (ibid. p. 32), but believe by focusing narrowly on the concept of perfect competition and equilibrium models the orthodoxy goes too far. What Nelson and Winter wish to look at is the competitive process (ibid.).

The basis of their evolutionary theory is that most business behaviour follows regular and predictable patterns. These patterns of behaviour they call 'routines'. It is these routines that play the same part in the economic evolutionary process that genes play in the biological theories of natural selection. It is the routines that enable firms to adjust to changes in the environment (ibid. pp. 134 ff.). These routines are classified into three types.

1 decisions concerning fixed quantities of factors (similar to Marshall's 'short-run');
2 decisions on periodical change in capital investment;
3 routines which modify decisions in class (1) over time.

The first class of routines are the day-to-day 'operating characteristics' of the firm. The second group provides the stochastic elements in the model, since investment is linked to profitability. Profitable firms will therefore expand, at the expense of unprofitable firms. The third category of routine Nelson and Winter call 'searches'. These are characterised by a 'routine-guided, routine-changing process'. The changing of routines enables firms to 'mutate', to use a biological analogy. The authors believe that this model of decision-making is sufficient to explain the dynamic evolutionary outcome of a competitive market. As they explain it, the current operating characteristics determine factor inputs and outputs. These decisions determine factor and product prices on the (given) market, which therefore determine profitability, which in turn affect investment. A new set of input and output levels are thereby generated from the new level of capital stock. All the while the operating characteristics are being slowly changed by the firms' search routines (ibid. pp. 14–19).

The organisational routines are similar to individual skills, according to Nelson and Winter. They believe that much of this skill is personal and tacit, and is not transferable, and cannot be widespread (ibid. pp. 76 ff.). It is for this reason that firms' reactions to a dynamically changing environment differ.

CRITIQUE

While much of Nelson and Winter's book is concerned with specific descriptions of the development of these routines, these need not detain us here. Our criticism of the evolutionary methodology will be at a more fundamental level. We can see how even Nelson and Winter – who are closest to the orthodox views of rationality – are relying upon *post hoc* explanation. There is no attempt at explanation of which routines are likely to be profitable, but merely something of an assumption that these exist. Similarly, in game theory there is no mention of just how organic institutions emerge through supergames, but only that such a process would be socially optimal.[14] Exactly what abilities are to be found in the leaders of hierarchies is not discussed by Williamson. The new institutionalist attempt at *post hoc* explanation is actually a *post hoc ergo propter hoc* fallacy, and by offering such a fallacy as a cause for events, they tend to offer undue justification for the *status quo*.

In fact, the new institutional economists use a very particular form of causal explanation. They explain not so much the historical emergence of institutions as the *'raison d'être'* for these institutions to exist (Langlois 1986 p. 21). They offer a functional explanation of institutional development – Williamson, in fact, often 're-interprets' historical institutions in logical terms (Dugger 1983 p. 102). But functional explanations have to be couched in terms of social benefit. The problem faced here – as with the positivism of the orthodox economists – is to show how this social optimum can be derived through methodological individualism. Either the historical institutions must be shown to be irrelevant for present choices, or the functional institutions must be traced from some sort of pre-institutional 'state of nature' (Rutherford 1989 p. 302), as Schotter sets out to do.[15]

Unfortunately, the presumed 'state of nature' is no more natural than the post-institutional world, which we can see very clearly when examining game theory. Recall that Schotter's neo-Austrian formulation was that the rules themselves were not regarded as institutional; the institutions emerged as the solution to the game problem. Nonetheless, game theory does take some rules or institutions as given. The notion of the supergame, for example, itself presumes that the game is capable of repetition (Rutherford 1989 p. 305). The supergame concept is inoperable if a non-optimal response is catastrophic (ibid. p. 308). Furthermore the entire structure is not so much abstract as artificial:

> Game theorists sometimes become so enamoured of the mechanics of the theory and the single-minded determination of their players to win that they lose sight of what any game-theoretic problem presupposes; the arena in which the players are to compete or cooperate . . . although one can investigate with game theory the dilemmas possibly faced by two prisoners, one should not expect from such a theory an explanation for why escape or insurrection is not part of the strategic space . . . the arena of any interactive game is partly determined by resources and technologies, but the social norms that pervade the atmosphere are an equally important characteristic of that arena.
>
> (Field 1984 p. 703)

Furthermore, the supergame must posit a constancy among the economic actors (Mirowski 1986 p. 252). Indeed, the 'rules' of the game, as we noted, posit very stringent restrictions on the information the players are presumed to obtain.

> Players are assumed to 'learn' from past players of the game but this learning is constrained to a very small sub-set of experience: they are

allowed neither threat strategies nor to be different from other players and cannot remember past the last immediate play of the game.

(Mirowski 1986 p. 251)

In fact, no real 'learning' is ever done. 'Schotter, like many other latter-day Austrians, shies away from explicitly discussing *learning*, as opposed to the transmission of a discrete and seemingly prepackaged commodity called *knowledge*, because the former suggests a social process, whereas the latter conjures up the grocer's dairy case' (ibid. p. 252; emphasis in original; cf. Field 1984) Game theory abstracts from the entire social and cultural elements of individuals, complete with customs, language and rules (Field 1984 p. 688 and *passim*). In fact, if game theory is to be consistent, these elements should also be explained in terms of efficiency. These 'basic' rules must be endogenised into the model. This it does not do (ibid. pp. 695–6). In fact, the individuals in the game theory models are just as abstract as the orthodox *homo oeconomicus*.

> In effect, Schotter defines the 'problem' to be so straight forward and unambiguous that only one choice can be made; it is not so much learning as it is mechanism . . . It is difficult to maintain that this model transcends the passive cooperation of the zombies found in conventional neo-classical general equilibrium.
>
> (Mirowski 1986 p. 252)

So in fact the economic actors never change throughout the supergame. In addition, the objectives and the environment are also given in the rules, and held to be constant. Actually no economic game is played at all and no problem solved: the rules, as for the orthodox theory, determine the outcome in advance.

> Given the fixed actors with their fixed objectives and fixed rules, the analyst (and *not the actors*) pre-reconciles the various sets, insists the pre-reconciled outcome is the one that will actually obtain and calls this a solution . . . The process in which the actors take part is irrelevant, because the deck has been stacked in a teleological manner.
>
> (Mirowski 1986 p. 253; emphasis in original)

And what is more, since the models assume this constancy, they cannot consider historical change (ibid. p. 255), which is precisely to say that they are unable to show the evolutionary adaptation to a changing environment which Schotter began by claiming is a necessary requisite of economics. In fact, the new institutionalist school relies upon essentially the same fundamentals as the orthodoxy it hoped to supplement (Hodgson 1989 p. 249). It still holds the same hedonistic approach, using a self-seeking and abstract individual, and may be no more dynamic than general equilibrium analysis. We have just seen how game theory, like general equilibrium, models an unchanging world. Similarly, Williamson actually has a notion of rationality not too dissimilar from that of the orthodoxy, particularly because he misunderstands Simon's concept of the bounded rationality (ibid. p. 254). Simon's point was that because human computational ability is limited, agents cannot maximise, and therefore strive for acceptable minima. The problem for Simon is not scarcity of information but of the complexity and quantity of information (Hodgson 1988 p. 81). The problem of information is not therefore simply that of its cost.

> 'satisficing' does not amount to cost-minimising behaviour. Clearly, the latter is just the dual of the standard assumptions of maximisation; if 'satisficing' was essentially a matter of minimising costs then it would amount to maximising behaviour of the orthodox type.

But this is clearly Williamson's interpretation:

> Williamson adopts the orthodox, cost-minimising interpretation of Simon and not the one which clearly prevails in Simon's work. In Williamson's work 'economizing on the transaction costs' is part of global, cost-minimizing behaviour, and this is inconsistent with Simon's idea of bounded rationality. Whilst Williamson recognizes some of the informational problems, the fact that the cost calculus remains supreme in his theory means he has not broken entirely from the orthodox assumption of maximization.
>
> (Hodgson 1988 p. 254)

Williamson therefore holds a similar notion of rationality to that found in orthodox models. He also employs the general equilibrium static concept of cost when he considers transaction costs. As we saw in Chapter 3, the entire problem of costs was that these were subjective. Yet in Williamson's treatment, they appear to be objective – in fact, they have been given primacy. It is unclear why this should be so.

> Following the lead of George Stigler's classic article (1961), search and information costs could be accommodated alongside, and treated similarly to, other costs in a probabilistic framework. In this approach information is treated just like any other commodity, and subject to the marginalist rule that its composition is optimal when the marginal cost of information and acquisition is equal to its expected marginal return.
>
> (Hodgson 1988 p. 201)

The 1930s 'London debate', it will be recalled, identified this question of costs as a pivotal issue. The whole argument stemmed from the Austrian critique that the minimal cost of production was unknown; it was therefore impossible to judge *a priori* how economic actors would behave. If the costs of production were objective, it was then conceded that production could in fact be centrally planned (cf. Hodgson 1989 p. 80). A similar criticism is raised by

Dugger, who points out that in the Williamson model it would be possible to extend the analysis to the state.

> Although not emphasised by Williamson this advantage of internal-isation over contracting out could be applied to numerous government purchases ... The state should not contract out to the private sector for goods and services so readily ... Yet, it must be noted, Williamson does not emphasise these public policy implications, though they are of immense practical import. This monumental omission in his transaction cost analysis yields a glimpse into his philosophical orientation. Al-though he views the firm as an efficient transaction-cost economiser he does not extend his vision to include the state.
>
> (Dugger 1983 pp. 99–100)[16]

Williamson differs from other practitioners of transaction-cost analysis in this. Although Williamson claims to go beyond as it were the seminal work of Coase (1937), it rather appears that his concept of transaction costs are derived in an entirely different manner, and different conclusions can be drawn from each author. Coase suggests that costs form an intrinsic part of each and every transaction. He claims, following Dahlman, that all trans-actions involve search and information costs, bargaining and decision costs, and policing and enforcement costs (Dahlman 1979 p. 148). It is due to the existence of these costs that firms exist, and also these costs are why markets exist (Coase 1988 p. 7 ff.). Both emerge so as to cut down on transaction costs. Whereas in Williamson's analysis transaction costs emerge due to lying and oligopoly, Coase is more concerned with the problems of discovering relevant prices and with the desirability for firms to avoid a myriad of contracts for each production activity. For Coase it is the large number of contracts which are the problem, not a small number, and it is processing all the price information which is available that is problematic, not dealing with false information. Firms exist simply to cut down on the need to make a new contract each time a service is required.

The reasons Coase gives for limits to the size of firms are unconvincing, however. He suggests that there are decreasing returns to the entrepreneurial function[17] (Coase 1937 p. 340), yet it is far from clear why these should exist. And indeed, in 1960 Coase, in contradistinction to Williamson, claimed that 'The government is, in a sense, a super-firm' (Coase 1960 p. 497). For Coase, the analysis is as applicable to the state as it is to firms.[18]

The suspicion remains that the concept of transaction costs is simply a gloss, or at best a respecification, of what used to be known simply as market failures.[19] Nonetheless, as will be argued in the next chapter, the presence of large transaction costs means that the initial distribution of resources is actually of vital importance – resources may not be allocated through markets in an efficient manner, and we have to consider the problem of economic power. This is largely absent from the analysis of Coase, and totally absent from Williamson. Returning for a moment to the Austrian critique, it will be recalled that the significance of markets, especially markets in capital was to ensure control over management. Yet Williamson necessarily maintains that this control is inadequate due to 'information compactness' (Williamson 1975 p. 142). Yet without even the market or the state as a regulator, it is far from clear what is to stop corporate power running amok.

> If not anti-trust and the market, if not the public purpose and planning, *then what* ? Is any kind of social control over corporate power needed . . .
>
> (Dugger 1983 p. 107; emphasis in original)

Indeed, any notion of power is non-existent in both Williamson's formulation and the new institutionalists in general (ibid. p. 108). At no time do the market institutions coerce or influence either individual actors or the social or political institutions. The new institutional economics attempts to entirely remove the possibility of power – all multinational conglomerates are serving the public interest by minimising costs; legal institutions emerge because they are the most efficient at distributing property rights; and optimum government will necessarily emerge by rational choice. The entire programme takes on an air of unreality – try telling 'em about 'efficient property rights' in Soweto.[20] What the new institutional programme amounts to is an attempt to endogenise institutions (Rutherford 1989 pp. 301–2, Hodgson 1989 p. 252),[21] thereby eliminating all possibility of power. All decisions are deemed to be the result of rational action. Nonetheless, the new institutionalists only consider J.R. Commons treatment of institutions – collective action as a restraint. They do not look at the Veblenian psychological critique of rationality, but rather take the view that

> the individual can be 'taken for granted'. To put it another way, the individual, along with his or her assumed behavioural characteristics, is taken as the elemental building block in the theory of the social or economic system.
>
> (Hodgson 1989 p. 250)

The possibility that the individual behaviour may be malleable is never met by the new institutionalists, and in this sense 'the assumption of the abstract individual which is fundamental to classic liberalism is fundamental to the "new institutional economics" as well' (ibid. p. 252), as it is for the Austrians (ibid. p. 253). They are not therefore able to consider conspicuous expenditure, cultural manipulation, the production of waste and the other machinations of the business class that Veblen discusses. Douglas North, for example, recognises and attempts to accommodate the need to include 'ideology' in economic analysis. But North's concept of ideology is not that of Marx or Veblen. His concept is endogenous and evolutionary. Ideology is 'derived from the experiences people have. If all the people had the same experiences, we could expect that their perspectives about the world around them would be the same' (North 1984 p. 35). The sole role of ideology was as a method of deciding on the fairness of institutions (ibid.).[22] No exogenous manipulation of ideology is considered.

In effect, the new institutionalism is more deterministic than the old institutionalism it seeks to replace. If the new institutionalism is indeed attempting to offer a supplement to the orthodox analysis it has to explain how a social optimum is obtained from the individuals acting selfishly. In evolutionary theories which, as we have seen, the school invariably adopts, this necessarily takes the form of an efficiency argument (Langlois 1986 p. 21). But as noted before, this is not an explanation of the origin of an institution but 'at best an explanation of the persistence of the institution and only then if the feedback mechanism is specified' (Langlois 1989 pp. 293–4). Our critique earlier was precisely that the feedback mechanism is indeed unspecified. Their theory is Darwinian in nature; the explanations always fall short of a complete specification of the reason of maintenance of an institution. As a result the school's proponents become simply apologists for the *status quo*.

The orthodox analysis purported to show how a social optimal could be derived from individual actions – this was the idea of the 'invisible hand'. The new institutionalists have replaced the 'positive' economics of the orthodoxy with an 'evolutionary' functional explanation which is derived from *post hoc* observation. As we mentioned in Chapter 1, methodologically this involves moving to theories which are explanatory but not predictive. But as we saw in Chapter 1, the justification for a science of society was precisely this predictive nature of scientific thought. It was the ability to control and manipulate the social arena to advantage that was the *raison d'être* for the entire enterprise. The basis of the orthodoxy was that it was able to show how the 'best' policy could be determined; it was a tool for the policy scientist to use. Now that prediction has been rejected, and only *post hoc* explanations are being mooted, there is no possibility of policy being derived at all – even a policy of *laissez-faire*, since no explanation of the origin of present-day institutions is given.

What is lacking is what Langlois calls a 'compositional' principle. We need to show how individual behaviour links together to form an aggregate result (Langlois 1989 p. 281). He believed it was carelessness concerning this principle that caused errors in the work of the new institutionalists (ibid. p. 293). Our critique would go further, since we saw earlier that the economic compositional principle – the derivation of the social optimum from the individual action – consisted in the theory of value. What is lacking in the new institutional economics is a value theory.[23] Although the analysis may show how institutions could be organic, it can no longer show that these organic institutions would be optimal nor that the market complete with organic institutional supplement would be optimal.

When push comes to shove, the new institutionalists simply give us the flip side of the same methodological individualist coin as the orthodox economists. The orthodox analysis tried to ignore the social and the political by abstracting such aspects from their purely economic theory. This resulted in an unrealistic and virtually useless theory. The reason that value theory is essential to this scheme is that it enables them to arrive at a social optimum from their individualist analysis. The new institutional economists accept that the exclusion of the political and social is not sustainable, but they attempt to reduce these to economic activities. Again, this will manifest itself in value theory, which is either ignored (Williamson, Nelson and Winter) or the values are given (Schotter). None actually meet the problems raised by the theories of market failure which motivated the new theories. The orthodox economists gave us an unrealistic theory which showed how a social optimum could be derived. The new institutionalists have chosen the other path and attempted to give a realistic theory, but in so doing they cannot show that the outcome will be socially optimal. When they attempt to do so, their theory loses touch with reality, and often becomes orthodox in nature. In the last analysis the new institutionalists are unable to provide a viable alternative to orthodox economics.

6

NEW SOCIAL MOVEMENTS

The quest for a positive science of economics has ended in failure. We have shown in Chapter 2 that the utilitarian philosophy of science was impossible to put into practice. The alternative positivist economic theory – the idea of a planned economy – was shown in Chapter 3 also to be inoperable. Furthermore, in Chapter 4 we have shown how the economic cannot be separated from the political and the social. The Veblenian critique was that individual wants are socially manipulated, and it is therefore futile to demonstrate how aggregate satisfaction can be maximised by markets: both are created by the vested interests. In Galbraith's phrase

> it is the process of satisfying wants that creates the wants ... the individual who urges the importance of production to satisfy these wants is precisely in the position of the onlooker who applauds the efforts of the squirrel to keep abreast of the wheel that is propelled by its own efforts.
>
> (Galbraith 1958 p. 149)

Moreover Mitchell and Commons showed how markets were themselves dependent on the social institutions of money and also of law and property rights. It is therefore not the case that the problems of economy are indeed universal for all societies, as was claimed by Robbins and others. The economic is itself defined by the society, and to claim that the 'economic problem' is universal is in fact reification.

With the inability to separate the economic from the social and the polity, the possibility of economics providing a policy science is also removed. It is not the case that the economic scientist can inform us which policies will best promote our political ends, since the operation of 'the economy' will vary according to the institutional set. Our interest should centre on this institutional set, not only upon the economy. What the optimum institutional set would consist of will be the question considered in this chapter.

It is worth recalling from Chapter 1 that the justification of positive social science was precisely that it did offer the possibility of policy science, the ability to control social life. This was possible because of two facets of positive

145

science – the ability to predict and the provision of objective knowledge. We have shown that the predictive ability of microeconomics is so limited as to be useless, and we have seen that the predictive ability of all areas of economic science has been brought into question. While *laissez-faire* cannot be defended by employing a positivist metatheory, the rejection of positivism will necessarily involve accounting for the social and the political. The Austrian theory provided a critique of central planning based on the concept of subjective value, disseminated information and a Darwinian, evolutionary theory of distribution. The new institutionalist school accepted the concept of institutions, but attempted to endogenise these into their economic models. As we saw, all of the attempts at incorporating the political, social and legal into a methodological individualist framework were inadequate.

In this chapter we will consider how best to move beyond the inadequacies of the New Right and orthodox theories, and will examine some of the emerging schools of thought in an attempt to ascertain the most promising threads for the development of social and political economy. Our focus here will be on two main schools: firstly on the green movement and the question of environment, and secondly on what I have termed the new market socialists. We will see that although the two schools of thought arose from critiques of different theories and have slightly different goals, there are significant similarities and paths of convergence between them. We will also point out aspects of the analysis pertinent to ecofeminism, which as a social movement bridges both these schools. In particular, we will be discussing the notion that there may be many aspects of 'the good' – many elements valuable for a good society – which do not take the form of commodities. This idea had formed part of the feminist critique for some time. In addition, we will suggest that the masculine conception of 'rational economic man' should be discarded, and a more feminine 'ethic of care'[1] based in a conception of citizenship, should be used.

THE GREEN MOVEMENT

Hirsch

Much green political economy has emerged as a reaction to both the inherent political theory of positive economics and the associated modernist principle of judging social value by pecuniary quantification. While environmental concerns have a long pedigree, it could be argued that the contemporary debate began with the publication of the Club of Rome report, *The Limits to Growth* (Meadows *et al.* 1972). To the extent that this is the case, it is not without irony. The message from the Club of Rome was that present rates of growth of consumption were unsustainable, since the resources to fuel and supply this growth and the capacity to absorb the waste products of the exponential growth would be exhausted in the foreseeable future. The evidence for this view was derived from projections based upon a complex causal model of a large variety of variables; that is to say, the argument is positivist. This positivist argument subsequently set off a debate which has seen the rise of a green social movement which has to a large extent rejected the value-neutral positive approaches to science and the bias to quantification of the modernism it is associated with.

While ironic, perhaps the chain of events should not, with the benefit of hindsight, be regarded as particularly surprising. It would be much harder for so-called positive economists to ignore positive arguments (although as we have said several times they have displayed a remarkable capacity for this in the past). But possibly the main reason why *Limits to Growth* acted as such a catalyst for environmental debate was that it revealed the extent to which the whole orthodox economic 'package', and more particularly the centralised policy-science-based political theory that is inherent within it, is inextricably bound up with the concept of growth. On the face of it, an orthodox economics concerned mainly with equilibrium ought not to be overly concerned with growth. Unfortunately, growth becomes a vital issue because of the lack of an adequate (or indeed any) distributional theory within mainstream economics. It is then far from clear what tools the positive policy scientist is to use to analyse the optimal distribution set. In practise economic growth has acted to deflect questions of redistribution (Hirsch 1977 p. 7). Posing a limit to growth causes the whole problem of distribution to rise to the surface again, and the further matter of limitations of orthodox economics to rise with it.

Hirsch's point of departure has also formed one of the main themes of the present book (which is why the present title recalls Hirsch's work). Hirsch questions the process of aggregation within orthodox economic theory. The basis of modern economic analysis Hirsch believes, is that it 'adds up', it attempts to provide 'a theoretical basis and an associated accounting frame for the aggregation of economic activity within an integrated system' (ibid. p. 15).

By claiming to show how the economic activity of individuals can be added up, Hirsch believes that orthodox economic theory has wielded considerable political influence. He believes that the prospect of statistical measurement of national income has a direct influence on both economic and political expectations. Nonetheless, these expectations are based on a conception of the ultimate objective of economic activity as being the consumption of scarce goods and services (ibid. p. 16). It therefore follows that growth in these elements of consumption will increase economic welfare.

Hirsch believes this is a misconception. The objectives of economic activity are far from straightforward. Economic output is actually deeply ambiguous (ibid. 1977 p. 55). Hirsch (echoing Myrdal) points out that basing economic theory on a distinction between ends and means à la Robbins is misguided, since means cannot be separated from ends. Often the item consumed is simply the means to a further end – petrol is a means to travel. Hirsch refers to these as 'intermediate' goods, which are not consumed in their own right but as a means of consuming other goods or services. Hirsch suggests that we could view consumer intermediate goods as 'regrettable necessities' or 'defensive' goods (ibid. p. 55 ff.). A rise in expenditure on defensive goods does not mean that overall benefit has been increased. Intermediate, defensive goods should be regarded more as a cost than a benefit. They derive their value 'only from the existence of the negative factor that is being countered' (ibid. p. 57).

An increase in expenditure does not therefore necessarily correspond with an increase in benefits, but may simply be a cost associated with a change in circumstances. We may gain no benefit from, say, increased expenditure on fuel, but this may simply be the result of increased congestion, and should rightly be regarded as a cost rather than a benefit.

It is therefore no longer the case that economic activity corresponds to economic output. In order to make judgements about economic output we must consider what the economic activity is for. This question is not amenable to quantification, particularly pecuniary quantification (we will consider alternative quantifiers later). That is to say that orthodox economics, based on the dichotomy of ends and means, is unable to get a handle on defensive expenditures, and 'for the purpose of economic measurement, then, the question remains unoperative' (Hirsch 1977 p. 59). The idea of intermediate goods and defensive expenditures bursts the banks of orthodox economic theory.

The analysis of defensive expenditures is similar in many ways to the Austrian critique of the orthodoxy. Both are claiming that what ought to be (to some degree) a subjective concept is being used as an objective, quantifiable concept. The whole point of the Austrian concept of opportunity cost, the measurement of value *by* cost, is precisely to deny legitimacy to quantification, so as to show why economic planning will not work. One of the corollaries of the Austrian approach is the denial of the legitimacy of economic aggregates. If economic data is subjective and only available at the individual level, economic aggregates are meaningless. The entire thrust of the Austrian theory is that only the individual is aware of the value of purchases. Inflation, for example, is purported to be a measure of rising costs. Yet the Austrian conception of opportunity cost was precisely that economic cost could not be measured by money, but only by the value of opportunities foregone, which only the individual knew. Opportunity costs were only known by the person on the spot. Indeed, the Austrians would deny that the economic goods which are being aggregated can ever be homogeneous; each is capable of an infinite number of variations, and the function of the entrepreneur, it will be recalled, was precisely to develop new goods. While the prices of goods can be collated, aggregated and indexed, such indices tell us nothing worthwhile.

Furthermore, employing costs as an objective measure of value, which is

148

what is done by aggregates such as GNP, leads to paradoxes. Spending more on petrol because of congestion raises GNP, even though the same amount of travel is undertaken. Money spent on expensive technologies to counteract the effect of pollution ('clean-up' technology) adds to GNP, even though all they achieve is to return the world to the same state as before. If technology is employed that cost the same but did not pollute in the first place (clean technology) GNP would be lower, not higher. Even though the same amount of benefit is yielded, less 'growth' occurs.

The same phenomenon can be seen to occur when activity is withdrawn from the monetary sphere. If, for example, a homeowner decides to work less paid overtime and do her/his own plumbing rather than pay for a plumber, the same end result occurs even though the national income goes down. Note that the point in question is not whether the individuals are better or worse off, but the fact that the aggregate measures are of activity and not value.

Increased economic activity, which is often referred to as economic growth, may therefore not correspond to an increase in economic 'welfare', and the standard economic aggregate such as GNP do not inform us of the level of economic welfare.

There may be other reasons why economic activity differs from economic welfare. We may recall the discussion earlier concerning game theory, whereby it was suggested that in many situations some form of external coordination to individual activity would be mutually beneficial. These were termed positive-sum games. However, it is also possible to have zero-sum games, whereby protagonists can only gain at another's expense. These situations will ensue whenever the goods and services available are subject to an absolute fixed quantity. Hirsch identifies two such causes of absolute scarcity; physical and social scarcity. We will consider physical scarcity more closely later, but Hirsch's main focus is on social scarcity. This occurs when the scarcities themselves are objects of consumption, either directly (e.g. fashion) or indirectly through being effected by the extent to which they are used by others (e.g. congestion, leadership positions) (Hirsch 1977 p. 20). Socially scarce goods are goods whose value depends on their exclusiveness. Such 'goods' as traffic space, for example, diminish in value as they are consumed by others. An empty road yields a higher value than a congested road (ibid. p. 23).

If they are not to be debased (Hirsch refers to this as 'crowding'), all goods subject to an absolute fixed quantity of supply must be subject to some process of allocation. Hirsch identifies two main allocation processes, auctions and screening (ibid. p. 30).[2] The latter consists of social and political decision-making as to who should have access to the socially scarce resources, processes which we would suggest may vary in form and may be either benign (such as credentials for academic posts or even elections for politicians) or malign (such as petty racism).[3]

Hirsch refers to goods which are socially scarce as 'positional' goods.

Access to the goods will always depend on one's position in the 'pecking order' – in the auction or in the screening process. The existence of positional goods has two main consequences for our previous arguments. The first is that the attempt to obtain positional goods may involve increased defensive expenditures (ibid. p. 64). The price of positional goods may be bid up by auction, or the screening processes may cause individuals to take unwanted actions: for example, taking extra education, or living further away from work to avoid city-centre crowding. In addition, the problem of positional goods is bound up with the question of distribution in several ways. Although the positional goods may be allocated by auction by reference to the distribution of income and wealth, the distribution set at any one time is itself positional. In addition, we shall see how raising the question of distribution moves us towards the political arena.

Because of the ways in which the distribution of income and wealth is tied up with the positional economy, it would seem that economics has to offer a theory of distribution. Of course, such a theory is expressly excluded from the orthodoxy. As a result of this, orthodox economics has no advice to offer policy-makers on this crucial question. Yet the existence of both physical and social scarcity throws distributional issues into sharp relief. As we maintained earlier, the traditional method for politicians and policy-makers to avoid debates over distribution was to promise economic 'growth'. Yet we have seen that this promise is empty. Many goods are positional, and cannot by their very nature be supplied to everyone. The promise of everyone obtaining such goods is false; 'they embody a false hope of what economic growth means for the individual. By promising to satisfy individuals demand for what only some among them can have, the processes distort the pattern of output within the market economy' (Hirsch 1977 p. 32). Individuals my strive and still get nowhere. In addition, they may well see what has been termed economic 'growth', and yet feel no better off than before. The undeliverable promise of growth is a recipe for continuing resentment.

Environmental economics

Much of Hirsch's analysis will apply to environmental resources, which are absolutely fixed in supply, and which may be collective in character. Hirsch acknowledges the work of Galbraith and others in questioning the extent to which the preferences of consumers are transmitted to producers through market mechanisms, and the further failure of market processes to signal demand for public or collective goods, which are available to groups rather than individuals. He also acknowledges that there is a recognition among economists of the existence of market imperfections and market failures, although there is no consensus on their relative significance, on the extent to which individual valuations are misleading. He notes, however, that the qualifications to market mechanisms

150

are concerned essentially with perfecting the transmissions from the preferences of the individual consumer to the delivery mechanism of the market and governmental suppliers. If both consumer preferences and full social costs could be correctly passed on to producers, fulfilment of these preferences of individual consumers would be the accepted goal of the system.

(Hirsch 1977 p. 17)

Hirsch has pointed out that the matter goes deeper than this. The essential problem, as Daly and Cobb recognise, is the total inability of both orthodox and Austrian economics to so much as conceive of a collective good (Daly and Cobb 1990 p. 159). All goods must be reducible to individual values in order for the methodological individualist economic schema to be able to take cognizance of them. This is why social costs or benefits are regarded as 'externalities'. The problem is conceived in terms of the 'external' effects of what should otherwise be regarded as an individual choice; there is no mechanism for conceiving of a social good as such.

It is important to realise that the 'problem' of environmental resources is not one of externalities. This is only the interpretation placed upon it by economists. The 'problem' is how to allocate scare resources which are

1 social;
2 positional;
3 not commodities;
4 often depleted some time after consumption.

For any or all of these reasons, environmental resources, or indeed other social resources, may not be traded, or the trading prices may not reflect social values.[4] The response of orthodox economics is either to attempt to treat untraded goods as if they were traded (Ball 1979 p. 68), or to suggest adjustments in market pricing by taxation or subsidies to alter the price of environmental resources to their 'correct' levels. This latter also involves some notion of non-market valuation of environmental resources. Cost-benefit analysis (CBA) adopts these approaches. By using techniques such as shadow pricing (following a supposedly 'parallel' market to the environmental good in question), or contingent valuation (an elaborate survey method using pecuniary valuation rather than scaled responses), the economist claims to obtain a non-market value for resources.

In fact, what is occurring is that orthodox economics has resorted to planning. A planning 'supplement' is being suggested for a predominantly market-oriented system. Prices and values are being arrived at without recourse to market mechanisms, and these are being viewed as objective valuations. The tradability of scarce objects is not, it would seem, being viewed as necessary for their valuation.

Given that the proponents of CBA are claiming that non-market, objective

151

pecuniary valuations can be obtained, we may ask why we should stop at valuations of environmental resources. It is unclear why we cannot obtain these objective valuations for all traded goods, and thereby plan the entire economy. As we have seen throughout, there is no reason why objective economic values cannot be used for planning. If techniques for obtaining economic values without the need for trade have been devised, it is far from clear why these cannot be employed for economic planning. The boundary between the planned environmental sector and the unplanned market sector appears arbitrary and unnecessary.

The debate over environment can be viewed as a contemporary counterpoint to the 1930s' debate on socialist calculation. If we accept the existence of objective values, then it is hard to deny the possibility of a planned economy. By the same token, critiques of planning must also involve criticisms of the planning supplement being proposed for the valuation of environmental resources. Furthermore, as we saw earlier, the critique of objective values also means that aggregate economic indicators are not of use. We have already criticised indicators such as GNP. The same criticism would also hold for other indices of objective social welfare. A natural response to the inadequacies of measures of economic activity as indicators of welfare is to attempt to measure welfare 'directly'. This invariably involves using a variety of 'social indicators' as surrogates for pecuniary values. Daly and Cobb include the 'value' of loss of wetlands and farmland for example, as well as women's household labour and an estimate of defensive expenditures (Daly and Cobb 1990 pp. 401 ff.). Hirsch points up two problems which this approach is likely to run into. Firstly, there will inevitably be difficulties in obtaining measurable proxies for economic output. In addition, he suggests that there is an 'absence of any common unit of measurement to link and aggregate the separate measures, comparable to that of money in GNP' (Hirsch 1977 p. 64). The decision as to which indicators to include in the index and what weighting to give them would be highly contentious issues, and can never be resolved objectively.

The construction of alternative indices such as these has exercised the minds of many in the green movement,[5] yet the approach can be seen to be fundamentally flawed. The social and political questions concerning resources remain. All such a process achieves is to restate the problem of aggregating individual valuations in a numeric format. Such indices amount to political and social decisions with numbers attached to them, but these decisions are made by policy scientists whom it is difficult to bring to account. Indeed, we can see here precisely what is meant by the scientisation of politics and the political theory of policy science. The political decisions concerning distribution, the use of scarce resources, which objects should be commodified and which should not and how the commodities are to be valued, are all presented as technical questions and decided upon by the policy scientist. They are thereby effectively removed from the political agenda.

Nonetheless, we would suggest that some sort of pecuniary valuation is necessary for the efficient allocation of environmental – and other – resources. Without this valuation it is impossible to gauge the ratios of exchange of one scarce resource *vis-à-vis* another, even, for example, the cost of insulation relative to fuel. What is being claimed here is that this valuation is the result of political and social processes, and it is these processes that we should consider.

If the debate over environmental economics is reminiscent of the 1930s' debate, then our criticisms of the Austrian position on environment should be similar. The Austrian approach invokes some of the ideas of the new institutionalists, and revolves around the concept of property rights. The claim is that the 'externalities' emerge because property rights have been inadequately defined. If these rights were given out, then they could be traded, and a correct valuation would emerge. The seminal article on this approach is from Coase (1960).[6] Coase adds to the orthodox analysis the institutionalist concepts of transaction costs and property rights. He claims that so called 'social' cost is really a matter of reciprocal dispute.

> The traditional approach has tended to obscure the nature of the choice that has to be made. The question is commonly thought of as one in which A inflicts harm on B and what has to be decided is: how should we restrain A? But this is wrong. We are dealing with a problem of a reciprocal nature. To avoid the harm to B would inflict harm on A. The real question to be decided is: should A be allowed to harm B or should B be allowed to harm A? The problem is to avoid the more serious harm.
>
> (Coase 1960 p. 485)

In other words, the so-called question of social costs is actually a question of who has rights over the resources. If a polluter has, say, no right to pollute (use) clean air, then the polluter would have to compensate those who do have this right. By the same token, if a polluter does enjoy a right to create, say, noise pollution, then the polluter could claim compensation for giving up this right. The question is who enjoys the right to use environmental resources.

The distribution of these property rights notwithstanding, Coase then goes on to show that, if the market mechanism is 'working smoothly', which Coase takes to mean that the operation of the pricing system is without cost (Coase 1960 p. 486), then the final allocation of the hitherto untraded goods will, after trading, be identical regardless of the initial distribution of the property rights. That is, because of trade, the final allocation of property rights will be unaffected by their initial distribution, *if* markets are costless (ibid. pp. 485–95). This is what has generally become known as the 'Coase theory'. It has often been taken by the New Right to mean that environmental problems should be dealt with by the (random) allocation of tradable rights in environmental resources, after which market mechanisms can be left to achieve an optimal allocation of these resources.

153

Coase himself does not subscribe to the 'Coase theory' however, or rather he regards the theory as trivial, since markets and the transactions that take place within them are never costless. Coase believes that transactions always involve cost – transactions costs are never zero – and that speculation as to what occurs in their absence is futile. As Coase puts it 'a world without transaction costs has very peculiar properties' and is 'as strange as the physical world would be without friction' (Coase 1988 p. 14). Coase suggests 'it would not seem worthwhile to spend much time investigating the properties of such a world'. Among other things, firms would not exist, neither would insurance companies, and monopolies would be compensated to act like competitors (ibid.). The point Coase was trying to make in 1960 was that transaction costs must be accounted for if we are to make any sense whatsoever of the empirical world in general, and social costs in particular. 'What my argument does suggest', he explains, 'is the need to introduce positive transaction costs explicitly into economic analysis so that we can study the world that exists' (Coase 1960 p. 15). Coase further believes that 'we will not be able to do this unless we first discard the approach at present used by most economists' (ibid. p. 16).

At any event, Coase is clear that the conclusion reached when transaction costs are ignored – that the distribution of rights to 'social' resources are irrelevant to their final allocation – does not hold in the 'real world' where transaction costs have to be take into account. Under these conditions 'the initial delimitation of legal rights does have an effect on the efficiency with which the economic system operates' (ibid. p. 496). If the costs of market transactions are high, then it may be too costly to transact exchanges of rights; if, for instance, a myriad of transactions would be required to reallocate the resource (as with air pollution for example), this may well prove an impossible exercise. In this instance the initial distribution of resources if vital.

> But when transaction costs are substantial, as is usually the case, the allocation of property rights is critical. One of the main pillars of traditional neoclassical economics – the separability of equity and efficiency – breaks down under these circumstances: the terms and conditions of contracts in various transactions, which directly affect the efficiency of resource allocation, now depend crucially on ownership structures and property relations.
>
> (Bardhan 1989 p. 5)

Instead of showing how *laissez-faire* can be relied upon to deal with environmental resources, the introduction of the question of property rights suggests that government intervention may be necessary in order to secure best distribution and use of those resources. In fact, the questions go further than Coase has taken them. Discussions of rights must also involve consideration of the legal and ethical, as well as the economic. As Bromley maintains, legal relations have to be reciprocal, and a component of a legal system which is (following J.R. Commons's usage) part of the 'working rules' which create the social order necessary to society. (Bromley 1991 p. 14).

The reciprocity of rights was touched upon in the Coasean analysis. Bromley (following Hohfield) observes that the existence of a right involves a duty on others to behave in a specific way. A tenant's right to quiet enjoyment of a rented property corresponds to a duty on the landlady not to harass the tenant. By the same token an absence of legal right for a party means a corresponding privilege is enjoyed whereby others actions need have no regard to that party's interests. Therefore I enjoy the legal privilege to mow my lawn in the afternoon, even if this wakes up the night-shift worker next door; my neighbour has no legal right to stop me mowing.

Rights are therefore only as secure as the duties of others to respect them: they are meaningless unless enforced by the state (Bromley 1991 p. 22). The question of management of resources is therefore, Bromley suggests, a question of which 'regime' of property rights is optimal. He outlines four such regimes – state, private, common (more accurately, group) and 'open access'. Bromley suggests that much of the debate over environmental resources has confused the last two. In fact, open access regimes are actually the absence of property rights – everyone has privilege over the resource, and no duty in respect of it. It does not follow from this that any of the three other regimes will necessarily be more desirable, also it is important not to confuse group (common) regimes, where property rights are owned collectively, with an open access regime where no rights exist.

Property regimes, 'whether private property, state property or common property' are, Bromley believes, 'complex constellations of rights, duties, privileges, and exposures to the rights of others'. Because of the existence of transaction costs, the choice of regimes and the distribution of rights is of great significance. It is far from being the case that a private property regime will necessarily lead to an optimal allocation of rights. Bromley points out that the very existence of 'externalities' points towards the existence of transaction costs (ibid. p. 63). Furthermore, the particular types of legal entitlement which are enacted will themselves affect the transaction costs, since they affect who is to undergo the information costs and (particularly) the bargaining costs (ibid. pp. 41 ff.).

In fact, the problems of environment often stem from the fact that appropriate legal rights are hard to define. In particular, environmental resources may be indivisible, either physically or socially (they may be public goods). In addition, a process of individual contracting may be inappropriate if the processes are irreversible (ibid. p. 20). In these instances some other regime of rights will be appropriate.

In addition to these reservations, it should be recalled that the ability to change property rights may be uneven (ibid. p. 17). One party may be able *de facto* to force a change in property rights regarding another party. The distribution of rights over resources therefore becomes far from trivial to the allocation of property rights, regardless of the ethical implications involved. The libertarian analysis of property rights excludes the concept of power.

The ethical implication of rights cannot simply be ignored though. The rights over many environmental resources are, unfortunately or not, decidedly ambiguous, and the ethics of distributing these is fraught with dilemmas. Indeed, once we see that all transactions are in fact based on political decisions concerning property rights and regimes, the entire economic domain now takes on a moral dimension. This is the point of departure for the new market socialists.

NEW MARKET SOCIALISTS

Positive freedom

The imperative for political, subjective analysis does not in itself preclude a policy of *laissez-faire*, but means that such a justification must be political as well as economic. Indeed, the most successful defence of *laissez-faire* has been conducted in precisely these terms. The point of departure for the New Right, derived from Austrian theory, is precisely that markets will maximise the freedom of individuals. In this view it is precisely the fact that markets allow the individual 'free choice' that makes market allocation preferable to any collective allocation (Hodgson 1984 Ch. 3). The information concerning the wants and desires of individuals is necessarily dispersed throughout the economy, and any interference with the freedom of individuals to exchange will, they suggest, lead to a sub-optimal allocation of resources. Central planning, redistributive taxes and for some even legal tender are all unwarranted infringements on individual liberty.

The social institution of the market is therefore justified not only in terms of efficiency, but because only through markets can individuals obtain 'freedom'.[7] That is, the free market obtains a moral justification (ibid.). We would note though, that a particular conception of freedom is being mooted here. This conception of freedom is often known, following Berlin (1969) as *negative* freedom. A person is free when she or he is 'not subject to coercion by the arbitrary will of another or others' (Hayek 1960 p. 11). Freedom is simply the ability to act 'according to our own decisions' (ibid. p. 12). Only deliberate infringements on the right to make our own decisions is relevant in the denial of freedom; the ability to procure the desired results of our decisions is not pertinent to this view of freedom.

> In this sense 'freedom' refers solely to a relation of men to other men, and the only infringement on it is coercion by men. This means, in particular, that the range of physical possibilities from which a person can choose at a given moment has no direct relevance to freedom.
>
> (Hayek 1960 p. 12)

The point of this conception of freedom is to attempt an ethical justification of distribution. The inability to consider distribution adequately was one of the main failings of orthodox economics. Here *laissez-faire* distribution is justified on the grounds of individual liberty. What is important for the libertarians is not whether I am able to give effect to my desires, but that I am able to make my own choices: 'The question of how many courses of action are open to a person is, of course, very important. But it is a different question from that of how far in acting he can follow his own plans and intentions' (ibid. p. 13).

The New Right often call upon a difference between freedom and ability. Simply because I am unable to climb Mount Everest does not reflect on my freedom to try. Conversely, I am not free (at present) to enter the White House, even though I am able. Ability is regarded as a natural obstacle, and there is no obligation to remove such a natural obstacle. The only relevant denial of freedom occurs when I am intentionally stopped from doing something I am able to do (see Miller 1989a pp. 31 ff.). The results of market exchanges are viewed as precisely such a natural element, and are claimed to be the *unintentional* result of action, and therefore not a restraint on liberty. The outcomes of market exchange can be viewed as no more unjust than the consequences of the weather (Plant 1989 p. 54).

The New Right would also deny that moral questions can be given an objective basis. The point about market exchange, they would claim, is that it requires only a subjective view. The only commitment is to the exchange procedure – no end-state, such as equality, is being morally justified. Individuals are following their own values in the market (ibid. p. 58). It is for this reason that equality is claimed to be a denial of liberty (Held 1986 p. 26).

The American institutional school posed a significant challenge to this libertarian position, for it suggested that markets were themselves coercive, and that social institutions could be formative of individual liberty. In particular, J.R. Commons' use of institutions as 'collective action in control, liberation and expansion of individual action' (Commons 1931 p. 644) would be of special concern for the libertarians, since it destroys the neat causal link between individual freedom and the absence of coercion. Commons was suggesting that some level of coercion may be necessary for individual liberty to exist.[8]

The reason for the emphasis of the New Right on organic institutions is precisely that they wish to show that such institutions can occur through choice: no coercion need be involved. Our previous analysis showed that the development of these organic institutions was unlikely. We need not therefore reject market 'intervention' (indeed, it is unclear that the phrase has meaning, since the polity and the society establish markets in the first place), nor deliberate restraint on individual action. The question is what intervention and what restraints would be best.

We may also wish to query the exclusive reliance on negative freedom of the New Right. Indeed, we may well ask why we should have any interest in negative freedom at all. What is it about coercion which is so repugnant to us?

> The answer must surely be that, if we are free from coercion, we are then able to live a life shaped by our own desires and preferences and not those of another, and that is part of what the distinctively valuable features of human life consist in. However, in order to realize what is valuable about liberty, we have to be able to pursue values of our own, and to do this we have to have abilities resources and opportunities – that is to say, some command over resources so that we can live life in our own way.
>
> (Plant 1989 p. 65)

In fact, very few libertarians would hold rigidly to a notion of exclusively negative freedom, and most would accept a right to positive freedoms in extreme cases. It would be perverse to regard maximum liberty to be the sole criterion for judging the plight of the starving children of Africa or of the homeless of New York and few of the New Right would do so. Most would concede that there is some obligation to interfere with property rights in cases of catastrophes.[9] Yet as Miller points out, limiting this obligation to extreme cases is arbitrary. It is not made clear why a right to a minimum command over these resources should be confined to life-and-death situations (Miller 1989a p. 44). To limit the right to resources to extreme cases or only to basic resources is arbitrary. We cannot say which resources are basic and which are not.[10] We have to accept that all resources can contribute to the effective freedom of individuals (Abell 1989 p. 84). Although we should accept the need for negative freedom, we should not rely exclusively upon it (ibid. p. 83). The choice is not between market or state. Rather, we should view the two types of freedom – negative and positive – as complementary, and attempt to derive the optimal balance (Miller 1989a p. 25). It is this balance that we will look at now.

We saw in Chapter 3 that attempts at central planning – even using markets – foundered because they did not recognise that goods were produced in order to satisfy unknown and inscrutable wants. This aspect of the exchange mechanism is beneficial and should be defended. Market mechanisms are an efficient method of coordinating decentralised decision-making (Le Grand and Estrin 1989 p. 1). Markets are 'an efficient way of producing and distributing a very large number of mundane items, from tomatoes to transistor radios' (Miller and Estrin 1986 p. 3). Furthermore, we should take seriously the liberal emphasis on individual choice.

> Markets give their participants a certain kind of freedom. They tend to expand the range of choices that may be made, and they give each person a variety of partners with whom to deal. [Furthermore] if I am buying

for cash, I have no need to explain or justify a request for a large consignment of salami, and this freedom to arrange my personal life in the way I happen to prefer is one whose value should not be under-estimated.

(Miller and Estrin 1986 p. 4)

This is to say that 'people on the whole should be left to determine their own idea of the "good" and indeed of the "good life"' (LeGrand and Estrin 1989 p. 7). Furthermore, comptitive markets tend to disperse personal power over the positive freedoms which we held to be important, so that we do not have to deal with petty bureaucrats (Miller and Estrin 1986 p. 4) or even discriminatory practices.

Public provision of positive freedoms should not be regarded as an end in itself, but rather justified either in terms of comparative efficiency (Miller 1989b p. 31) or on the grounds that 'the good' in this particular instance goes beyond the limitations of money measurement. We should be especially wary of confusing the allocative results of exchange with the distribution effects of inequalities of wealth and income. As we mentioned in our earlier discussion, the exchange function of markets already presumes a given distribution; it was in attempting to theorise distribution that both orthodox analysis and Austrian theory failed as complete social theories. It should be realised that 'it is important to distinguish between the unjustifiable consequences of markets *per se* and those consequences which arise as a result of the different endowments which people bring to production' (Abell 1989 p. 80). That is to say that we must bear in mind that the lack of distributional theory in the conventional economic approach results in the need for a political decision concerning distribution as a preliminary to establishing a socially optimal allocation of goods and resources through markets. Only after the question of distribution has been adequately decided will a market allocation system deliver an optimum solution. By the same token, we must be careful not to confuse problems caused by inadequate distribution with those which are the consequences of market allocation.

Market limitations

Market mechanisms can have many unjustifiable consequences though, and require the existence of J.R. Commons-style deliberative institutions in order for their efficient operation. We should stress the idea that markets are in no sense natural or 'free', and that the conception of markets as being somehow separate from the polity is reification. In a sense referring to 'The Market' (using the definitive article) is incorrect – all markets are set up by the society, and require a large set of laws and decisions by the polity and society for their operation, all of which alter the characteristics of a market exchange mechanism. We have already mentioned the need for a distributive mechanism to supplement the market exchange mechanism, and we will be examining this issue in greater depth shortly. We have also touched upon the relatively uncontentious desire to ensure a minimum provision of facilities for the abolition of poverty and to provide minimum standards of health and welfare. That is to say, we do have some notions of end-states which we wish to achieve. Although it may be possible to achieve some of the desired end-states through markets, the entire argument for markets becomes dubious when the user of the resources has insufficient information to make informed judgement on the good or services provided.[11] Health is the usual example cited, although there may be others.[12] As Miller points out, such goods and services will invariably require public monitoring or regulation.[13] As the need for this becomes greater, the difference between public and market provision becomes smaller, and in the end there may prove to be very little difference between a public system and a highly constrained private system (Miller 1989a p. 317).

We have seen other aspects of markets which may be undesirable. We have already mentioned the problem of induced wants and the conspicuous expenditure raised by Veblen. We would reject the strict determinism of Veblen though. Veblen appeared to regard individuals as completely determined by institutions which were controlled by the vested interests. It was this that enabled him to suggest a Darwinian evolutionary approach to economics, which we view as untenable. We also rejected his view that it was only this institutional control which was the cause of scarcity. Furthermore, even if overall scarcity may not ensue, the decision of what should be produced remains, as we saw in Chapter 3, problematic.

What we can gain from Veblen is firstly that the economy cannot be studied in isolation. We will need to widen our horizons to include both the cultural and the political, to establish to what extent 'wants' are formulated, and to control power over institutions. But although we may consider individuals as to some extent malleable, we should also consider that basically people are self-determining, and that subject to suitable regulation we should take their expressed wants as achieving some correspondence with welfare. After all, we cannot read minds. Unless we are to presume knowledge of individual wants – and then plan for these *à la* Veblen – then we are left with markets, problematic though they may be (Miller 1989a p. 146).

It should also be realised, following from this invocation of property rights, that there are many aspects of rights over property. We may wish to separate the right of possession from the right of use, or the right of use from the right to alienate (right to the capital). There is no *a priori* reason to support full ownership of rights as opposed to other combinations (Honore 1961, cited Miller 1989a). This means that the particular forms of property rights must themselves be decided upon by the polity, even before we invoke market exchange mechanism. Recall, as Commons pointed out, that it is the legal transaction which we are concerned with, not the physical act of exchange.

The polity has to make a meaningful decision as to what legal rights will be exchangeable, as well as who will have initial rights to resources.

This is particularly significant when we look at the other limitation of markets which was implicit in our discussion. Both the orthodox 'externality' and the neo-Austrian 'property rights' treatment of 'commons' hinged on the notion that everything has got a price. This has not actually been demonstrated. There may well be what Miller refers to as non-commodity elements or conceptions of 'the good'. We may well regard, say, cruelty to animals or the promotion of the arts in the light. Health, education and especially unpaid women's housework and child-rearing, may also be viewed as bordering on this. These non-commodity elements may involve particular conceptions of property rights. We may wish to limit the right to dispose of pets as the owners wish, or the right to bargain over health. The somewhat incongruous Austrian treatment of 'commons' has obscured this difference between commodity-based and non-commodity elements of 'the good', because it blurs the usual distinction between what is tradable and what is not. We may simply regard it as bizarre that, for example, a picturesque view or beautiful architecture should be regarded as commodities,[14] and absurd that they should require a monetary value. We might well suggest that clean air or public health, or caring for the elderly or children contribute to 'the good' in their own right, and reject as perverse any suggestion that they should be tradable in the first place.

It is important to note the distinction between these non-commodity elements and our previous conception of end-states. We are not setting out, say, the preservation of picturesque views as an end in itself. Different people may have different conceptions of which non-commodity elements contribute to 'the good life'. What we are suggesting is that market exchange mechanisms will either not take cognisance of non-commodity wants, or more probably will price them disproportionately high, since these non-commodity elements would not exchange for much in a market. Miller points to the market for part-time labour as a case in hand – the ability to work part-time is usually bought at a premium (Miller 1989a pp. 94–5). This obviously introduces a sex bias into the economy. Similarly, a high premium may be charged for job satisfaction or even for the lowering of health risks at work. We may well need to alter market mechanisms to provide such elements of 'the good life'; indeed, many people would suggest that this is the major function of the polity.

Given this lack of provision of non-commodity elements, and also considering the problem of induced wants, we may well decide not to follow the received wisdom of orthodox economics and attempt to maximise production (as measured by money). Rather, we will wish to obtain a mix of commodity and non-commodity elements. In particular, political economists such as Gorz would stress the increase of leisure as a major part of policy (Gorz 1975, 1980). Others stress the need for individual 'development' (Hodgson 1984 p. 31), which for authors such as Ivan Illich would necessarily involve the rejection of most of the consumer and capital goods presently produced. It also reinforces the requirement to base distribution on some other footing than the contribution to the production process.

It is in the sphere of distribution that the main failing of *laissez-faire* can be said to occur. What we must concern ourselves with is ensuring that individuals obtain sufficient resources 'in order to enter markets in an effective manner' (Plant 1989 p. 66). We must be concerned with 'the conditions of freedom for the individuals who enter markets and with ensuring that these conditions embody in their institutional form the highest degree of freedom of choice' (ibid. p. 68).

This emphasis on freedom of choice was, of course, the original right-wing justification for *laissez-faire* . One of our critiques of the libertarian emphasis of negative freedom was that the existence of such a *laissez-faire* social order required the derivation of social institutions – money, legal rights in property, rights in technical knowledge and innovation and so on. We then discussed the possibility of these institutions being derived unintentionally or 'organic-ally'. We will now turn to another criticism of the invocation of organic institutions which will lead us to a basis for distribution. This concerns the emphasis placed on the spontaneity of organic institutions, on the fact that they lead to unintended consequences, which suggests that such institutions would not be coercive.

In the first place, it is far from clear why the intentions of others should be relevant to *my* freedom. If my freedom to act is curtailed then it remains curtailed whether or not this occurred by accident or by design, indeed the distinction is not always clear cut. Much depends on whether we believe the outcome, even though unintentional, could have been reasonably forseen. The implication of the libertarians is that because outcomes are unintended, nothing can be done about the result, but if the outcome of the social order is predictable, then we can influence the consequences and we may be regarded as being instrumental in the final outcome (see Miller 1989a p. 35). Plant suggests that although we may be unable to foresee which individuals will be worse off from the market exchange mechanism, we can foresee that the poorest group will derive least benefit (Plant 1989 p. 65).

The relevant question is not, therefore, what outcomes are intentional, but which we should act upon. Miller suggests that we must hold an idea of 'moral responsibility' to answer this question. We must have some notion of 'what people can reasonably demand of one another'. Causal analysis is insufficient. We also need some ethical judgement about behaviour (Miller 1989a p. 35). Constraints on action (or inaction) can be justified morally; the debate is really over moral responsibility (ibid. p. 36).

Turning to the distribution of wealth and income, we can conclude that the distributive consequences of *laissez-faire* cannot be justified on grounds of freedom, since the results are broadly predictable and can obviously be influenced by government action. We therefore require a moral justification of our distribution set. As Miller terms it, we must defend distribution in terms of justice (ibid. p. 58 ff.). Indeed, we need to do this even to defend *laissez-faire*.

> Even complete *laissez-faire* is a governmental economic policy; and capitalist governments escape ideological responsibility for its full consequences only by fostering a naturalised or prescriptive conception of property rights
>
> (Dunn 1986 p. 37)

whereas if we conceive of property rights in an instrumental fashion, the state becomes the 'locus' of questions of distribution (ibid.).

The question of distribution cannot be regarded as a technical question, as we saw in Chapter 2. We must regard the matter as an ethical question of justice which pervades all areas of economic activity. Since the question of distribution is ethical, it cannot be decided through a market exchange mechanism but must ultimately be regarded as the responsibility of the polity.

Participation

We must therefore reject what in Chapter 1 Fay termed a 'policy science'. What is required to answer the ethical questions of distribution, to resolve disputes over externalities, to promote non-commodity elements of 'the good' and to regulate instances of market failure is what he called a participatory theory. We need to put forward a theory of politics. We should not assume as Commons did that the legal and political structures will automatically dispense an appropriate distributive justice (see Miller 1989a p. 227), not least because this justice is far from straightforward. We cannot separate distribution from market or consider an equitable distribution (or even an equal distribution) without an effective exchange mechanism (Miller 1989b p. 32).[15] Although the state may be the locus of distribution, and should accept responsibility for the distribution, it is not a solution to distribution (Dunn 1986 p. 38). The task of the state is to set up the market framework so as to achieve the optimal balance between economy and polity.

This is especially relevant if we believe that the polity extends beyond the state apparatus. We may well hold the view such that

> Politics is a phenomenon found in between all groups, institutions, (formal and informal) and societies, cutting across public and private life. It is involved in all the relations, institutions and structures which are implicated in the activities of production and reproduction in the life of societies. It is expressed in all the activities of co-operation, negotiation, and struggle over the use and distribution of resources which this entails ... Thus, politics is about power, about the forces

which influence and reflect its distribution and use, and about the effect of this on resource use and distribution . . .

This means that individual autonomy or independence can actually only be achieved through political participation.

> If politics is understood in this way, then, the specification of the conditions of enactment of the principle of autonomy amounts to the specification of the conditions for the participation of citizens about the use and distribution of resources in relation to affairs that are important to them (i.e. us) . . . We should strive towards a state of affairs in which political life – democratically organised, is an essential part of all peoples lives.
>
> (Held 1986 pp. 25–6)

This suggests participation in and democratisation of both state and market (Paine 1986 p. 54). Furthermore, since we must consider both commodity and non-commodity elements, or as Paine terms it, 'a socially just distribution of "life chances"', these being 'not just income and assets, but also non-monetary components of the quality of life', we cannot make *a priori* judgements on the relationship between the polity and the economy, but this must be continually re-assessed as part of the participatory process. We need to constantly monitor the political economy to ensure neutrality between commodity and non-commodity elements of 'the good':

> a neutral framework cannot be specified in advance of knowing something about the conceptions of the good that people actually hold, and this is a contingent matter. Since the point of the framework is to balance competing claims on social resources, broadly conceived, we cannot sensibly say anything about its shape until we know what claims it has to accommodate . . . Furthermore, since conceptions of the good change historically, the appropriate framework cannot be designed in a once-and-for-all manner. We need a political forum in which new demands can be heard, and the framework revised accordingly.
>
> (Miller 1989a p. 96)

We would therefore reject any idea of a 'blueprint' for the optimal political economy. Not only will the conceptions (and realisations) of 'the good' constantly alter, but 'there is no simple way of measuring more equal rights nor participatory decision-making, and more social justice' (Paine 1986 p. 55). Nonetheless, we would hope to be able to show that a participatory political economy would be feasible, and the main elements we would expect it to consist of.

Most 'communitarian' (as opposed to libertarian) political economists, following Nove (1983), would place an emphasis on individual and co-operative enterprises. These would be supplemented by state utilities where needed and by quasi-autonomous state enterprises. The models usually allow for some level of employment, varying from small-scale enterprises (Nove 1983), through to informal employment only (Breitenbach *et al.* 1990).

Before we make a brief examination of these models, we should note that the emphasis on small-scale production is more than just an attempt at breaking market power. We should regard it as a necessary part of participation within the economic process. The cooperative format both extends democracy to the workplace, and gives workers a direct reward for the progress of their firm. Not only does the emphasis on cooperation and small-scale production reduce as much as possible the alienation of the workers from the production process caused by large production lines and a hierarchical management structure, but it also is likely to increase productivity through the work-force having a greater incentive for the profitability of the firm. Although we will not have space here for a full investigation of cooperative economics, we will briefly mention several questions concerning the model of competing small-scale cooperatives which would require resolution.[16] The first which we have already mentioned is the possibility of hiring labour. If the economy is not to revert to a capitalist system, this must be curtailed or restricted in some way – some would even abolish it altogether.

A more awkward organisational problem concerns investment. We can identify two forms of investment strategies; mutual investment or external investment. The former is prevalent in the US and UK; members pool resources and are the exclusive owners of the firm's assets. The latter form of investment is based on the (former) Yugoslav model; all capital is leased at market prices,[17] in other words all firms have a 100 per cent gearing (Estrin 1989 p. 172).

The difference between the two models is not only one of finance. The real question is of the property rights in capital. In the high-geared model the co-operative members have rights of use of capital, but do not have the right to dispose of it or to depreciate it. In the variable geared model, which historically had to compete with limited liabilities, the capital is owned by the co-op. The co-op itself is not necessarily 'owned' by anyone though. Although co-ops are by definition managed democratically by the members (one member one vote), in some models a variable share holding is allowed, which gives members individual rights to the capital (finance by non-voting shares, as it were). These are the Co-operative Producer Federation rules. The alternative (Industrial Common Ownership Movement rules) is to allow only a 'membership fee' to join the co-op; no additional equity is allowed and all assets are held collectively (ibid. 1989 p. 173).

We will consider the variable gearing model first. This has the same full ownership rights as present private limited liability companies since the co-ops are in competition with them. The fact that profits are shared equally among all members may well act as a restraint on the raising of equity though, since raising equity necessarily involves the dissolution of profits among a larger membership, resulting in a tendency to under-capitalise. In addition, co-operative members may be reluctant to risk both income and capital should the firm fail (Miller 1989a p. 87). This places the co-operatives at a disadvantage compared to limited-liability companies (ibid.). It may also lead to problems raising loan finance, as the commercial banks would be unwilling to lend to small producer co-operatives to the same extent as private companies (Vanek 1975 p. 455). This may well occur through more than prejudice, since the higher the gearing the higher the risk involved,[18] and could make the establishment of a 100 per cent geared companies tremendously difficult if they have to compete with private companies, particularly since the larger companies would be better suited to risk spreading.

This suggests that a large co-operative sector cannot emerge from the present market mechanism in competition with limited-liability companies. A move towards a largely self-managed economy will only come into existence as a result of deliberate political intervention and will invariably be highly geared: the polity will probably adopt a 100 per cent gearing model. This means considerable changes in company law, to ensure that most companies are self-managed firms, but more importantly would require some method of organising the banking sector to ensure appropriate investment. Opinions differ as to whether some form of state-run enterprise or oligopoly should be envisaged if the investment banking sector should be private (or substantially private), or precisely what mixture of these should exist.[19]

Other areas for political decision will arise over sectors where economies of scale are likely to occur and indeed judgements will be required as to which these are. The technical question of the scale of production (as opposed to the economic question of risk) would probably not be a problem in general. As Miller points out, it is feasible for co-operatives to retain the size of the individual plants that at present pertain under private firms. There may be particular areas which will require large-scale operation or investment though – in particular, technological research and development may well require large financial commitments. We would be wrong to rely exclusively on co-operatives for all production, and a variety of labour-managed organisations could be expected to emerge (labour/capital partnerships for example, or even co-operatives with both producers and consumers). It should also be restated that maximising production is not necessarily the object being pursued. Maximising investment may therefore not be of primary importance: the level of production will be a political decision.

The appropriate market structures are not likely to emerge through the present market system, but will require a drastic alteration of the legal foundations of markets by the state. The state will also need to arrive at a decision as to how the inevitable inequalities which will emerge from a market-based economy will be handled: how much inequality should be tolerated and how excess inequality should be stopped. The state would also be responsible for meeting that element of positive freedoms that are to be based on need, for the provision of public goods and the regulation of externalities.

Having shown that polity and economy are necessarily interlinked, and having considered the form of economic organisation which we believe to be optimal, we can now go on to look at the polity. This will necessarily involve some consideration of our view of *homo politicus*. Our critique of libertarian political economy centred around the idea that the pursuit of rational self-interest was not sufficient to ensure the derivation of institutions. If we are to suggest that the democratic polity is to install such an institutional set, we have to maintain that the individuals are guided by a different motivation. As Schumpeter amongst others has pointed out, to simply move rational self-interest into the political sphere solves nothing – in fact, the lack of a budget constraint will mitigate against proper political management (see Schumpeter 1942).

Miller refers to this rationalist conception of political behaviour as 'interest aggregation'. The participants are viewed as attempting to promote their individual interest or the interests of the group they represent,[20] and to guide necessary collective action towards this end. There will of course be many such competing interests, and in this view politics is a process of aggregating these interests into one (Miller 1989a p. 254). In this respect politics is analogous to economics, in that it acts as a method of deriving an aggregate conclusion from individual wants.[21]

Miller contrasts this with what he calls 'dialogue'. Individuals enter the political process not to press their individual interests, but to voice opinion on 'matters of general concern'. They then enter into dialogue in which they attempt to persuade others, but can also be persuaded in turn. Viewpoints are constantly altered until a consensus emerges (ibid. p. 255). This is to say that people can act as citizens, being concerned with the public interest and the communal good, instead of only acting as selfish consumers (Saghoff 1988 p. 8), and in what some commentators believe is a 'feminine' manner, concerned with their relations to and connections with others, employing an ethic of care which is contingent (cf. Nelson 1993 p. 125).

A fairly stock response to a dialogue view of politics is that it is naive, but we could also venture a criticism of the liability of the interest-aggregation view. We might actually wonder more about the concept of self-seeking: it would seem most likely that total self-seeking would destroy virtually all modern societies – it would certainly destroy any democracy (among other things, no one would vote [qv. Downes 1957]). Indeed, the orthodox economists have to indulge in strange contortions of the rationality concept involving 'direct utility' and suchlike to explain the commonplace non-self actions such as parenthood, charity and so on.[22] It would be hard to avoid the idea that some level of altruism must exist at present.

Interest-aggregation politics will invariably contain all the same problems of its economic sibling. Unless all interests are equally represented the process will not be optimal. Also, the promotion and bargaining process measures the cost of the failure of the lobbying, rather than the quality (value?) of the interests. At any event, the aggregation procedures will suffer from all the social choice problems we outlined at the end of Chapter 2: intransitivity and the other problems of Arrow's impossibility theory (Miller 1989a p. 257). In fact, such a mode of politics may well require a considerable amount of coercion to enforce the decisions reached – exactly the opposite of the original New Right claim (ibid. p. 25).

There are two aspects to the conception of politics as dialogue. The first concerns the individual as a social being, willing and able to take part in communal activity. The second element is that the dialogue process is itself likely to result in superior decisions being made; 'The aim of dialogue is not simply to allow participants to air their views, but to reach the best possible decision on matters of general concern' (ibid. p. 285).

The aim of the economy could be seen as providing the necessary security to enable people to develop and follow altruistic aims (see Abell 1989 p. 88). We would also suggest that a major concern would be to free resources to enable the equality of opportunity for participation in the political process, in terms of time and human development (education, training and so forth). It should be noted here that the conception of the altruistic individual does not involve any notion of sacrificing the individual wants for the greater good or some such. Our conception is of community, where 'each person identifies with the social group in the sense of seeing both his origins and his destiny as bound up with those of the group as a whole' (Miller 1989a p. 229). The individual should also not be viewed as entirely formed by the community: the community attachment is partial. This conception goes beyond the idea of passive 'traditional' ties, but is a positive notion that we can organise and control the social world (ibid. p. 235).

This leaves us two areas for consideration. The first is what is to form the basis for this community – what is to form the group cohesion and why will individuals identify with the group. The second consideration is what the limits should be on the community ties, and which matters should be regarded as individual affairs.

If we are to suggest that individuals will be able to identify their well-being with that of the community, then this community will require a point of reference. 'If a community is to make a claim on my allegiance, it must represent a distinct way of life; there must be something about the community and its members that makes it *my* community' (Miller 1989a p. 231; emphasis in original). Nonetheless, the different communities will also require non-communitarian links between each other (otherwise the communities would not be distinctive) and will need to be sufficient size to exert control over their environment. This suggests that there is a play-off between small communities with a greater participation and tighter ties or larger groups with more control and internalised links but a weaker sense of identity (ibid. pp. 231–6). The difficulty is to decide the balance.

Miller believes that the common identity has to be based on nationality and citizenship. He points out that only distribution at this level would be equitable given regional variations, and that this distribution will necessarily require an ideology based on the nation-state: he does not believe that the links between smaller communities would be strong enough to invoke agreement to redistribute wealth (ibid. p. 237). He also believes that, at any event, current identities are actually national – regardless of the lack of substance to this national identity – and that we must start with the existing identities (ibid. p. 239).[23] This would be a point of contention between Miller and many in the green movement, whose vision of community is more federal. Many in the green (and socialist) movement might question this attempt to collapse the concept of community into that of the state. They would suggest that individuals are more likely to identify their community in their locality, rather than in their nationality. In addition, the green movement, because of the environmental standpoint, would place greater emphasis on the 'international', intercommunity relationships.

We may in this respect wonder if Miller would be able to limit the sphere of national identity in quite the manner he wishes. Recall that the community was only a part of the individual identity. We would be keen to protect areas which need not be planned from interference by the polity: we are not proposing a totalitarian state. But given Miller's appeal to national citizenship as a focus for community, it may – as Veblen recognised – be difficult to avoid nationalistic tendencies emerging (that is, an unswerving allegiance to the nation, together with an hostility towards other nations and towards minorities, and so on). Miller recognises this problem, but does not show how it can be avoided.[24]

We can therefore see a convergence between the green movement and the Left. Both are beginning to accept the usefulness of markets in economic organisation, while realising that markets need to be initiated and controlled by the polity and the society. Furthermore, the new market socialists are invoking the concept of community, which has been a principle focus of the green movement since its earliest inception. The main areas of disagreement would seem to be over the conception and the size of the sphere of the community.

SUMMARY AND CONCLUSION

While both the new market socialists and most of the green movement[25] agree upon the employment of market mechanisms, the argument of this book is that the former are correct in refusing to de-link the economic from the political and the social, and that the attempt of many in the green movement to do so is an error. The notion that some objective evaluations of environmental damage can be used to 'tweak' the economy or that objective social indicators can be used to decide upon policy is mistaken. Instead emphasis should be given to placing the political decisions concerning resource distribution and allocation back on to the political agenda.

While these decisions are undoubtedly political, the political process whereby the decisions are taken may be somewhat oblique. What we have pointed out is that the economic process should be viewed as part of the political process, and can be used to make some, though not all, political decisions concerning resource allocation. It is suggested that some form of exchange mechanism is necessary in order that resources can be easily allocated to their best use; people are far more likely to get what they are after if they can swap things. Furthermore, an exchange mechanism is grossly inefficient without money to act as a measure of value and a medium of exchange. We must accept that some form of money-based market exchange mechanism is inevitable in a viable political economy.

The point to be made is that these market exchange mechanisms need to be set up and supported by both the polity and the society. All that is being exchanged in markets are legal claims to property, not the physical goods themselves (this may indeed require a further act of exchange). These rights are dependent for their existence upon the duty of others to respect the right being upheld, with sanctions against those who do not exercise their duty being enforced. However, rights are many and various, and one of the decisions to be made by the political process is what particular set of rights should be sanctioned. The Right often use the concept of the 'minimal state' to describe a state which only enforces property rights. It can be seen that this concept is somewhat hollow: rights in property have to be created by the state in the first place, which also decide on how they are to be exchanged – what the contract laws should be. The concept of the minimal state is more to do with the other constraints which the state is to work under than whether it should go 'beyond' the maintenance of property rights. All this is to say that market mechanisms can have many different shapes and forms, and it is a major task of the polity to decide among these. The polity will in particular have to decide on the following:

Constitution of rights and legal formats of exchange mechanisms

As we have just stated, the polity is responsible for decisions as to the form of property rights and corresponding duties, as well as the format of contract law. These two concepts are connected but the extent to which the latter is a vital element of market mechanisms is often unrecognised. The repeal of trademark laws, for example, would entirely transform the economy at a stroke, as would the repeal of health and safety legislation. All of these laws

170

and rights/duties require proactive decisions by the legislature, in addition to decisions concerning money, banking and so on.

Scope of exchange mechanisms

A major constraint upon the decisions regarding property rights and contract law are questions as to the scope of market exchange mechanisms. What should be provided by markets, and what should be provided by alternative means, and indeed what should not be provided at all, would form the major part of the political agenda in the absence of the scientisation of politics. We have argued that the optimal method of allocation is contingent and will vary according to the particular resource under consideration. In addition it will vary both with circumstance and with the decisions concerning the format of exchange mechanisms. Although in some cases the decision will be guided by purely ethical considerations or considerations based purely on efficiency in others, in many instances the analysis as to the correct allocative mechanism will be a complex mixture of efficiency and ethical questions.

Labour laws and industrial organisations

Of particular importance regarding the scope of market exchange mechanisms is the question of labour. Socialists have traditionally been antithetical to the notion of private employers, and even many of the new market socialists have seen fit to make prescriptions on the forms of industrial organisation and the types and levels of employment that should be allowed by the state.

The present author is more circumspect about the utility of making such prescriptions in advance. Which forms of organisation, and which corresponding employment laws would be desirable is as much contingent as the questions concerning the domain of market exchange mechanisms. This is particularly so given the fluidity of the entire set of property rights. At the back of this position is an argument that the state and the community have sufficient leverage and are able to exercise sufficient control over the economy so as to remove many or all of the undesirable elements involved in present employer–employee relations; in particular, the undesirable effect of market power. It would none the less be unsurprising to see a fully democratic polity attempting to increase democracy in the workplace, in particular by encouraging co-operative forms of industrial organisation.

Distribution

Much of the above discussion is underpined by the issue of distribution, which we have argued is a key political decision. The distribution of income and wealth should be regarded as an input into allocative market mechanisms, rather than a result of these mechanisms.

Obviously, the distributive mechanism and the particular levels of individual income and wealth will have a considerable effect on the operation of market mechanisms, especially upon employment. If, for example, part of the distribution of income was undertaken directly by the polity, as suggested by Lerner and Lange, perhaps in the form of some sort of flat-rate basic income, this would obviously act as a baseline for such wage levels as exist to be judged against. The actual effect would be dependent upon a range of other variables, not least the levels of market power. It is doubtful that a basic income scheme would have much effect at present if instigated in most Western capitalist countries.[26]

As well as the distributive mechanism, decisions will need to be made concerning the redistributive effects on any wage economy which exist, especially such obvious matters as taxation levels.

The thorniest questions will probably not be in these areas, however, but will be questions concerning the distribution of capital. Decisions as to whether the capital is to be distributed by a market process, and if so what that process will be (and for that matter how it is to be distributed otherwise) will be vital questions for any democratic economy. It may well be that markets for capital, and even high interest rates, will prove the only viable method of allocation.

Value of non-commodity desiderata

Part of the question of distribution concerns the valuation (explicit or implicit) of elements of 'The Good' which either cannot be formulated as commodities or which it has been decided will not be so formulated. Many environmental resources will fall into this category, as will activities such as child-rearing and caring.

Even if the valuation of these non-commodity desiderata is implicit and not pecuniary, it ought to be realised that such a valuation is indeed implied and that it might be advantageous if it were possible to make the valuation explicit. This is not to say, of course, that this explicit valuation would be in any sense objective.

Action on positional goods

Commodities which are subjected to a maximum quantity of supply are, it will be recalled, termed 'positional goods'. Positional goods can be physically limited or socially scarce. Given that such commodities are by definition not generally available for everyone, decisions as to their allocation have to be made. We have mentioned Hirsch's two main techniques for allocating positional goods; these were auction or screening. Which of these methods is to be used, and how any screening is to be operated will often be vital questions. Again, many environmental resources will fall into this category, as will many commodities which use environmental resources.

Inter-community and inter-state decisions

In addition to the above list, all of which are interrelated, it will be obvious that decision-making cannot be limited to either the community or the state. Many of the decisions will have effects which go beyond national borders, particularly concerning environment and trade, but obviously the present set of decisions concerning international politics will remain important.

Nonetheless, a democratically run economy need not be committed to international trade any more than it need be committed to internal trade. Daly and Cobb show how (even under the assumptions of orthodox economists) the received wisdom of 'free' trade is only valid under an unrealistic assumption of capital immobility. They suggest that 'balanced trade' may be more beneficial (Daly and Cobb 1990 pp. 209–35). While a full discussion on international trade is beyond the scope of the present work, our analysis clearly suggests some such course.

Given that these political decisions have to be made and implemented in order for an economy to exist at all, participation in the political process becomes paramount. All of the matters above are mixtures of ethical and efficiency problems; all must be decided through the political process; they are all interrelated and all of them are vital. What is required is to show how the democracy can be structured to be as fully participatory as possible, and how it is possible to generate a democracy in which constituents participate as citizens. This will require in turn an understanding of what communities are, how they can be generated or regenerated, and how they can be incorporated into the nation and hence into the world political order.

These factors tend to suggest that the days of formalised economic analysis based upon narrow conceptions of rationality are numbered. It has long been recognised that the world of perfect knowledge inhabited by the orthodox economists bore little relation to reality, but we have seen that the theory is incapable of relaxing the increasingly stringent assumptions that are necessary for social policy to be derived. The orthodox theory is analytic in nature, and cannot be used to obtain policy recommendations – even if the legal and environmental boundaries of the theory are ignored. Such a science cannot be justified. Indeed, it is very notable how the 'right-wing' politicians invariably invoke Austrian theory in preference to the orthodoxy when they attempt polemical justification of their political policies, a good example of this being the former British Prime Minister's invocation of negative freedom as a defence of *laissez-faire*, and her denial of the very existence of such a thing as 'society'. Apart from anything else, there appears to be a clear perception of a political theory behind the policy recommendations, and a belief that the economics involved is not neutral.

It is often forgotten that Fritz Schumacher subtitled his most famous book 'Economics as if people mattered'. The message in this book is that in order to have an economics as if people mattered, we have to find out what matters to people.

NOTES

1 THE POLITICS OF POSITIVE ECONOMICS

1 For example:

> all the coins in my pocket are shillings
> This coin is in my pocket
> Therefore it is a shilling
> (Hempel 1966 p. 56, cf. Benton 1977 p. 10).

2 i.e.: If not A then not B.

3 Fay disagrees with this analysis (1975 p. 37).

4 Fay also argues that statistical explanations of mass events are as much explanatory as deductive models, and that this would maintain the symmetry of explanation and prediction (1975 pp. 37 ff.). Although we do not have space to discuss this question here, we would suggest that this form of 'explanation' is somewhat empty.

5 It is important to note that the term 'instrumentalism' has a different meaning here to that we used in our discussion of Fay's work. The term can have many different meanings – instruments have different functions. What is meant here is methodological instrumentalism, that theories are instruments in generating predictions. This should be distinguished from policy instrumentalism, which concerns the use of science to generate policies. The two views are, however, linked (Keat and Urry 1975 p. 63).

6 Keat and Urry consider instrumentalism as a form of conventionalism, but they note that it has many similarities with extreme views of positivism, and it is easy to move from one to the other. Moreover, they lead to similar forms of activity (Keat and Urry 1975 p. 64). Hollis and Nell (in their discussion of Friedman) seem to place instrumentalism in a similar position, but they also maintain that pragmatism is a form of positivism (Hollis and Nell 1975 p. 4): they seem to have little space for conventionalism at all. In this, they follow Kolakowski (1972 p. 181). Possibly the more empathetic analysis is from Benton (1977 p. 68), who suggests that there are different forms of the instrumentalist methodology.

7 Streeten's 1958 translation uses 'cause' for propelling cause and 'teleology' for final cause (German *final*). This seems to be an error, although I am happy to be corrected on this matter.

8 For a review of Austrian methodology see Hutchison (1981 chs 6–7). The discrepancies between the Austrians and Robbins also carried over into the substantive theoretical concepts: see Chapter 3.

9 This is the conception of science as consisting of refutable statements. The body of scientific knowledge at any one time consists of the set of unrefuted statements.

175

For a brief synopsis of Popparian falsification see Caldwell (1982) or Blaug (1980 pp. 10 ff.).

10 Note in particular Mises: 'The starting point of praxeology is a self-evident truth, the cognition of action, that is, the cognition of the fact that there is such a thing as consciously aiming at ends' (Mises 1962 pp. 5–6).

11 Machlup criticises Friedman on this point (Machlup 1955 p. 17).

12 The response of Machlup was to suggest that ordinal utility was part of the Austrian heritage (Machlup 1956 p. 491). We will see the inadequacy of this reply in our survey of value theory.

13 Although in the 'Rejoinder' Machlup seems to place this rationality postulate alongside all the other instrumental theories. If a suitable alternative model comes up 'then the Assumption will have outlived its usefulness and will be sent to the limbo of "disconfirmed propositions"' (Machlup 1956 p. 489). This seems to take Machlup closer to Friedman.

14 See the next chapter.

15 This appears to be what Friedman is trying to say, especially in the light of the corresponding footnote, where he adds the rider that unrealistic assumptions do not guarantee a useful theory. His phrasing of the point is a bit clumsy though – he almost appears to regard unrealism as a virtue. This was later caricatured by Samuelson.

16 This of course throws some light on the Hutchison/Machlup debate.

17 The three senses of unrealistic assumption outlined by Nagel seem to correspond to that of Musgrave (Nagel 1963 pp. 214–15).

18 See Chapter 4.

19 Samuelson's methodological naivety is noted by Caldwell (1982). Certainly he has not understood the instrumentalist methodology.

20 Although the differences between the theories turn out to be largely semantic.

21 This claim is made by Samuelson after a rather weak attempt at refuting Hempel's contrary position (Samuelson 1965 p. 1167). For a refutation of the empiricist position Samuelson identifies with, see Benton (1977 p. 50) and citations therein: 'No number of observation statements can ever be equivalent to the statement "The sparrow is cleaning itself"' (ibid.).

22 Although Boland and Frazer do argue for an 'alignment' of Friedman's methodology with Popper's philosophy (Boland and Frazer 1983).

23 q.v. Hammond: 'Popper ... formulated and rejected the anti-realist instrumentalism of which Friedman's essay is said to be an example' (Hammond 1990 p. 204).

24 For an explanation of how this squares with arguments for *laissez-faire* see the analysis in Chapter 2.

2 FROM UTILITY TO WELFARE: THE TRAJECTORY OF ORTHODOX ECONOMICS

1 This is not to say that planning cannot be criticised or that *laissez-faire* cannot be defended, but simply that this would require a non-positivist approach. We will consider one such approach in the next chapter.

2 More accurately exchange value: see the analysis below.

3 For an explanation of the differences between various formulations of the differential approach to utility see Mitchell (1969 p. 55).

4 The original text was von Neumann and Morgenstern (1947 [1944]).

5 'He saw, that is, how closely dependent microeconomic maximisation theorems

are on the 'perfect competition' postulate. He even went so far as to argue that in a regime of general monopoly (and, presumably of oligopoly) 'abstract economists would be deprived of their occupation, the investigation of the conditions which determine value. There would survive only the empirical school, flourishing in a chaos ...' (Edgeworth *Collected Papers*, vol. 1 pp. 138–9, cited Hutchison 1953 p. 112).

6 Edgeworth's formulation involved the ability to recontract: this would ensure an unique equilibrium price (Hutchinson 1881 p. 18).

7 This may well have been based on Marshall from his *Pure Theory of Domestic Values and of Foreign Trade* (Hutchison 1953 p. 114).

8 References to the 8th edition (1920) are taken from the Variorum edition, London, Macmillan 1961.

9 In particular, Marshall held a vague notion of human capital. The improvement of the conditions of the working class would help the material wealth of the country (Marshall 1920 p. 562). Marshall believed that 'The most valuable of all capital is that invested in human beings' (ibid. p. 564). The improvement of the effectiveness of the labour force – especially through education (ibid. p. 212, 562 ff.) – was one of the keys to growth. Indeed, Marshall believed that investment in human capital may itself end class distinctions (Dasgupta 1985 p. 118).

10 See also Hutchison (1953) p. 71.

11 See the footnotes in the Variorum edition (Marshall 1920) for references.

12 Marshall's marginal notes are misleading here.

13 This should be compared with the institutionalist critique of the economic assumptions concerning human action which began to emerge in America about the time of the sixth edition of the *Principles*, with the work of Veblen and Mitchell. We will look at the institutionalist school in Chapter 4.

14 With the possible exception of Pigou (we are concerned, of course, only with microeconomics).

15 Marshall defined the consumers' surplus as 'the excess of the price which (the consumer) would be willing to pay rather than go without the thing, over that which he actually does pay' (Marshall 1920 p. 124). This amount will be less the more units are actually consumed, and will be zero at the market clearing price, since the marginal utility diminishes with each additional unit. If it were possible to sell the consumer units at a higher price than the subsequent units, then the producer could take some of this surplus (in a competitive market this is not possible – the consumer would buy elsewhere, at the lower equilibrium price).

16 Hicks also believes this is a requisite for an industry demand curve (Hicks 1939 p. 26).

17 His reaction is ambiguous (cf. Hutchison 1953 p. 84 ff.).

18 Or as Mitchell was shortly to suggest, business cycles.

19 'My conclusions ... are identical with those established thirty years ago by Dr. Marshall' (Pigou 1924 p. 30).

20 Pigou suggests that freeloading could also occur when durable capital is leased rather than owned. The tenants may not receive adequate compensation for investment (Pigou 1920 p. 176), in particular this could apply to tenant farmers (ibid. p. 177). He believes that a case could be made for compensation to be paid for investment in capital made by tenants (he notes that penalties are often levied for damage to capital) (ibid. p. 179), but also that all such compensation schemes have shortcomings.

21 And also, of course, dispensable: cf. Robinson (1962), who also believes that 'value' is metaphysical, but believes that metaphysics is a necessary complement to science.

22 For an outline of Pareto's sociology see Aron (1970). Pareto's sociology actually

appears to be more an exercise in political theory, in which case a positivist philosophy is an inappropriate guide. We shall be considering our own approach to political theory in Chapter 6.

23 Although, as we shall see later, ordinal utility and indifference analysis tend towards static theories.

24 cf. Cooter and Rappoport: 'John Hicks and R.G.D. Allen ... supplied the technical basis for a behaviourist account of consumer theory. Their article reconstructed consumer theory by isolating and developing those parts that did not rely on cardinality ... A concept that described mental impulses (marginal utility) was replaced by a behaviourist concept (marginal rate of substitution)' (Cooter and Rappoport 1984 p. 523).

25 Hicks attempted to reconstruct the theory of consumer's surplus in his article. For a critique see Samuelson (1947).

26 Recall that Pareto took his indifference curves simply as data. 'As we have seen, by the time he wrote the *Manuel*, Pareto had adopted Edgeworth's indifference curve techniques. However unlike Edgeworth he did not derive the curves from an existent cardinal utility function. On the contrary, he worked his way from indifference maps to the preference function. In this manner he did away with the need of considering any measurability of utility and interpersonal comparisons of utility as well' (Cirillo 1979 p. 100).

27 For a full list of the conditions for Pareto-efficiency see Nath (1969 p. 28).

28 This was, of course, the distinctive element in the Pigouvian analysis. Pigou was happy to consider distribution, up to a point.

29 Although cf. Scitovsky's *The Joyless Economy* (Scitovsky 1976).

3 MARKET SOCIALISM

1 Although the early market socialists were also influenced by Marshall.

2 Pareto also made some contributions to this question, although as we have seen his work is equivocal.

3 Bradley (1981 p. 23) and Vaughn (1980 p. 542) both note what Bradley terms a 'retreat from a pure advocacy of Marxist socialism to a compromise watered down with "competitive" infusions'. In fact this was an explicit admission by Lange. Several decades later, however, Lange qualified this somewhat, by claiming that the only reason market mechanisms were needed was because of the limitations in calculating ability at the time. He suggested that this is close to being remedied, and that the advent of computing power would enable central planning of all prices, q.v. the discussion below.

4 Useful summaries of the early market socialist models can be found in Vaughn (1980) and Vaughn (1981).

5 Although the similarity of the two schemes was pointed out by Hayek (1935b), Dickinson actually mentioned the problem of 'linked' prices requiring a general equilibrium approach himself, but did not draw out the corollaries of this (Dickinson 1933 p. 240).

6 Although this was something of a red herring, as we shall see presently.

7 It should be pointed out that many of these managerial rules are based on 'conventional' economic analysis of the firm, assuming U-shaped cost curves and so on.

8 See for example Dobb (1937 ch. viii), and more recently the debate between Nove and Mandel in the *New Left Review* (Mandel 1986, Nove 1987).

9 Halm was also concerned that the 'rate of accumulation' would be entirely arbitrary, since any interest rate would be arbitrary. There is no non-arbitrary

method to determine the level of industrial investments (Halm 1935 pp. 161 ff.). This affected the possibility of developing new production techniques so as to lower costs. See the argument below.

10 The reader will recall Marshall's extensive discussion on economies of scale.

11 Actually the problem of interconnected utilities was noted by Roper in his 1931 book (Roper 1931, see Hoff 1938 p. 126).

12 It is worth remembering that Lange is the only participant in the 1930s' 'London debate' to explicitly endorse the Marxist theory of history.

13 See e.g. Nove (1980), and Nove (1984).

14 In many ways the system resembled that proposed by Veblen; see Chapter 4 below.

15 It is worth noting that Marshall's scheme was different: he was looking at 'well-being'. He believed this was capable of some measure of objectivity.

16 and in some of Popper's work.

17 Neither Hayek or, as Shand points out, Rothbard, hold *a priori* theories (Shand 1990 p. 12).

18 Even Hayek distances himself from uncritical support of the present distributional set (1935a pp. 22–3), but offers no re-allocational scheme to remedy the faults. Indeed, none would be possible under the Austrian theory – presumably this is incorporated in the 'evolutionary' distributional theory.

4 AMERICAN INSTITUTIONALISM

1 Nabers points out that both the classics and the neo-classics supported the *status quo* for the most part. Certainly not much in the way of new policies was derived for business or for the state, and the analysis of the relation of the individual to the economy was similar (Nabers 1958 p. 78). See also Chapter 2.

2 i.e. propelling cause.

3 See Veblen (1914 p. 25, 1918 p. 5). Nabers (1958 p. 84) and others put the predation among the instincts, possibly because of the use of the term in the *Theory of the Leisure Class* (Veblen also refers to the 'instinct of sportsmanship'). This was an early work, however, and contains some loose terminology. Veblen makes several references to predatory 'culture' and predatory 'habit' (cf. Veblen (1899 pp. 7, 14 and 36), see also chapter headings 'Dress as an expression of the Pecuniary Culture', (ibid. ch. vii), 'The Technology of the Predatory Culture', (1914 Ch. 4). The concept of a predatory instinct would also contradict the non-predatory nature of savage societies mentioned in the *Leisure Class* (Veblen 1899 p. 24) and the *Instinct of Workmanship* (Veblen 1914 p. 101) (Rutherford 1979 p. 122).

4 In fact, many social scientists also use similar classifications.

5 For a discussion of Marxian critiques of Veblen see Simlich and Tilman (1982).

6 cf. Gruchy (1972 p. 45):

Mitchell believed that detailed, quantitative studies of the business cycle would enable economists to have a better understanding of the qualitative aspects of the money economy. He felt that in the early decades of this century there was more to be gained from quantitative than qualitative economic analysis. His inquiries might be 'more intensive and tamer' than Veblen's broad speculative studies, but in Mitchell's opinion this was the way to advance beyond Veblen on the path that the latter had staked out.

7 The two-volume publication Types of Economic Theory (Mitchell 1969) was edited from Mitchell's lecture notes for this course.

8 McDougall treats pain and pleasure as modifying influences on instinctive behaviour (Mitchell 1910 p. 103).

9 Mitchell used the same units of economic activity as the neo-classical authors (Vining 1951).
10 Cf. Vining (1951) *passim*. Vining suggests that this is in fact the main motive of all economic theory.
11 The Knight/Ayres debate does indeed seem to be a confusion, as suggested by the titles of the articles. If morality becomes objective, then indeed no moral judgements need be made. The difference is over the content of value theory, not over the inclusion of ethics in economics.
12 See references in Dickson (1974) and Rose and Rose (1976). Both Marxists and Greens would reject the idea of neutral technology: see for example the works of Habermas, Illich and others.
13 Also J.K.Galbraith.
14 Qv. Chapter 5.

5 NEW INSTITUTIONALISM

1 'There is, we are regularly told, a "crisis" in economic theory. Indeed, over the past 20 years this crisis has been almost permanently evident because it seems to have been the favourite theme for the Presidential Address to the Royal Economic Society and the American Economic Association.'

(Whynes 1984 p. 3)

For a listing see Nelson and Winter (1984 p. 4).
2 The term was coined by Oliver Williamson. The NIE are not to be confused with modern 'neo-institutionalists', who are followers of the American Institutional tradition: see Dugger (1983 n. 1) and the discussion below.
3 See Chapter 1.
4 Although Schotter and, of course, Menger are Austrian rather than neo-classic, we will show that the game theory approach actually collapses into an orthodox position. We will consider the Austrian normative theory at greater length in the second part of this chapter.
5 The model is usually simplified to a two-player, two strategy model.
6 The following examples of a prisoner's dilemma game are taken from Rutherford (1989): This matrix shows the basis of the prisoner's dilemma game. Each player (prisoner) has a choice of two options: cooperation with the police or a refusal to cooperate. The right-hand numbers are the pay-offs accruing to player A, the left-hand numbers are the pay-offs to player B.

		Player A	
		Co-operate	Don't co-operate
Player B	Cooperate	5\5	0\8
	Don't cooperate	8\0	2\2

There is no possibility of communicating or contracting between the players. Each protagonist benefits most if, while the other player co-operates, they refuse to do so, so that while the best joint strategy is to cooperate, the result of each single round is that the worst joint strategy – mutual non-cooperation – ensues.

7 This is an example of a coordination game:

Player A

		Co-operate	Don't co-operate
Player B	Cooperate	3\3	0\0
	Don't Cooperate	0\0	3\3

Unlike the prisoner's dilemma there is an incentive to find a coordinated solution: the problem here is simply to ensure that the protagonists coordinate their action. In this example both the pay-offs are equal pairs, but this need not be the case: in some situations a 4\3: 3\4 pay-off may occur, in which case considerable bargaining may ensue.

8 Schotter points out the similarity of this approach to that of Nozick (1974). See also the analysis below.

9 Schotter differs in this from, for example, Martin Shubik (see Mirowski 1986 p. 248).

10 Cf. Buchanan (1975).

11 See the argument below.

12 Williamson does suggest that some peer groups may be desired 'for themselves', presuming the loss of efficiency is not too great (Williamson 1975 p. 55).

13 Nelson and Winter's methodology is not Darwinian but Lamarkian, stressing adaptation and 'inheritance of acquired characteristics' (Nelson and Winter 1982 p. 11).

14 See below on 'learning'.

15 Nelson and Winter actually seem closer to the marginalist position of simply abstracting from institutions.

16 It could presumably be suggested that the argument concerning hierarchies could be extended to the political sphere, whereby competing governments attempt to economise on 'bounded rationality' by instigating hierarchies. Williamson mentions that his approach is well suited to the analysis of non-market organisations: this 'social Darwinism' would be an extension of that. Certainly, the domain of the transaction-cost model has not been specified. See also Olson (1965) for an extension of economic concepts into the polity.

17 More accurately the managerial function.

18 Indeed, unlike Williamson, Coase does not appear to be entirely against state economic organisation. cf. the discussion in the next chapter.

19 As Canterbury and Marvasti put it, 'the market never fails; rather, transaction costs are simply excessive' (Canterbury and Marvasti 1992 p. 1183).

20 This is a reference to the theory put forward in North and Thomas (1973), that changes in relative prices cause more efficient institutions to emerge. Later on North abandoned this view (North 1990 p. 7).

21 Langlois points out that Coase and Williamson come from a more neo-classic (sic) position, and as such do not attempt this endogenisation of all institutions (Langlois 1989 p. 292). We would view this as a weakness rather than a strength though. The question of legal and political institutions and the lack of con-ceptualisation of power are glaring omissions in the transaction-cost analysis.

22 North is also happy to extend the subsequent 'fair' contracting to an analysis of political institutions. Since no other influences on decisions are brooked, this

appears legitimate. A more radical approach would suggest that it is ideology that affects our experiences, rather than vice versa. The contracting approach then looks far more sinister.

23 This is Dugger's criticism of Williamson (Dugger 1983 p. 110), but we would suggest it is generalisable.

6 NEW SOCIAL MOVEMENTS

1 See Nelson (1993).
2 We might also add a third allocation process: rationing. It is precisely because market mechanisms are not good at allocating resources in fixed supply that rationing is usually invoked during wartime.
3 They may even be arbitrary, as with some methods for shortlisting job applications.
4 This is particularly relevant to the work involved in housekeeping and child-rearing. Not only are these not valued in an exchange economy, but their exclusion may also mean that the commodities which housekeepers and child-rearers are able to exchange, such as part-time labour in particular, are artificially devalued. See the discussion below.
5 Note especially the work of the New Economics Foundation, e.g. Anderson (1991).
6 In fact, given that what has become known as the 'Coase theory' is not really capable of extension, supporters of this approach rarely go beyond citing the article with approval. In a sense, once the conclusion has been reached there is nothing more to be said.
7 Although the freedom argument invariably conflates into arguments concerning efficiency. As we will see below, both negative and positive freedom are required in any realistic conception of 'the good life'.
8 Furubotn and Pejovich (somewhat grudgingly) admit that a theory of property rights cannot be truly complete without a theory of the state. They also, somewhat surprisingly, believe that 'no such theory exists at present' (Furubotn and Pejovich 1972 p. 1140). Given that numerous such theories exist, albeit few that are sympathetic to the New Right authors cited in their article, it would seem a damning admission on the part of the authors of the limitations of New Right theory.
9 If a protagonist does insist on maintaining an ethical argument regardless, then as Miller and others have pointed out, it is impossible to prove this argument wrong. All we can simply say is that it is ludicrous or perverse.
10 Some formulations of the Austrian theory stress the notion that ownership of resources is irrelevant, since access is the relevant aspect. This presumes in particular completely free access to credit markets, which is simply ludicrous.
11 It may also be the case that the requisite information may need to be the subject of regulation to ensure adequate distribution.
12 The subject of health also raises the problem of non-commodity conceptions of 'the good'. See the argument below.
13 Or possibly even banning, as in the case of hard narcotics.
14 Although, of course, a room with a view may be regarded as such. The point being made is not that picturesque scenery may not be the subject of rights, but that many people would regard these as perverse.
15 A similar point was made by Little (1950).
16 For a full investigation of the economics of co-operatives, see Vanek (1970) and (1975), and the references in Miller (1989a p. 83).

17 One of the main problems with the Yugoslav economy is thought to be that the interest rate was well below market price, so that capital was quickly swallowed up in inefficient ventures (Miller 1989a p. 14).

18 Although many large companies presently have gearing well in excess of 100 per cent.

19 See Breitenbach *et al.* (1990 pp. 50–1), Miller (1989a p. 310), Estrin (1989 pp. 187–90).

20 This need not be rational self-interest in the narrow sense of orthodox economics. They may, for instance, attempt to seek to further a religious cause.

21 Hence Hodgson's term 'economics of politics'. The process actually described by Miller is sometimes referred to as 'log-rolling', whereby the parties bargain until a compromise position is reached which commands a majority.

22 For a critique along these lines see Sen (1977).

23 Given this appeal to empirical evidence, we may wonder what idea of 'nation' Miller has in mind. Most of the existing states are either having or have had severe disputes over the question of nationality. It could be suggested that this problematic question is as much an issue as the other questions we have dealt with.

24 He actually likens the connection between nationality and nationalism to that between a football fan and football hooligans. Reading this for the first time during the 1990 World Cup it seemed an unfortunate example – combating nationalist-based football hooliganism was a very topical problem.

25 Although not all – the position of some eco-anarchists, for example, may differ.

26 Actually this point is made by many conservatives who believe a basic income scheme to be a good method of organising welfare payments. They claim that wage rates will simply adjust downwards to negate the redistribution of income. Nonetheless, to say that basic income will have little effect on overall redistribution is not to deny that it will have some effect on social welfare. Such a policy may well make a vital difference to many people in need and should be considered on that basis alone.

REFERENCES

Abell P. (1989) 'An Equitarian Market Socialism', in Le Grand and Estrin (1989).

Anderson V. (1991) *Alternative Economic Indicators*, London: Routledge.

Aron R. (1970) *Main Currents in Sociological Thought, Vol. 2*, Harmondsworth: Penguin.

Arrow K.J. (1951) *Social Choice and Individual Values*, New York: Wiley.

Ayres C.E. (1944) *The Theory of Economic Progress*, 2nd edn, New York: Schocken, 1962.

—— (1953) 'Role of Technology in Economic Theory', *American Economic Review*, vol. 43, p. 279–87.

—— (1958) 'Veblen's Theory of Instincts Reconsidered', in Dowd (1958).

—— (1961) *Towards a Reasonable Society*, Austin: University of Texas Press.

—— (1962) 'Foreword' to *Theory of Economic Progress*, 2nd edn, New York: Schocken.

Ball M. (1979) 'Cost-Benefit Analysis: A Critique', in Green F. and Nore P. (eds), *Issues in Political Economy*, London: Macmillan.

Bardhan P. (1989) *The Economic Theory of Agrarian Institutions*, Oxford: Clarendon.

Barone E. (1908) 'The Ministry of Production in the Collectivist State', in Hayek (1935).

Barry N.P. (1984) 'The Austrian Perspective', in Whynes (1984).

Bentham J. (1789) *Introduction to the Principles of Morals and Legislation*, from *Collected Works*, (eds Burns J.H. and Hart H.L.A.) London: Athlone, 1970.

Benton T. (1977) *The Philosophical Foundations of the Three Sociologies*, London: Routledge & Kegan Paul.

Bergson A. (1948) 'Socialist Economics', in Ellis (ed.), *A Survey of Contemporary Economics*, Illinois: American Economic Review/Irwin.

—— (1967) 'Market Socialism Revisited', *Journal of Political Economy*, vol. 73, pp. 655–73.

Berlin I. (1969) 'Two Concepts of Liberty', in *Four Essays on Liberty*, Oxford: Oxford University Press.

Blackhouse R. (1985) *A History of Modern Economic Analysis*, Oxford: Blackwell.

Blaug M. (1962) *Economic Theory in Retrospect*, Cambridge: Cambridge University Press.

—— (1980) *The Methodology of Economics*, Cambridge: Cambridge University Press.

Boland L. (1979) 'A Critique of Friedman's Critics', *Journal of Economic Literature*, vol. 17 (ii), pp. 503–22.

—— (1980) 'Friedman's Methodology v Conventional Empiricism: A reply to Rotwein', *Journal of Economic Literature*, vol. 18 (iv) (December), pp. 1555–7.

Boland L. and Frazer W.J. (1983) 'An Essay on the Foundation of Friedman's Methodology', *American Economic Review*, vol. 73, pp. 23–39.

Bradley R. (1981) 'Market Socialism: A Subjectivist Evaluation', *Journal of Libertarian Studies*, vol. 5 (i), pp. 23–40.

Breitenbach H. *et al.* (1990) *Features of a Viable Socialism*, London: Harvester.

Bromley D.W. (1991) *Environment and Economy*, Oxford: Blackwell.

Buchanan J.M. (1975) *The Limits of Liberty*, Chicago: Chicago University Press.

Burns A. (1952) *Wesley C. Mitchell, The Economic Scientist*, New York: NBER.

Cairnes J.E. (1875) *The Character and Logical Method of Political Economy*, 2nd edn, London: Cass.

Caldwell B. (1980) 'The Positivist Philosophy of Science and the Methodology of Economics', *Journal of Economic Issues*, vol. 14, pp. 53–76.

—— (1982) *Beyond Positivism*, London: Allen & Unwin.

Canterbury E.R. and Marvasti A. (1992) 'The Coase Theorum as a Negative Externality', *Journal of Economic Issues*, Vol. 26 (ii), p. 1179–88.

Chung P. (1978) 'Clarence Ayres and the Socialist Planning Debate', *Journal of Economic Issues*, vol. 12 (i), pp. 115–23.

Cirillo R. (1979) *The Economics of Vilfredo Pareto*, London: Cass.

Clapham J.H. (1922) 'Of Empty Economic Boxes', *Economic Journal*, vol. 32, pp. 305–14.

Coase R.H. (1937) 'The Nature of the Firm', *Economica*, n.s. vol. 4, pp. 386–405.

—— (1960) 'The Problem of Social Cost', *Journal of Law and Economics*, vol. 3, pp. 1–44, reprinted in Breit and Hochman (eds) *Readings in Microeconomics*, Hinsdale Illinois: Dryden, 1971.

—— (1975) 'Marshall on Method', *Journal of Law and Economics*, vol. 18, pp. 25–31.

—— (1988) *The Firm, the Market and the Law*, Chicago: University Chicago Press.

Coddington A. (1972) 'Positive Economics', *Canadian Journal of Economics*, vol. 5, pp. 1–15.

Commons J.R. (1924) *Legal Foundations of Capitalism*, New York: Macmillan.

—— (1925) Law and Economics, *Yale Law Journal*, vol. 34, pp. 371–82.

—— (1931) Institutional Economics, *American Economic Review*, vol. 21, pp. 648–57.

—— (1934) *Institutional Economics*, New York: Macmillian.

—— (1936) 'Institutional Economics: Discussion', *American Economic Review Supplement*, vol. 26, pp. 237–54.

—— (1950) *The Economics of Collective Action*, (ed. Parsons K.H.) New York: Macmillan.

Cooter R. and Rappoport P. (1984) 'Were the Ordinalists wrong about Welfare Economics?', *Journal of Economic Literature*, (ii) (June) pp. 507–30.

Copeland M.A. (1958) 'On the Scope & Method of Economics', in Dowd (1958).

Cottrell A. and Cockshott P. (1993) Calculation, Complexity and Planning: The Socialist Calculation Debate Once Again, *Review of Political Economy*, vol. 5 (i), pp. 73–112.

Dahlman C.J. (1979) 'The problem of Externality', *Journal of Law and Economics*, vol. 22, (i) pp. 141–62.

Daly H.E. and Cobb J.B. (1990) *For the Common Good*, London: Green Print.

Dasgupta A.K. (1985) *Epochs of Economic Theory*, Oxford: Blackwell.

DeMarchi N. (ed.) (1988) *The Popperian Legacy in Economics*, Cambridge: Cambridge University Press.

Dickinson H.D. (1933) 'Price Formation in a Socialist Community', *Economic Journal*, vol. 43, p. 237–50.

Dickson D. (1974) *Alternative Technology*, London: Fontana.

Dobb M. (1937) *Political Economy and Capitalism*, London: Routledge & Kegan Paul.

Dowd D.F. (1958) *Thorstein Veblen: A Critical Re-Appraisal*, Ithaca: Cornell University Press.

Downes A. (1957) *An Economic Theory of Democracy*, New York: Harper & Brothers.

Dugger W.(1979) 'The Reform Method of John R. Commons', *Journal of Economic Issues*, vol. 13, (ii), pp. 369–81.

—— (1983) 'The Transaction-Cost Analysis of Oliver Williamson', *Journal of Economic Issues*, vol. 17, (i), pp. 95–114.

Dunn J. (1986) 'Defining a Defensible Socialism for Britain Today', in Nolan and Paine (1986).

Durbin E.F.M (1936) 'Economic Calculus in a Planned Economy', *Economic Journal*, reprinted in *Problems of Economic Planning*, London: Routledge & Kegan Paul 1949.

Edgeworth F.Y. (1877) *New and Old Methods of Ethics*, Oxford and London.

—— (1881) *Mathematical Psychics* (1967 reprint), New York: Kelly.

Estrin S. (1989) 'Workers Co-operatives: Their Merits and their Limitations', in Le Grand and Estrin (1989).

Fay B. (1975) *Social Theory and Political Practice*, London: Unwin.

Field A.J. (1984) 'Microeconomics, Norms and Rationality', *Economic Development and Cultural Change*, vol. 32, pp. 682–711.

Friedman M. (1953) 'The Methodology of Positive Economics', in *Essays in Positive Economics*, Chicago: Chicago University Press.

Furubotn E. and Pejovich S. (1972) 'Property Rights and Economic Theory', *Journal of Economic Literature* vol. 10, p. 1137–62.

Galbraith J.K. (1958) *The Affluent Society*, 2nd edn, Harmondsworth: Penguin, 1970.

Gordon R.A. (1976) 'Rigour and Relevance in a Changing Institutional Setting', *American Economic Review*, vol. 66 (i), pp. 1–13.

Gorz A. (1975) *Ecology as Politics*, London: Pluto.

—— (1980) *Farewell to the Working Class*, London: Pluto.

Gramm W.S. (1988) 'The Movement from Real to Abstract Value Theory 1817–1957, *Cambridge Journal of Economics*, vol. 12, pp. 225–46.

Gruchy A.V. (1972) *Contemporary Economic Thought*, London: Macmillan.

—— (1987) *The Reconstruction of Economics*, New York: Greenwood Press.

Habermas J. (1969) *Towards a Rational Society*, trans. J. Shapiro, London: Heinemann, 1971.

Halévy E. (1901) *La Formation du Radicalisme Philosophique*, trans. as 'The Growth of Philosophic Radicalism' by Morris M., London: Faber, 1952.

Halm G. (1935) 'Further Considerations on the Possibility of Adequate Calculation in a Socialist Community', in Hayek (1935).

Hammond J.D (1990) 'Realism in Friedman's Essays in Positive Economics', in Moggridge D.E. (ed.) *Perspectives on the History of Economic Thought, Vol. iv*, Aldershot: Elgar.

Hayek H.A. (ed.) (1935) *Collectivist Economic Planning*, London: Routledge & Kegan Paul.

—— (1935a) 'The Nature and History of the Problem', in Hayek (1935).

—— (1935b) 'The Present State of the Debate', in Hayek (1935).

—— (1940) 'The Competitive Solution', *Economica*, reprinted in Hayek (1947).

—— (1945) 'The Use of Knowledge in Society', *American Economic Review*, reprinted in Hayek (1947).

—— (1946) 'The Meaning of Competition', in Hayek (1947).

—— (1947) *Individualism and Economic Order*, London: Routledge & Kegan Paul.

—— (1955) *The Counter Revolution of Science*, Glencoe: Free Press.

—— (1960) *The Constitution of Liberty*, London: Routledge & Kegan Paul.

Held D. (1986) 'Liberalism, Marxism and the Future Direction of Public Policy', in Nolan and Paine (1986).

Hempel C. (1966) *Philosophy of Natural Science*, New York: Prentice-Hall.

Hicks J.R. (1939) 'The Foundations of Welfare Economics', *Economic Journal*, reprinted in Hicks (1981).

—— (1946) *Value and Capital* 2nd edn (1st edn 1939) Oxford: Oxford University Press.

—— (1975) 'The Scope and Status of Welfare Economies', *Oxford Economic Papers*, reprinted in Hicks (1981).

—— (1981) *Wealth and Welfare*, Oxford: Blackwell.

Hicks J. and Allen R.G.D. (1934) 'A Reconsideration of the Theory of Value', reprinted in Hicks (1981).

Hirsch A. and DeMarchi N. (1984) 'Methodology: A Comment on Frazer and Boland, I', *American Economic Review*, vol. 74, pp. 782–88.

Hirsch F. (1977) *Social Limits to Growth*, London: Routledge & Kegan Paul.

Hodgson G. (1984) *The Democratic Economy*, Harmondsworth: Penguin.

—— (1988) *Economics and Institutions*, Oxford: Polity.

—— (1989) 'Institutional Economic Theory: The Old versus the New', *Review of Political Economy*, vol. 1, (iii), pp. 249–69.

Hoff T.J.B. (1938) *Economic Calculation in the Socialist Society*, London: Hodge.

Hollis M. and Nell E. (1975) *Rational Economic Man*, Cambridge: Cambridge University Press.

Homan P.T. (1928) 'Contemporary Economic Thought', reprinted in Burns (1952).

Honoré A.M. (1961) 'Ownership', in Guest A.G. (ed.), *Oxford Essays in Jurisprudence*, Oxford: Oxford University Press.

Hoover K.D. (1984) 'Methodology: A Comment on Frazer and Boland, II', *American Economic Review*, vol. 74, pp. 789–92.

Humphreys D.S. (1987) 'The Idea of Economic Planning', Unpublished PhD. thesis, Aberystwith University.

Hunt E.K. (1979) The Importance of Thorstein Veblen for Contemporary Marxism', *Journal of Economic Issues*, vol. 13, pp. 113–40.

Hutchison T.W. (1938) *The Signifciance and Basic Postulates of Economic Theory*, London: Macmillan.

—— (1953) *A Review of Economic Doctrines 1870–1929*, New York: New York University Press.

—— (1956) 'Professor Machlup on Verification', *Southern Economic Journal* vol. 22, p. 476–83.

—— (1981) *The Politics and Philosophy of Economics*, New York: New York University Press.

Jevons W.S. (1871) *Theory of Political Economy*, 5th edn, New York: Kelly 1957.

Jones E. (1977) 'Positive Economics or What?', *Economic Record*, vol. 53, pp. 350–63.

Kaldor N. (1939) 'Welfare Propositions of Economics and Interpersonal Comparisons of Utilities', *Economic Journal*, vol. 49, p. 549–52.

Keat R. and Urry J. (1975) *Social Theory as Science*, London: Routledge & Kegan Paul.

Keizer W. (1989) 'Recent Reinterpretations of the Socialist Calculation Debate', *Journal of Economic Studies*, vol. 16 (ii), pp. 63–83.

Keynes J.N. (1890) *The Scope and Method of Political Economy*, 4th edn, New York: Kelly 1917.

Kirzner I. M. (1988) Some Ethical Implications for Capitalism of the Socialist Calculation Debate', *Social Philosophy and Policy*, vol. 6 (i), pp. 165–82.

Knight F. (1920) Review of Veblen (1919a) *Journal of Political Economy*, vol. 28, pp. 518–20.

—— (1940) Review of Hutchison (1938), *Journal of Political Economy*, reprinted in *On the History and Method of Economics*, Chicago: Chicago University Press, 1956.

Kolakowski L. (1972) *Positive Philosophy*, Harmondsworth: Penguin.

Koopmans T.C. (1947) *Three Essays on the State of Economic Science*, New York: McGraw-Hill.

Kornai J. (1986) 'The Hungarian Reform Process', *Journal of Economic Literature*, vol. 26 (iv.), p. 1720–37.

Kuhn (1962) *The Structure of Scientific Revolutions* 2nd edn, Chicago: Chicago University Press 1970.

Lachmann L.M. (1990) 'Austrian Economics: A Hermeneutic Approach', in D. Lavoie (ed.) *Economics and Hermeneutics*, London: Routledge.

Laidler D.E. (1982) *Introduction to Microeconomics*, London: Philip Allen.

Lange O. (1934) 'Marxian Economics and Modern Economic Theory', *Review of Economic Studies*, vol. 2, pp. 189–201.

—— (1938) 'On the Economic Theory of Socialism', *Review of Economic Studies*, vol. 4 (1936), reprinted with corrections in Lippincott (1938).

—— (1945) 'The Scope and Method of Economics', *Review of Economic Studies*, vol. 13, p. 19–32.

—— (1967) 'The Computer and the Market', in Feinstein C. (ed.) *Socialism, Capitalism and Economic Growth*, Cambridge: Cambridge University Press.

Langlois R.N. (1986) *Economics as a Process*, Cambridge: Cambridge University Press.

—— (1989) 'What was Wrong with the Old Institutional Economics?', *Review of Political Economy*, vol. 1, pp. 270–98.

Lavoie D. (1985) *Rivalry and Central Planning*, Cambridge: Cambridge University Press.

Le Grand J. (1982) *The Strategy of Equality*, London: Allen & Unwin.

—— (1989) 'Markets Welfare and Equality', in Le Grand and Estrin (1989).

Le Grand J. and Estrin S. (eds) (1989) *Market Socialism*, Oxford: Oxford University Press.

Leipert C. (1986) Social Costs of Economic Growth, *Journal of Economic Issues*, vol. 20, pp. 109–32.

Leontief W. (1971) 'Theoretical Assumptions and Nonobserved Facts', *American Economic Review*, vol. 61, p. 1–7.

Lerner A.P. (1937) 'Statics and Dynamics in Socialist Economics', *Economic Journal*, vol. 47, pp. 253–70.

Lerner M. (ed.) (1948) *The Portable Veblen*, New York: Viking Press.

Lippincott B.E. (ed.) (1938) *On the Economic Theory of Socialism*, Minneapolis: University of Minneapolis Press.

Lipsey R. (1975) *Introduction to Positive Economics*, 5th. edn Weidenfield & Nicholson.

Lipsey R. and Lancaster K.J. (1956) 'The General Theory of Second Best', *Review of Economic Studies*, reprinted in Farrell (ed.), *Readings in Welfare Economics*, London: Macmillan, 1973.

Little I.M. (1950) *A Critique of Welfare Economics*, Oxford: Clarendon.

Loasby B.J. (1978) 'Whatever Happened to Marshall's Theory of Value?', *Scottish Journal of Political Economy*, vol. 25, pp. 1–12.

McFarland F.B. (1985) 'Thorstein Veblen versus the Institutionalists', *Review of Radical Political Economy*, vol. 17 (iv), pp. 95–105.

Machlup F. (1955) 'The Problem of Verification in Economics', *Southern Economic Journal*, vol. 22, pp. 271–84.

—— (1956) 'Rejoinder to a Reluctant Ultra-empiricist, *Southern Economic Journal*, vol. 22, p. 483–93.

—— (1964) 'Professor Samuelson on Theory and Realism', *American Economic Review*, vol. 54, pp. 733–5.

McLachlan H.V. and Swales J.K. (1978) 'The Positive/Normative Distinction in Economics', Working Paper 78/3, University of Strathclyde.

McLachlan H.V. and Swales J.K. (1982) 'Friedman's Methodology: A Comment on Boland', *Journal of Economic Studies*, vol. 9, pp. 19–34.

Mandel E. (1986) 'In Defence of Socialist Planning', *New Left Review* 159, pp. 5–38.

Marshall A. (1879) *Pure Theory of Foreign Trade and Domestic Value*, reprinted London: LSE, 1930.

—— (1920) *Principles of Economics* 8th edn (1st edn 1890), London: Macmillan.

Marshall A. and Marshall M. (1879) *The Economics of Industry*, London: Macmillan.

Mason W.E. (1980) 'Some Negative Thoughts on Friedman's Positive Economics', *Journal of Post-Keynsian Economics*, vol. 3, pp. 235–55.

Meadows D.L. *et al.* (1972) *The Limits to Growth*, London: Earth Island.

Meek R. (1956) *Studies in the Labour Theory of Value*, London: Lawrence & Wishart.

Melitz J. (1965) Friedman and Machlup on the Significance of Testing Economic Assumptions', *Journal of Political Economy*, vol. 73, pp. 37–60.

Menger C. (1883) *Problems in Economics and Sociology*, trans. Nock. F., Urbana: University of Illinois Press, 1963.

Mill J.S. (1836) 'Definition and Method of Political Economy', in *Essays on some Unsettled Questions of Political Economy*, London: Parker 1844 (reprint, London: LSE, 1968).

Miller D. (1989a) *Market, State and Community*, Oxford: Oxford University Press.

—— (1989b) 'Why Markets?' in Le Grand and Estrin (1989).

Miller D. and Estrin S. (1986) 'Market Socialism: A Policy for Socialists', in Forbes I. (ed.), *Market Socialism: Whose Choice?*, Fabian Pamphlet 516, London: Fabian Society.

Mirowski P. (1986) 'Institutions as a Solution Concept in a Game Theory Context', in Mirowski P. (ed.) *The Reconstruction of Economic Theory*, Boston: Kluwer.

—— (1990) 'The Philosophical Bases of Institutional Economics', in Lavoie D. (ed.) *Economics and Hermenuetics*, London: Routledge.

Mises L. von (1920) 'Economic Calculation in the Socialist Commonwealth', reproduced in Hayek (1935).

—— (1922) *Socialism*, Indianapolis: Liberty.

—— (1962) *The Ultimate Foundations of Economic Science*, Kansas: Sheed.

Mitchell W.C. (1910) 'Rationality of Economic Activity', *Journal of Political Economy*, vol. 18, pp. 97–113; 197–216.

—— (1912) 'The Backward Art of Spending Money', *American Economic Review*, vol. 2, pp. 269–81.

—— (1913) *Business Cycles*, Berkerly: University of California Press.

—— (1916) 'The Role of Money in Economic Theory', *American Economic Review*, vol. 6 (Mar) sup. pp. 149–76.

—— (1918) 'Benthams Felicific Calculus', *Political Science Quarterly*, vol. 34 (ii), pp. 161–83.

—— (1944) 'Facts and Values in Economics', *Journal of Philosophy*, vol. 41, p. 212–19.

—— (1967) *Types of Economic Theory, Vol. 1*, New York: Kelly.

—— (1969) *Types of Economic Theory, Vol. 2* New York: Kelly.

Murrell P. (1983) 'Did the Theory of Market Socialism Answer the Challenge of Ludwig von Mises?', *History of Political Economy*, vol. 15, pp. 92–105.

Musgrave A. (1981) 'Unreal Assumptions in Economic Theory: The F-Twist Untwisted', *Kyklos*, vol. 34, pp. 377–87.

Myrdal G. (1929) *The Political Element in the Development of Economic Theory*, trans. Streeten P.), London: Routledge & Kegan Paul, 1958.

—— (1933) 'Ends and Means' in Myrdal G., *Value in Social Theory*, London: Routledge & Kegan Paul, 1958.

—— (1953) 'The Relation between Social Theory and Social Policy', *British Journal of Sociology*, vol. 4, pp. 210–42.

Nabers L. (1958) 'Veblen's Critique of the Orthodox Economic Tradition', in Dowd (1958).

Nagel E. (1963) 'Assumptions in Economic Theory', *American Economic Review Papers and Procedures*, vol. 53, pp. 211–19.

Nath S. (1969) *A Reappraisal of Welfare Economics*, London: Routledge & Kegan Paul.

Nelson J.A. (1993) 'Value-Free or Valueless? Notes on the Pursuit of Detachment in Economics', *History of Political Economy* vol. 25, pp. 120–45

Nelson R. R. and Winter S.G. (1982) *An Evolutionary Theory of Economic Change*, Cambridge: Belknap.

Nolan P. and Paine S. (eds.) (1986) *Rethinking Socialist Economics*, Oxford: Polity.

North D. (1984) 'Three approaches to the Study of Institutions', in Colander D.C. (ed.), *Neoclassical Political Economy*, Cambridge, MA: Ballinger.

—— (1990) *Institutions, Institutional Change and Economic Performance*, Cambridge: Cambridge University Press.

North D. and Thomas R. (1973) *The Rise of the Western World*, Cambridge: Cambridge University Press.

Nove A. (1980) 'The Soviet Economy: Problems and Prospects', *New Left Review*, 119, pp. 3–19.

—— (1983) *The Economics of Feasible Socialism*, London: Allen & Unwin.

—— (1987) 'Markets and Socialism: Comment', *New Left Review* 161, pp. 98–104.

Nozick R. (1974) *Anarchy State and Utopia*, Oxford: Blackwell.

Olson M. (1965) *The Logic of Collective Action*, Cambridge, MA: Harvard University Press.

Ormerod P. (1992a) 'Waiting for Newton', *New Statesman and Society*, 28 August, pp. 12–13.

—— (1992b) 'Crisis in the Exchange Rate', *Times Higher Education Supplement*, 18 September 1992, p. 16.

Page A. (ed.) (1968) *Utility Theory: A Book of Readings*, New York: Wiley.

Paine S. (1986) 'Notes on late Twentieth-Century Socialism' in Nolan P. and Paine S. (eds.) (1986)

Pareto V. (1896) *Cours d'Economie Politique*, Geneva: Droz 1964.

—— (1901) 'On the Economic Principle', *International Economic Papers*, 3 (1953) pp. 203–7.

—— (1909) *Manuel d'economique Politique*, trans. as 'Manual of Political Economy' by Schwier A. and Page A., New York: Kelly 1971.

—— (1916) *Mind and Society*, trans. Bongiorno A. and Livingston A., New York: Dover Publications 1935.

Parsons K.H. (1942) 'John R. Commons' Point of View', *Journal of Land and Public Utility Economics*, vol xviii, pp. 245–66, reprinted in Commons (1950), Appendix iii.

Parsons T. (1937) *The Structure of Social Action*, New York: Free Press.

Phelps-Brown E.H. (1972) 'The Underdevelopment of Economics', *Economics Journal*, vol. 82 (i), pp. 1–10.

Pierson N.G. (1902) 'The Problem of Value in the Socialist Society', in Hayek (1935).

Pigou A.C. (1920) *The Economics of Welfare*, London: Macmillan.

—— (1924) 'Comment' on D.H. Robertson 'Those Empty Boxes', *Economic Journal*, vol. 34 pp. 30–1.

—— (ed.) (1925) *Memorials of Alfred Marshall*, London: Macmillan.

Plant R. (1989) 'Socialism, Markets and End States', in Le Grand and Estrin (1989).

Pluta J.E. and Leathers C.G. (1978) 'Veblen and Modern Radical Economics', *Journal of Economic Issues* vol. 12, pp. 125–46.

Popper K. (1934) *Logic of Scientific Discovery*, (English edn), Hutchinson 1959.

Ramstad Y. (1986) A Pragmatist's Quest for Holistic Knowledge: The Scientific Methodology of John R. Commons, *Journal of Economic Issues*, vol. 20, pp. 1067–105.

Robbins L. (1933) *The Great Depression*, London: Macmillan.

—— (1935) *The Nature and Significance of Economics* 2nd edn, reprinted in 3rd edn, London: Macmillan, 1981.

Robinson J. (1962) *Economic Philosophy*, Harmondsworth: Penguin.

Roper W.C. (1931) *The Problem of Pricing in a Socialist State*, Cambridge, MA, Harvard University Press.

Rose H. and Rose S. (eds) (1976) *The Political Economy of Science*, London: Macmillan.

Rostow W.W. (1976) 'Technology and the Price System', in Breit and Culbertson (eds) *Science and Ceremony*, Austin: University of Texas Press.

Rotwein E. (1980) 'Friedman's Critics: A Critic's Reply to Boland', *Journal of Economic Literature*, vol. 81 (iv) December, pp. 789–92.

Rutherford M. (1981) 'Clarence Ayres and the Instrumental Theory of Value', *Journal of Economic Issues*, vol. 15, pp. 721–44.

—— (1983) 'J.R. Commons' Institutional Economics', *Journal of Economic Issues*, vol. 15, pp. 721–44.

—— (1984) 'Thornstein Veblen and the Process of Institutional Change', *History of Political Economy*, vol. 15 (16) pp. 331–48.

—— (1989) What is Wrong with the New Institutional Economics?', *Review of Political Economy*, vol. 1, pp. 299–318.

Rutherford M.H. (1979) *The Development of Institutional Economics*, Unpublished PhD. Thesis, Durham University.

Saghoff M. (1988) *Economics of the Earth*, Cambridge: Cambridge University Press.

Samuels W. (1974) *Pareto on Policy*, Amsterdam: Elsever.

Samuelson P. (1938) 'The Pure Theory of Consumer's Behaviour', *Economica*, n.s. vol. 5 (Feb.), pp. 61–71.

—— (1947) *Foundations of Economic Analysis*, London: Harvard University Press.

—— (1950) 'Evaluation of Real National Income', *Oxford Economic Papers*, n.s. vol. 5, pp. 1–29.

—— (1963) (Discussion), *American Economic Review Papers and Proc.*, vol. 53, pp. 231–36.

—— (1964) 'Theory and Realism: A Reply', *American Economic Review*, vol. 54, pp. 736–39.

—— (1965) 'Professor Samuelson on Theory and Realism: A Reply', *American Economic Review*, vol. 55, pp. 1164–72.

Schoeffler S. (1955) *The Failures of Economics*, Cambridge, MA: Harvard University Press.

Schotter A. (1981) *The Economic Theory of Social Institutions*, Cambridge: Cambridge University Press.

Schumpeter J.A. (1942) *Capitalism, Socialism and Democracy*, London: Allen & Unwin.

Scitovsky T. de (1941) 'A Note on Welfare Propositions in Economics', *Review of Economic Studies*, vol. 9, pp. 77–88.

—— (1976) *The Joyless Economy*, Oxford: Oxford University Press.

Sen A. (1973) *Behaviour and the Concept of Preference*, London: LSE.

—— (1976) Rational Fools, *Philosophy and Public Affairs*, vol. 6, pp. 317–44.

—— (1979) 'Personal Utilities and Public Judgements', *Economic Journal*, vol. 89, pp. 463–89.

Shand A. (1984) *The Capitalist Alternative*, Brighton, Wheatsheaf.

—— (1990) *Free Market Morality*, London: Routledge.

Simlich J.L. and Tilman R. (1982) 'Thorstein Veblen and his Marxist Critics: An Interpretive View', *History of Political Economy*, vol. 14, pp. 323–41.

Simon H.A. (1959) 'Theories of Decision-Making in Economic and Behavioural Sciences', *American Economic Review*, vol. 49, pp. 253–83.

—— (1976) 'From Substantive to Procedural Rationality', in Latsis S. (ed.) *Method and Appraisal in Economics*, Cambridge: Cambridge University Press.

Smyth R.L. (1962) *Essays in Economic Method*, London: Duckworth.

Starr M.E. (1983) *The Political Economy of American Institutionalism*, Unpublished PhD. Thesis, University of Wisconsin.

Steele D.R. (1981) 'Posing the Problem: The Impossibility of Economic Calculation under Socialism', *Journal of Libertarian Studies*, vol. 5 (i), pp. 7–22.

Stigler G. (1950) 'The Development of Utility Theory', *Journal of Political Economy*, reprinted in Page (1968).

—— (1961) 'The Economics of Information', *Journal of Political Economy*, vol. 69, pp. 213–25.

Streeten P. (1958) Introduction to Myrdal (1929).

Tarascio V.J. (1966) *Pareto's Methodological Approach to Economics*, Chapel Hill: University of North Carolina Press.

—— (1967) 'Vilfredo Pareto and Marginalism', *History of Political Economy*, vol. 4, pp. 406–25.

Taylor F. (1929) 'The Guidance of Production in a Socialist State', *American Economic Review*, reprinted in Lippincott (1938).

Tollison R.J. (1982) Rent-Seeking: A Survey', *Kyklos*, vol. 35, pp. 575–602.

Tugwell R.G. (1937) 'Wesley Mitchell: An Evaluation', *New Republic*, vol. 92, 6 October, pp. 238–40.

Vanek J. (1970) *The General Theory of Labor-Managed Market Economies*, Ithaca: Cornell University Press.

—— (1975) 'The Basic Theory of Financing of Participatory Firms', in Vanek (ed.), *Self Management*, Harmondsworth: Penguin.

Vaughn K.I. (1980) 'Economic Calculation under Socialism', *Economic Inquiry*, vol. 18, p. 535–54.

—— (1981) Introduction to Hoff (1929), Indianapolis: Liberty.

Veblen T. (1898) 'Why is Economics not an Evolutionary Science? *Quarterly Journal of Economics*, reprinted in Veblen (1919a).

—— (1899) *The Theory of the Leisure Class*, New York: Macmillan.

—— (1904) *The Theory of Business Enterprise*, New York: Kelly.

—— (1906) 'The Socialist Economics of Karl Marx', *Quarterly Journal of Economics*, reprinted in Lerner (1948).

—— (1909) 'The Limitations of Marginal Utility', *Journal of Political Economy*, reprinted in Lerner (1948).

—— (1914) *The Instinct of Workmanship*, New York: Kelly.

—— (1917) *An Inquiry into The Nature of Peace and the Terms of its Perpetuation*, New York: Kelly.

—— (1918) *The Higher Learning in America*, New York: Kelly.

—— (1919a) *The Place of Science in Modern Civilisation and other Essays*, New York: Macmillan.

REFERENCES

—— (1919b) *The Vested Interests*, New York: Kelly.

—— (1921) *The Engineers and the Price System*, New York: Kelly.

—— (1923) *Absentee Ownership and Business Enterprise in Recent Times*, New York: Kelly.

Viner J. (1925) 'The Utility Concept in Value Theory and its Critics', *Journal of Political Economy*, reprinted in Page (1968).

Vining R. (1951) 'Economic Theory and quantitative research: A Broad Interpretation of the Mitchell Position', *American Economic Review Papers and Procedures*, vol. 41, pp. 108–18.

Von Neumann J. and Morgenstern O. (1947) *The Theory of Games and Economic Behaviour*, 2nd edn., Princetown; Princetown University Press.

Walker D.A. (1978) 'Economic Policy Proposals of Clarence Ayres', *Southern Economic Journal*, vol. 44, pp. 616–28.

—— (1979) 'The Institutionalist Economic Theories of Clarence Ayres', *Economic Inquiry*, vol. 17, pp. 519–38.

Walker D.A. (1980) 'Clarence Ayers' Critique of Orthodox Economic Theory', *Journal of Economic Issues*, vol. 14, pp. 649–80.

Warnock M. (1962) *Utilitarianism*, London: Fount Paperbacks.

Whynes D.K. (1984) *What is Political Economy?*, Oxford: Blackwell.

Wicksteed P. (1913) 'The Scope and Method of Political Econonomy in the Light of the "Marginal" Theory of Value', reprinted in Smyth (1962).

Williamson O. (1975) *Markets and Hierarchies*, New York: Free Press.

Wolfe A.B. (1939) 'Thoughts on Perusal of Wesley Mitchell's Collected Essays', *Journal of Political Economy*, reprinted in Burns (1952).

Worswick G.D.N. (1972) 'Is progress in Economic Science possible?', *Economic Journal*, vol. 82 (i), pp. 73–86.

Wong S. (1973) 'The F-Twist and the Methodology of Paul Samuelson', *American Economic Review*, vol. 62, pp. 312–25.

—— (1978) *The Foundations of Paul Samuelson's Revealed Preference Theory*, London: Routledge & Kegan Paul.

Zingler E.K. (1974) 'Veblen vs. Commons: A Comparative Evaluation', *Kyklos*, vol. 27, (ii), pp. 322–44.

INDEX

Note: pages in **bold** indicate main references

Abell, P. 159
ability 157
abundance 123
accidental generalisations 14
action 23, 37, 48, 50–1, 62, 97; cognition
    of 176; collective 124; constraints on
    162; human 100; individual 100, 101,
    122, 131; participatory 36
aggregation 43, 100, 147, 149, 167–8
Allen, R.G.D. 178
allocation process, auction and
    screening 149–50
American Economic association 1
Anderson, V. 182
approximation to reality 20
Aron, R. 177
Arrow, K.J. 72
'as if' 23, 24
The Assumption 27–8, 176
assumptions 24–5, 176; heuristic 25, 27;
    negligibility of 24, 27; unrealistic 25
Austrian school 4, 7, 7–9, 19–20, 35–6,
    73, 96–100, 130, 133, 148, 151, 156,
    159, 173, 175, 179, 183; critique **80–93**
Ayres, C.E. 101, 107, 110, 116–21, 128,
    180

Ball, M. 151
Bardhan, P. 154
bargaining costs 155
Barone, E. 75, 78, 82, 86
Barry, N.P. 82, 83, 89, 93, 95
behaviour 45; analysis of 121; business
    137; economic 102; human 102–3,
    118; institutional/ceremonial 118, 119
behaviourism 63, 64

Bentham, J. 38–40, 42, 44, 102, 120
Benton, T. 5, 13, 175
Bergson, A. 91
Berlin, I. 156
Blackhouse, R. 57
Blaug, M. 17, 18, 41, 176
Boland, L. 25–6, 26, 27; and Frazer,
    W.J. 27, 176
bourgeois economics 76–7
Bradley, R. 80, 82, 84, 86, 88, 89, 90, 94,
    95, 178
Breitenbach, H. 183; *et al.* 165
bridge principles 14, 22
British Association 2
Bromley, D.W. 154–5
Buchanan, J.M. 181
business 104–6, 113
business class 106, 107, 109
business cycles 110, 114, 128, 177, 179

Cairnes, J.E. 17–18
calculation argument 86–7
Caldwell, B. 13, 19, 29, 176
Canterbury, E.R. and Marvasti, A. 182
capital 116, 117, 172
capital markets 97–8; as open-ended 98,
    155
capitalism 94, 127
Cassel, 67
causality 13–14, 37, 162
choice 64–5, 66, 79, 89, 94–5, 96, 156,
    158–9, 162
Chung, P. 117, 120
Cirillo, R. 60, 61, 178
Clapham, J.H. 23, 57–8
Clark, J.B. 55, 57

class theory 106–7
Club of Rome 146–7
Co-operative Producer Federation 165
Coase, R.H. 48, 50, 134, 141, 152–3, 182
Coase theory 154, 182
Coddington, A. 25, 26
coercion 157
commodities 87–8, 90, 161
common man 104, 106, 109
common sense 41, 50
Commons, J.R. 7, 121–7, 128, 131, 134,
    142, 145, 155, 157, 159
communitarian 164
community 168–9, 173
compensation 70–1
competition 46, 105; free 69; perfect 28,
    46, 53, 69–70, 79–80, 82–3, 107, 130,
    177
compositional principle 143
computation debate 86
consumers 65, 78, 84, 108, 167, 177;
    surplus 57
consumption, patterns of 104
contingent valuation 151
continuity 117
control 15, 32–3
conventionalism 11, 95, 175
cooperatives 165–6, 183
coordination problem 132, 181
Cooter, R. and Rappoport, P. 64, 178
Copeland, M.A. 102
correspondence rules see bridge
    principles
cost 52, 56, 58, 89, 134, 140, 148;
    calculation of 84; measurement of
    89–90, 95; reduction of 91
cost–benefit analysis (CBA) 151–2
Cottrell, A. and Cockshott, P. 81
counter-factual conditionals 14, 15
Cournot, 67
culture, as predatory 103, 179

Dahlman, C.J. 141
Daly, H.E. and Cobb, J.B. 41, 151, 152,
    173
Darwin, C. 103, 107, 125
Darwinian theory 97, 98, 102, 109, 110,
    143, 181
Dasgupta, A.K. 41, 42, 51, 52, 54, 55,
    177
data 112, 113
decision-making 96–7, 158; centralised
    135–6; inter-community/inter-state
173
DeMarchi, N. 1
depression 56
determinism, theories of **101–21**
Dewey, J. 26, 117
dialogue 167
Dickinson, H.D. 78, 80, 81, 178
Dickson, D. 180
diminishing returns 52–3
diminishing utility 41, 43, 55, 58, 64
direct utility 167
distribution 6, 35, 44, 45, 59–61, 66,
    70–1, 98, 105, 153, 154, 159–60,
    162–3, 171–2, 178; abstraction of 74;
    equitable 163
distributive efficiency 7
distributive justice (negative freedom) 7,
    156, 157–8, 162
disutility 44
Dobb, M. 81, 178
domination 10
Downes, A. 167
dual calculus 46
dualism 95
Dugger, W. 121, 138, 141–2, 182
Dunn, J. 163
Durbin, E.F.M. 80, 89

eco-anarchists 183
ecofeminism 146
economic human 18, 54
economic rationalism 112
'Economical Calculus' 45–6
economics, criticism of 1–3; defined
    131–2; as empirical science 21;
    history of 6; hypothetical method 21;
    justifications of 3–4; lack of realism
    in 3–4; limits of 69
economies of scale 88, 179
Edgeworth, F.Y. 45–7, 59, 60, 177
efficiency 123
empiricism 28, 176
employment 165
end-state 33, 36, 160, 161
end/means see means/end dichotomy
engineering approach 26, 27, 34, 123
'English debate' 74, 76–80
entrepreneurs 7, 83, 88, 97, 135, 141
environmental resources 150–6
equality 120
equilibrium 52–6, 60, 63, 68, 80, 81–2,
    113, 116, 177, 178; as static 82, 83–5,
    88, 94, see also general equilibrium

Estrin, S. 165, 183
ethic of care 146
ethics 19, 38, 122, 124
evolutionary theory 109, 125, 136, 179; critique of 137–44
excellence 120
exchange mechanism 83–4, 93, 157, 158, 160, 162, 170–1, 182; scope of 171
expenditure 148; conspicuous 160
explanation 11, 22, 29, 32, 42, 67, 109, 143; animistic and matter of fact 103; causal 37; centrality of 13; as deductive-nomological 13; evolutionary 96, 98, 136; functional 15, 136, 138; as inductive-statistical 14–15; of mass events 175; positive 16; post hoc 137, 143; why, how, what questions 95
externalities 59, 151, 153, 155, 161

fact/value dichotomy 17
falsification 19, 21, 30, 176
Fay, B. 11, 12, 32, 34, 36, 175
feedback mechanism 78–9, 143
Fictitious Mean 43
Field, A.J. 138, 139
final cause 17
the firm 136–7
Fisher, I. 67, 111
free enterprise 49
'free trade' 173
freedom 120, 156–9, 166–7, 182, see also distributive justice
Friedman, M. 15, 22, 23–5, 26–7, 27, 28, 30, 176
Furubotn, E. and Pejovich, S. 182–3

Galbraith, J.K. 145, 150, 180
game theory 126, 131–3, 137, 138–9, 149, 180–1
general equilibrium 82–92, 94, 129, 139–40, see also equilibrium
generalized utility function 46
German Historical school 23
GNP 4, 149, 152
the good 161, 163, 164, 172, 183
goods 89; access to 150; defensive 148; intermediate 148; positional 103, 150, 172–3
Gorz, A. 161
Gramm, W.S. 41, 42, 67
green movement 146–56, 169
growth 52, 53, 55, 147; economic 117, 150; industrial 117

Gruchy, A.V. 100, 106, 108, 118, 179

Habermas, J. 12, 33, 180
Halm, G. 178
Hammond, J.D. 26, 176
harmony of interests 124
Hayek, H.A. 75, 79, 82, 83, 85, 86–90, 92, 94, 95, 96, 132–3, 156, 178, 179
health 160
hedonism 38, 45, 47, 60, 67, 96, 101–2, 111, 112, 128
Held, D. 157, 164
Hempel, C. 13–14, 175, 176
Hicks, J., and Allen, R.G.D. 64
Hicks, J.R. 19, 64–5, 177, 178
hierarchies, analysis of 135
hierarchy of pleasures 44
Hirsch, A. and DeMarchi, N. 26
Hirsch, F. 103, 147–50, 151, 172
Hodgson, G. 92–3, 139, 140, 142, 161, 183
Hoff, T.J.B. 75, 90, 91, 179
Hohfield, 155
Hollis, M. and Nell, E. 20, 38, 68, 175
Homan, P.T. 112, 113, 114
Honoré, A.M. 160
Hoover, K.D. 26
human capital 177
human nature 129
Hume, D. 26, 66, 123
Humphreys, D.S. 91
Hunt, E.K. 106, 107
Hutchison, T.W. 20–2, 23, 29, 42, 45, 59, 68, 97, 175, 177
hypothesis 24, 33

ideal types 23, 25
identity 168–9; collective 36
ideology 142–3
Illich, I. 162, 180
impossibility theorem 72
incentives 84–5
income distribution 35, 57, 75, 77, 150, 162, 183
indifference analysis 39, 60, 178
indifference curves 178
individualism 42
inductive problem 26
industrial arts 108
Industrial Common Ownership Movement 165
Industrial Revolution 49
industry 104, 113

inequality 132–3
information 140, 156, 183; costs 155; decentralised and incomplete 87; impactness 135; insufficient 133–4
instincts 107, 116
institutionalism 100–27, 130–1
institutions 118–19, 124, 142, 157, 159; endogenisation of 142, 182
instrumentalism 15, 22, 23, 24, 120, 175; methodological 26, 27–9
interest-aggregation 167–8
interpersonal comparisons 44–5
intervention 157
investment 165–6, 177, 179
invisible hand 97, 105, 124

Jevons, W.S. 50–5, 59
Jones, E. 28
just price 105

Kaldor, N. 70, 71
Keat, R. and Urry, J. 5, 11, 13–14, 95, 96–7, 175
Keizer, W. 81
Keynes, J.N. 18
Kirzner, I.M. 81
Knight, F. 22, 108, 180
knowledge 13, 120; of alternatives 89; normative attitude towards 12; perfect 93, 129–30, 173
Kolakowski, L. 12, 175
Koopmans, T.C. 111
Kornai, J. 91–2
Kuhn, T. 5, 6

labour 171, 177
labour theory of value 43, 109
Lachmann, L.M. 96, 130
laissez-faire 4, 5–6, 27, 29, 33, 35–8, 56, 58, 73, 98, 126–9, 143, 146, 154, 156–7, 162–3, 173, 176; justification of 16–17, 22; side-effects of 48–9
Lamarkian theory 181
Lange, O. 76–7, 79–80, 80, 81, 82, 86, 90–1, 94, 172, 178
Langlois, R.N. 110, 130–1, 138, 143, 182
language 24
Lavoie, D. 82, 83, 86–7, 89–90, 94
law 44, 122–6, 127, 128, 134, 142, 145, 154–5, 160–1, 170–1; of indifference 43; labour 171
Le Grand, J. and Estrin, S. 158
leisure 161

leisure class 104
Leontief, W. 1, 72
Lerner, A.P. 80, 89–90, 101, 103, 104, 172
liberalism 118, 142
libertarianism 7
liberty 156, 157
life cycle 53, 56
Lipsey, R. 31; and Lancaster, K.J. 69–70
Little, I.M. 71, 183
Loasby, B.J. 52, 53
log-rolling 183
London Debate 140

McDougall, 112, 179
McFarland, F.B. 118–19
Mach, E. 13
Machlup, F. 22–3, 27, 28, 176
McLachlan, H.V. and Swales, J.K. 25, 30–1
managers 85, 89–92, 97, 178
Mandel, E. 81, 178
marginal costs 79–80, 89, 91
Marginal Productivity Theory 55
marginal products 57
marginal utility 41–2, 59, 101, 178
The Market 159
market socialists 6, 35, 74–80, 178
market/s 69, 83, 145; choice 62; exchange 8; limitation 159–3; mechanisms 158–63; significance of 142
Marshall, A. 18, 47–56, 57–8, 60, 62, 65, 68, 69, 82, 101, 111, 112, 137, 177, 178, 179
Marx, K. 41, 106, 109, 142
Marxism 75–7, 76, 91, 95, 109, 178
Mason, W.E. 25, 27–8
mathematics 45, 48
maximum universal utility 46
Meadows, D.L. et al. 146
means/end dichotomy 16–17, 19, 20, 33–6, 39, 115, 147
Meek, R. 67
Melitz, J. 24
Menger, C. 131, 180
metatheory 15, 19, 29, 31–2; justification of 37
methodology 5, 15, 18, 111; classical 18; hypothetical 21
militarism 105, 110
Mill, J.S. 17, 18, 20, 39, 41
Miller, D. 157, 158, 159, 160–1, 162–3,

164, 166–9, 183; and Estrin, S. 158–9
minimal state 170
Mirowski, P. 107, 138–9, 181
Mises, L. von 19, 75, 76, 77, 81–7, 92,
  94, 96, 98, 135, 176
Mitchell, W.C. 39–40, 42, 44, 45, 47, 51,
  60, 101, 110–16, 128, 145, 176, 177,
  179, 180
modernity 33
money 40, 51–2, 57, 59, 83, 112–15, 128,
  145, 149, 161, 170
monopolies 55, 76, 107, 130
motivation 112
Murrell, P. 84, 86, 93
Musgrave, A. 24–5, 68, 176
Myrdal, G. 16–17, 33–5, 39, 40, 43, 44,
  47, 67–8, 147

Nabers, L. 105, 108, 179
Nagel, E. 25, 26, 176
Nath, S. 69, 178
national dividend 57
nationalism 105, 110
nationality 183
natural order 105
natural science 10
negative freedom see distributive justice
Nelson, J.A. 167, 182
Nelson, R.R. and Winter, S.G. 129–30,
  136–7, 144, 180, 181
neo-classical theory 38, 47–60, 77, 81–2,
  117, 121
neo-institutionalists 180
new institutionalism 8, **128–44**, 146
new market socialists 8, 129, 156–69, 169
New Right 146, 153, 156, 157, 158, 183
non-commodity elements 161, 183;
  value of 172
normative theory 30–2, 93–9
North, D. 142–3; and Thomas, R. 182
Nove, A. 92–3, 164, 178
Nozick, R. 181

objective cost analysis 56
objective replacement theory 116
objective values 110, 152
objectivity 7, 13, 37
observation 18, 64–5
oligopoly 107, 135
oligopsony 135
Olson, M. 181
open access 155
opportunism 135

opportunity costs 80, 89, 148
ordinal utility 64–5, 66, 67, 176, 178
ordinalists **60–73**
organic institutions 131, 143, 157
Ormerod, P. 2–3
orthodox theory 33, 93–4, 97, 99, 105,
  109, 113–14, 121, 122, 130, 143, 144,
  146, 147

Paine, S. 164
Pareto, V. 60–3, 65, 68–9, 82, 115, 177,
  178
Pareto-optimum position 61–3, 68–9, 70
Parsons, K.H. 124, 126
participation 163–9
patriotism 105
pecuniary measure 39–40
Phelps-Brown, E.H. 2, 3
physical unit (non-pecuniary planning)
  75, 92
Pierson, N.G. 51, 75
Pigou, A.C. 48, 56–60, 82, 177
planning 28, 37, 56, 73, 116, 152, 176; as
  central 79, 81–2, 91–3, 94, 114, 140,
  156, 158
Plant, R. 157–8, 162
pleasure/pain 44, 46, 111, 179
Pluta, J.E. and Leathers, C.G. 106, 107,
  109
policy science 32, 163
political theory 6–7, 32–4, 45, 123
politics 163–9, 173
Popper, K. 19, 21, 22, 29–30, 176, 179
positive economics 16–29, 95
positive science 5–6, 10–16
positive-sum games 149
positivism 5–7, 9, 11–112, 19, 95–6, 99,
  129, 145–6; social theory of 29–36
positivist/policy dilemma 31–6, 43
power 124, 142, 182
pragmatism 7
prediction 7, 11, 25, 28, 32, 95; accuracy
  of 26
price 35, 41, 42, 44, 61, 66, 69, 71,
  78–81, 87, 113, 116–17, 133, 151;
  fixing 88
prisoner's dilemma 132, 180–1
Problem of Value 75
product specification 88
production 35, 55, 57, 58, 74, 85, 105,
  108–9, 140–1, 159, 161, 179; small-
  scale 165
propelling cause 17

property rights 123, 133, 145, 155–6, 160, 165, 170, 182
psychology 65, 67, 107, 112, 116
purposive theories 121–7

quantitative analysis 112

Ramstad, Y. 122
rational choice 29, 63
rational economic human 27, 72, 94, 136, 146
rationality 7, 20, 23, 27–9, 33, 67–8, 99, 100, 112, 140, 142, 167, 176; bounded 134–5, 181; procedural 134; substantive 134
rationing 182
real value 118, 120
real-world economics 93
realism 11, 95, 96
reasonable value 127
redistribution 147
regularities 21, 66
repeatable events 14
resources 172; allocation of 151–6
rights 170; constitution of 170–1; reciprocity of 155
Robbins, L. 19–21, 27, 63–4, 79, 82, 108, 117, 124, 131, 145, 147, 175
Robinson, J. 177
Roper, W.C. 179
Rose, H. and Rose, S. 180
Rostow, W.W. 116, 118
Rothbard, 179
Rotwein, E. 26
routines 137
Royal Economic association 2
Rutherford, M. 104, 107, 117, 119, 120, 124, 138, 142, 179, 180

Saghoff, M. 167
Samuels, W. 62
Samuelson, P. 28–9, 46, 65–8, 71, 74, 115, 176, 178
satisficing 140
scarcity 103–4, 108, 123, 126, 160; of means 19; physical and social 149
Schoeffler, S. 28
Schotter, A. 129–30, 131–3, 134, 136, 138, 139, 144, 180
Schumacher, F. 174
Schumpeter, J.A. 167
Schutz, 23
science 103, 120; defined 10–11; as

neutral 5; refutable statements 175; tripartite classification 11; as useful 31; value-free 10, 19
scientism 95
Scitovsky, T. de 71, 178
self-expression 101
self-interest 111, 112, 135, 136, 167, 183
Sen, A. 66, 67, 72, 183
Senior, N.W. 18
shadow pricing 151
Shand, A. 95, 96, 179
Shotter, 181
Shubik, M. 181
Sidgwick, H. 58
Simlich, J.L. and Tilman, R. 179
Simon, H.A. 134, 140
Smith, A. 41, 97, 124
social cost 153
social science 10, 12
social utility 69, 72–3
social value 47, 54–5, 122
social welfare 74, 115, 118, 147, 149, 152
Sombart 112
sovereignty 124, 126
Starr, M.E. 111, 121
the state 75, 77–8, 85, 106–7, 109, 126, 169
Stigler, G. 43, 46, 140
Streeten, P. 175
supergame 137, 138
superstition 103
supply and demand 53

Tarascio, V.J. 60–1, 62
Taylor, F. 77–8, 81, 91
technology 118–21, 128, 149
testing 14, 25; two-stage technique of 27
theory 20–3, 111–12; as essential 50; as irrelevant 30; as 'machine' 23; pure 111; rejected 28–9; two elements 24, see also named theories
time 52–3
trade 46, 153
trade-mark rules 8
Trading Body 42–3, 46
transaction-costs 133–6, 141, 153–5, 181
transactions 134, 154; bargaining 124–5; managerial 125; rationing 125
transfer of rights 123
trial and error 78–9, 84, 86, 90, 91
Tugwell, R.G. 111

ultimate causes 17–18

ultra-empiricism 23
uncertainty 105
uniformities 69
unity of value 120
utilitarianism 17–19, 38–47, 128, 145;
    mathematical conception of 45–7
utility 63

valuation 19
value 35, 44, 52, 53, 116, 117, 151–2; as
    metaphysical 177; notion of 60–1
value-free 32, 36
value-neutral approaches 7, 10, 32, 147
value-theory 60, 63, 67, 107–8, 110,
    111–12, 115, 120, 143–4, 176, 180
Vanek, J. 166, 183
variable gearing model 165–6
Vaughn, K.I. 82, 84–5, 88, 90, 178
Veblen, T. 15, 100, 101–10, 114, 116,
    117, 120, 125–6, 131, 142, 160, 169,
    177, 179
vested interests 104–5, 106, 108, 109
Viner, J. 42
Vining, R. 113, 114, 180
Von Neumann, J. and Morgenstern, O.
    176

Walker, D.A. 117, 119, 120
Walras, 60, 69, 79
wants 41, 160, 167
Warnock, M. 44
waste 104, 105
wealth 50, 51, 98, 103, 162, 169, 177;
    distribution 150; double meaning of
    123; positional 103, 104;
    redistribution of 43
Weber, M. 23, 96
welfare economics 57, 68–73, 82, 89, 93
well-being 51, 55, 58, 60, 68, 70, 72, 103,
    179
Whynes, D.K. 180
Wicksteed, P. 55, 79
Williamson, O. 129, 131, 133, 134–6,
    138, 140, 141–2, 144, 180, 181, 182
Wolfe, A.B. 111, 115, 116
Wong, S. 29, 65, 66
Worswick, G.D.N. 2, 3

Yugoslav model 165

zero-sum games 149
Zingler, E.K. 107, 108, 125, 126

7336

7335